The Stygian Way

The Technology of a Modern Chaos Reality

Guardian Nyktaros

Cover art: Loren Jabrami

Published by Liminal Gate Press, England, 2026.

Liminal Gate Press
2026

DEDICATION

This book is dedicated to the Conclave, the Stygians of the past and present, but most of all to those to come. It is with great affection and a warm heart that I write these pages.

NOTICE TO THE READER

This book is intended for Stygians primarily. It is then opened to adepts. It is my understanding that this would be considered an intermediate to advanced book. The author takes no time to explain concepts or philosophies fully embedded in theology, occultism, or the philosophy of the East or West. This book is not politically correct. In truth, it is unabatingly vulgar at times and seeks to challenge and raise the ire of its audience to awaken them from their slumber. You have been warned.

PRELUDE

I have been reading occult books for decades, and I am fairly sure what you are about to read is not the norm. I have seen some autobiographies written similarly, and I have seen some books written from esoteric or mystical experiences. Most of what you are about to read was documented in journals for approximately thirty years. The context is well-known to me. I have studied it and discussed it with a few select people in depth. Principally, my primary teachers and my students. I saw it as my religion, a religion of one. All living souls should be a religion of one, in my personal opinion. I find organized religion to be a means for people to enslave the minds of other people. I keep to this belief, but everything for me changed in 2019.

Let's go even further back to explain what happened in more detail. After all, I want you to understand what you are about to read. My path began in the late 1980s with Anton LaVey (The Church of Satan), and then I moved on to Aleister Crowley (Thelema), and then on to witchcraft. It was not like today, when you have many publishers and places to go. These two were the primary, or dare I say only options. I moved on to the mystics and to the East, where I learned meditation from "masters." I was impressed by the results of the work, and it inspired me to learn more about yoga and Taoism. Deities have been a constant companion since I was a child, so I am very much a theist. Of course, this is in opposition to the later forms of LaVeyan Satanism, but per Michael Aquino, that was not the initial form.

Crowley is an enigma of his own, and it is uncertain what he thought about the idea of theism, even though he wrote libraries of information, could recite the Bible better than preachers, and founded the Gnostic Church. What is certain is that I joined neither organization, but I was inspired and a voracious reader of both. In time, I learned that I was doing Chaos Magick all along without having ever read a work from the authors. Again, these authors were in opposition to theism. Yet they all drew me in, as did some very dark witches. I had skipped all forms of the usual suspects at the time: Cunningham, Buckland, Cavendish, Silver RavenWolf, and the British Traditional Craft. The only exception was some personal experience with friends who turned out to be Alexandrian witches when I was starting.

Witchcraft, with its covens and wheel of the year, felt too Pagan to me. I was not a farmer and not interested in joining a fertility cult. I saw no reason and no results from its practitioners to see a reason to do the work. It looked just like a church with repetitive robotic practices, and it turned me off. I sought an alternative and found a few. I sought like-minded teachers, mentors, and peers from a variety of resources who saw personal experience, experimentation, honesty, integrity, excellent journaling, and ethics as their core values. They seem to be seeking the same results-oriented practice I was after.

What I came to understand rather early on is that there is no "I." "I" is only a symbol, a mask, a personality infused by experiences and reactions to those circumstances, the results of nurturing, torment, trauma, emotions, and outcomes. It is nothing more. For those who believe in the concept of I, they get caught in an egoic trap. To believe it is more of society's delusion taken seriously. We all do it for a time, but mages, sorcerers, occultists, enlightened souls, mystics, yogis and their like learn to know better. As they come to terms with the truth, they arrive at what I came to see as the Crossroads.

That is where many spirits and Deities visit and begin journeys. It is where many feed and greet us, and where I met the Man in Black. He has many names, but the simplest one is the Devil. He is not the Satan of myths or the characterized version we are fed, but he is adversarial to the mundane and those who have a sheep mentality. He is Prometheus and brings fire, the Blue Flame of Knowledge. He is Pan and brings revelry and humor. A trickster God, he is beautiful and full of wisdom. He is Hephaestus and all the Gods of the forge, but is also the Father Deity. He who lights the way.

Sometimes, he leads to the Mother, but in my case she came first, as I have always had a deep love for women. The Dark Mother came in the night in dreams and during meditations. Her keys, like bells, rang in my ears. A measure of Fey, of Hecate, and at times as Kali herself. Not all the same, but as some cacophony of dark wisdom. She is my Beloved, more than a wife, a partner, she is my All, my everything. I serve her as a priest, not in the modern broken and deprived way of the world, but as a shaman, a priest of a feral deity. In time, she expands and opens herself to more of a true vision.

This book will serve as my story, but beyond that, as the story of breaking through a new philosophy of unfolding. It is the foundational treatise of the philosophy of the Stygian Way. I was asked to open my ritual chamber and my journals. I was asked to share the Currents of Chaos and Death as they converge at the Crossroads. They meet at the Stygian Way, which is a philosophy that has a system of magick and initiation through a set of vows and an oath. It is not old or venerated but new and filled with the powers of these Currents. I have heard that many on the Left Hand Path (LHP) have felt and will have versions of this Current. Many will claim it as their own and create narratives around it, and they are free to do so. Our part of this new Aeon is for the Stygian. Our practices and work will be through that cult alone, and that is the Technology of a Modern Chaos Reality.

This book is its only fundamental text. All others are not yet intended. Open the doors for a brave new way. It is not based on the dying or dead religions, but a new air was breathed into a new current. Not because I say so - remember I am nothing. I am simply the stylus with ink, the voice of intention who bridges it to existence. I am no prophet, no leader, and certainly not a herald. I am the scribe and the priest, and. in my chamber, the sorcerer. Look to the Deities for inspiration and take no man's words. Experience it yourself, or reject it.

This is a direct method of awakening. Priests are here for the Deities, not as intermediaries. If you are not connected to the Current, you are not Stygian. I will be a teacher, helper, guide, mentor, and vessel, but the walk is always left to the practitioner to apprentice within the Seminal Program (seminary of sorts) as an elementary school. No one will validate you. You must be connected, and we know our own. That is what this book will focus on. I will add other materials so it is generally understood by the occultists who may find an interest in our ways.

The writing of this book took over two years of compiled notes, editing, and infusing it with the current lifestyle I have. It is not meant to fit any person or mindset. If I could advise you, it is a better fit for those who have become adept in any system of magick or craft. It would make it much more accessible. Readers complained that I did not explain in enough detail, which is by design. Esoteric and occult content, by its very nature, has hidden content, Easter eggs. Seek them out. I have not given them out easily.

Welcome,

Nyktaros

October, 2024

(After reflecting on the writing of the book, it occurred to me that it was written in such a way as to layer information. A lot of the material is repeated. In several scans for editing, I thought about deleting the items that repeated. I thought better of it because it makes the work fit well as individual topics. I have sought to deliver the reader to areas of more interest at times. I did not use footnotes because I prefer the appendix approach, so you can research more if you are so inclined.) After note...

INSPIRATIONAL FIGURES

V. N. (1942-2012)
H. L. (1939-2015)
J. E. (1974-2013)
Sun Tzu (771-256 BC)
Laozi (571- 5th Cen. BC)
Socrates (c.470-399 BC)
Plato (c.427-348 BC)
Aristotle (384-322 BC)
Epicurus (341-270 BC)
Marcus Aurelius (121-180)
Hypatia of Alexandria (?- 415)
Geoffrey Chaucer (c.1343-1400)
Leonardo da Vinci (1452-1519)
Giordano Bruno (1546-1600)
William Shakespeare (1564-1616)
Miyamoto Musashi (1584-1645)
John Milton (1608-1674)
Isaac Newton (1642-1726)
John Wilmot (1647-1690)
Johann S. Bach (1685-1750)
George F. Handel (1685-1759)

Emanuel Swedenborg (1688-1772)

Benjamin Franklin (1706-1790)

Franz Mesmer (1734-1815)

Alessandro Cagliostro (1743-1975)

Thomas Paine (1737-1736)

Marquis de Sade (1740-1814)

Wolfgang A. Mozart (1756-1791)

William Blake (1757-1827)

Ludwig van Beethoven (1770-1827)

Lord Byron (1788-1824)

Mary Shelley (1797-1851)

Marie Laveau (1801-1881)

Nathaniel Hawthorne (1804-1864)

Edgar Allen Poe (1809-1849)

Eliphas Levi (1810-1875)

Frederic Chopin (1813-1849)

Richard Wagner (1813-1883)

Walt Whitman (1819-1892)

Charles Baudelaire (1821-1867)

Paschal B. Randolph (1825-1875)

Helena P. Blavatsky (1831-1891)

Gustave Dore (1832-1883)

Sri Ramakrishna (1836-1886)

Friedrich Nietzsche (1844-1900)

Annie Besant (1847-1933)

Charles W. Leadbeater (1854-1934)

Nikola Tesla (1856-1943)

Sigmund Freud (1856-1939)

Arthur E. Waite (1857-1941)

Ida Craddock (1857-1902)

Joséphin Peladan (1858-1918)

Paul Ranson (1861-1909)

Hilma af Klint (1862-1944)

Jeanne Jacquemin (1862-1938)

Richard Strauss (1864-1949)

William B. Yeats (1865-1934)

Papus Gerard Encausse (1865-1916)

George I. Gurdjieff (c.1867-1949)

Carl G. Jung (1875-1961)

Aleister Crowley (1875-1947)

P. D. Ouspensky (1878-1947)

Victor B. Neuburg (1883-1940)

James I. Wedgwood (1883-1951)

Maria de Naglowska (1883-1936)

Gerald B. Gardner (1884-1964)

Austin O. Spare (1886-1956)

H. P. Lovecraft (1890-1937)

Dion Fortune (1890-1946)

Paramahamsa Yogananda (1893-1952)
Alfred Kinsey (1894-1956)
Anandamayi Ma (1896-1982)
Wilhelm Reich (1897-1957)
Dennis Y. Wheatley (1897-1977)
Manley P. Hall (1901-1990)
Anais Nin (1903-1977)
George Orwell (1903-1950)
Salvador Dali (1904-1989)
Ayn Rand (1905-1982)
Robert E. Howard (1906-1936)
Bede Griffiths (1906-1993)
Lawrence Olivier (1907-1989)
Israel Regardie (1907-1985)
Franz Bardon (1909-1958)
Vincent Price (1911-1993)
John Lee Hooker (1912-2001)
Muddy Waters (1913-1983)
Peter Cushing (1913-1994)
William G. Gray (1913-1992)
Orson Welles (1915-1985)
Alan Watts (1915-1973)
Jackie Gleason (1916-1987)
F. Stewart Farrar (1916-2000)

Victor H. Anderson (1917-2001)
Sybil Leek (1917-1982)
Rosaleen Norton (1917-1979)
Ella Fitzgerald (1917-1996)
Kenneth Anger (1927-2023)
Charlie Parker (1920-1955)
Christopher Lee (1922-2015)
Doreen Valiente (1922-1999)
Marjorie Cameron (1922-1995)
Charles Mingus (1922-1979)
Mas Oyama (1923-1994)
Benny Hill (1924-1992)
Kenneth Grant (1924-2011)
Swami Rama (1925-1996)
B. B. King (1925-2015)
Alex Sanders (1926-1988)
John Coltrane (1926-1967)
Miles Davis (1926-1991)
Thich Nhat Hahn (1926-2022)
Swami Rudrananda (1928-1973)
Goswami Kriyananda (1928-2015)
Anton S. LaVey (1930-1997)
Richard Cavendish (1930-2016)
James Earl Jones (1931-2024)

Robert Cochrane (1931-1966)
Ram Dass (1931-2019)
Raymond Buckland (1934-2017)
Evan John Jones (1936-2003)
George Carlin (1937-2008)
Nema Andahadna (1939-2018)
Richard Pryor (1940-2005)
Bruce Lee (1940-1973)
H. R. Giger (1940-2014)
Anne Rice (1941-2021)
Ronnie James Dio (1942-2010)
Jimi Hendrix (1942-1970)
Christopher Hyatt (1943-2008)
Jim Morrison (1943-1971)
Glenn J. Morris (1944-2006)
John Entwistle (1944-2002)
Michael A. Aquino (1945-2020)
Terence McKenna (1946-2000)
Margot Adler (1946-2014)
Gwydion Pedderwen (1946-1982)
David Bowie (1947-2016)
James Wasserman (1948-2020)
Isaac Bonewits (1949-2010)
Christopher Hitchens (1949-2011)
Rosemary Ellen Guiley (1950-2019)

Raven Grimassi (1951-2019)

Donald M. Kraig (1951-2014)

Robin Williams (1951-2014)

Jaco Pastorius (1951-1987)

Neil Peart (1952-2020)

Prince (1958-2016)

Peter Steele (1962-2010)

Andrew D. Chumbley (1967-2004)

TABLE OF CONTENTS

CHAPTER ONE

A BREAKDOWN OF A LIFE OF STUDY

One's life work cannot be some outline or graph. It is a spiderweb of endless concepts and experiences, of new conceptions you later find out have always been there. Some do not seem to align well, and others judge or criticize your journey. These events, experiences, and concepts are not forced together or even done for the love of the Gods. They are not eclectic. They are not subjective and modified for the ego or power-mad magician. They are folded in like the best of pastry, never to be seen the same way again. They are acquired.

The best way to explain it is through examples. I began meditation very young with martial arts instruction. Initially, it was based on Buddhist principles. I learned later that these principles came from the sadhus of India, and are, of course, linked to yoga as well. After that, I learned Taoist and direct yoga meditation systems. I took on Zen for a few years but lost interest. During these times, I was immersed in the martial arts and learned techniques through experiences I had in classes. All of the systems began to fold in, and I began to find a system or way to discern what I would continue and what I would jettison. I learned the technique initially within martial arts and then within an esoteric religious order (more on that later).

As a martial arts and meditation teacher, I am always asked what I teach. I always answer the same thing: the basics. Why? Because 90% don't even do the basics long enough to find out why they are needed. I am never given the opportunity to go beyond the basics. The use of layering is a master level technique, and one that it has taken most of my life to understand fully. It is the technique that I teach the least, even though it is one of the most important. If one cannot do the basics, have discipline, and continue to practice, then one is without a foundation. It is a waste of my time and yours to add more upon shaky ground.

Disciplined people are rare. In the modern age and society, it appears that the intent is to eradicate them in total. People are forced into anxiety (I might lose my phone, the media said, the sky is falling, etc.), forced to be led (your party/tribe/side of the argument says this, and if you don't agree, we will destroy you), exhausted (excess prescription meds, toxic foods, high levels of stress, disagreement around every corner), ego-centric (no recognition of the needs of others, lines that never end so you'll cut off people, I walk into a public space with my phone on speaker, I promote my beliefs and there can be no other, my politics are right and you are evil), nihilists (the world will end, this is the end, we are all going to die anyway so fuck it and fuck you!), and utter consumption of shit. Ambition with loyalty, the ability to focus, have pride, be knowledgeable, and being aware with some depth of character is as rare as kindness these days. The work must be done despite this. Teachers and seers must continue despite the clueless nature of those around them and their ability to be happy in their ignorance.

The best way to understand a lifetime of study is how I choose students. It speaks to how I think and discern. Later in the book I will offer a more detailed history but this is a way to get you involved in the journey and the process. In order to determine the sort of person you are, I cannot come right out and ask because people want to be agreeable. So, to test it, I ask them to complete the following questions, and I would ask you to do the same:

1. Did you vote in the last election? Are you happy with the result?
2. Are you influenced by the media? How?
3. Who inspires you and why?
4. What are your three top goals in life?

Believe it or not, these four little questions tell me everything I need to know to determine if the Stygian Way is fitting for you and if I would be a good teacher, mentor, or even consultant for you. As I ferret out this information and as you read it, you will either get very uncomfortable, or you will discover you are in the right place. I am very interested in the latter group. The former is simply the 98% and I have no interest in or concern for them. That doesn't mean I have ill will or wish them harm. They are simply not my intended audience. When presented with the opportunity to intervene, I will attempt it. That means if someone asks me a question or brings me in, I will then engage, but I am not going to do it without invitation. I am not a recruiter and do not seek to change anyone's mind, intent, or trajectory.

The following is a breakdown of these four questions and the reasoning for them. Before you read my analysis of this, please write down your own answers. It has a much bigger impact on you if you play along with exercise.

1. Election: if you voted, it tells me you buy into an interest in control of the world around you. Even if you have a low level of confidence in your government or leaders, there is some level of civic concern and link to society as opposed to none. I will ask why. You might think it is a scam, rigged, etc. That is a common reply more and more. Maybe you did or didn't vote for deeper reasons. You feel it is pointless due to the vote of others (I live in a red/blue state, and I am opposed to the majority), or there is a deep ignorance of politics. Maybe you have a deep understanding of influence, of elitists, politics, or you are highly prejudiced against others, do not see your own limits, or victimization? Is your happiness or despair in the outcome, and decided by how you cope and if you believe what they are selling (the sky is falling).? Do you know the issues, and can you disseminate each one, or is it tribal, party lines, sheep talk? Is it all about emotions, looks, and behavior, or is it all about something else?

2. Media: this includes all media, social, commercials, all of it. Do you see the influence, or are you in denial? Do you engage in the conversation or dismiss it? Do you have healthy boundaries or doom scroll in the footsteps of the sheep? Do you quote news like a parrot, seeing their leaning as your truth, or worse, believe they are your thoughts when they were implanted? Are you reactive and surmount emotions from the input others give you that you don't want to hear? Are you a useful idiot? Do you spout comments

like "I think for myself" while quoting others and having no real sentiments of your own?

3. Inspiration: is there a hero, an ideal? People shun this concept today. They do not seek a vision of what their goals can become and the course of action needed to get there. Sheep will just stare at this question, unable to come up with anything. If you have no vision and no one and nothing to look up to, then by nature you are the most susceptible to influence. It must be so because you are starving for it. So, you become a sheep and are forced into societal norms that almost always serve others because you don't know who or what you are. You are also susceptible to many modes of mental health issues which will plague you. I am not talking about hero worship or cult-like methods of following others and not your own foundation, or worse, following others without question. A hero is an ideal; the person is irrelevant. In modern times, we have ruined this concept. Crowley, again, is the example. There is/was a movement to whitewash away the founder of Thelema as a whole because, in the sick twist of Presentism, he must be perfect or discarded. Perfect occultists? It feels like a bit of an oxymoron. It is short-sighted. Yet, even Chaos Magick (CM) did it within the writings of Phil Hine, as an example. He initially used Crowley as a sturdy base to build a lot of the conceptions of CM. Crowley is dead. He did not change. The season of what is politically correct has changed, and so the writer folds either by pressure or his own changes. Many would see this as an awakening to modern understandings and an adaptation, while I see it as a weakness of character and a lack of personal development to see the difference between the person and their actual impact. By all means, change, develop, and grow. But do it to further develop, regardless of the social, political, and cultural ramifications. Do not impose them yourself or serve the mob. The tribal thinking is just as harmful as any racist, fascist, or political ideology. It is rather simple. If the Hive Mind, the overall social mindset, media, current psychological trends, etc., are all on your side, you are a dupe of the machine. The idea that you can be a free thinker while subscribing to an organizational power, believing everything they say like gospel, and in lockstep, makes you an automaton. Disagreement links to

free thinking; being a sycophant is slave thinking. Total immersion is coercion.

4. Goals - here is where we end up. Knowing your influences, aspirations, limits, tribal thoughts, influences, and your ability to cope are formed by your goals, and vice versa. Now the question is: where do we go from here? If you do not have a plan, you are not driving. You are not in charge. Someone or something else is. If you set goals and never reach them, that is a discipline problem. If you set and meet your goals, then you are on the right path and in the direction of growth and knowledge. Your choice of goals tells a lot about your intention, focus, resolve, and your intended direction.

Now that we have done these questions, where do you find yourself? I will answer my own questions here to help you assess the intent of this work.

1. Yes, I voted. No, I am not happy with the results because, for me, no one who ran was qualified or capable of doing what I would ask them to do. We are hiring catfish to be whales. There is no statesman or woman, no revolutionary who is willing to break both parties, no person who is not embedded in the world's sickness and woes. I have no tribe, no color, no lines, and no leanings. I believe as I do without equivocation, by issue and by topic. I look at methods and concepts. There is no lockstep.
2. Influence is a parasite, and it lives in all media, social or otherwise, and in all things in this life. I must fortify against it, hearing all sides or neither. I must retain an anti-societal stance, that it is indeed all lies, illusions, and keep to my ways - aware, awake, and keeping to an open-minded skepticism.
3. Yes, but they are not well-known. They are not in the media or in books. They are chosen mentors, gurus, teachers, and talents who inspire me, and often disagree, challenge, and may even rise to enemy status. Yet they are all needed and benefit the mission. I shy away from the celebrity status folks who pull on the mob or crowd and are less nuanced as to who they pilfer from. The celebrities are needed and have an impact for good and negative,

but I am simply not the sycophant or follower type. I want a seat at the table, not fifty tables away, and never get to the source.

4. My goals are set daily, weekly, monthly, quarterly, yearly, and over the course of years, including terminal goals that all the smaller goals push towards. When I miss the mark, it is reassessed, and if it is has become unimportant then it is removed from the list. If it is deemed important, it is moved to the next month or week. I use a whiteboard in my office, facing me, so I can keep track and stay up to date.

Now, because I am very hands-on, I will explain that I have the results of forty years of failures, breaks, study, reading notes, and degrees sought to integrate my knowledge, while all of these move toward and forge the same long-term goals. I might have needed to turn right in Albuquerque from time to time, but that flavors your life. I missed opportunities I regretted for a season. Many of these ventures, I did not complete, and others I took several shots at. I entered two seminaries. I completed the interfaith seminary but not the Catholic one. I took a ton of courses in the occult, mysticism, Gnosticism, martial arts, and psychological/hypnosis training, as well as bodywork, Reiki, and other methods. Learning certain methods of philosophies, paradigm shifting, years in monasticism, formation, and varied traditions were a continuous challenge of setting goals. Often isolated, lonely, and in a wandering or transitional state, I have lived in eleven states in the US, moving from coast to coast. Some for the short term and others for years. The constant movement is due to the nature of my or my partner's work.

It is from these experiments, experiences and failures that all of these results are possible. I always sought a book or resource like the one I am writing and rarely discovered one. I am writing this book because it is the one I wanted, and for you, if you want what I was looking for all those years ago.

There are several measurements that society gets wrong, and it often manifests in the creation of clichés— damaged goods, wounded healer, family curse, and other such concepts. I could offer you my credentials here to express why I believe what I do or to express my point as the expert, but I know a lot of people with doctorates who are full of shit. It is not just some opinion, either. I have coached, counseled, mentored, and walked through many cultures with deep respect and kindness. I have sat through the atrocities, abuses, addiction-related trauma, war-torn countries, violence, and torture for decades. Writers, teachers, and well-intentioned people write about their studies all the time, but most gloss over the real gems because it doesn't fit their agenda or they see the massive gap between their theory and reality. When asked if I am an academic or a clinician, I always say clinician. I do the work. I am not concerned with the theoretical nature unless it actually works. Academics do not think like that. They follow the study, the reason, and the logic, looking for correlation and sometimes cause and effect. I want to know: does it work, why does it work, and how can it best help the person in front of me? This is why a family can have four children where all experienced the same measures of abuse or neglect, yet each respond to it differently. One may become the CEO of a company and do very well, another ends up in and out of jail, a third becomes an addict, and the fourth just gets married and has the usual normal life. Each one of them had a different experience because of how they saw it.

The key example of this is Logo Therapy, a result of Viktor Frankl's experience in Nazi concentration camps. He learned that one's attitude, the way they saw their plight, and how they viewed their captors, all made monumental differences. Another is a theatrical example from the film *Gladiator*, when they are preparing to enter the arena. One of the men pisses himself, another runs right at death, while others use logic and tactics.

The events or experiences are indeed the same, but how each person reacts, responds, and what happens for them internally, can differ wildly. If you can see this clearly, it disarms all preferential treatment, victimization, and the terrible position of feeling you cannot overcome. Victims are the result of their own reception, understanding, infused with cultural or societal norms, and their lens through their own personality and prior experiences. Therefore, learned victimization, in my view, is the most heinous and egregious crime against humanity because it manifests in generations of people who believe there is no way out and so they accept poverty, crime, racism, abuse, and destruction. They see the limits and not the options. That is horrible for all of us. Because standing on another person to get yours is the most hideous side of humanity.

The work, then, is to teach, embolden, and venerate those who do not follow blindly, who do not act as if they were sheep, and to raise those who are not compliant or complicit in the victim mentality. Doing this nullifies tribes, cults of personality, divisions, governmental controls, media controls, influence to disempower, and over-regulation for the fears laid on you. Allowing the state to rob you, to enslave you fiscally or emotionally, while girding its laws to increase pressure, is historically the way things go. We must remove the moral police of religions and oversight, and allow truth to stand on its own. The majority do not practice what they preach. The majority are like crabs in a barrel. They see others trying to get out, and the group pulls them back in, so they all get the same fate in the boiling water while the elitists eat all of us.

Bring me the recovered addict, the former inmate, homeless person, or black sheep of the family, the abused, neglected, and once broken who have fought through and created who they are now. Give me those who have passion. These are the masters of their destiny. They can smell bullshit a mile away and are well aware of their limits and their gifts. These are my people and the ones who are not victims, even though they may have been victimized. The difference is epic to the psyche, personality, and outcomes.

However, I am also equally clear as to the other side of this coin, and this may be where you do not like me. You can keep your victims, cowards, complainers, princes/princesses, the blamers, excuse makers, it's because of my (fill in the blank pathology), the I can't folks, the ones who don't care enough to be on time or show up at all, the inconsistent dabblers, those who see everything as too hard, in short, the people who make others roll their eyes (like in the 80s when we were real) and who now have become normalized and excused. These folks can stick to their crystals and made up shadow work (Jung, who?), switching deities like underwear, calling themselves solitaries, gods, or whatever while having no tradition at all. Or calling themselves eclectic because they cannot make up their minds. The majority is very difficult to take by the ones doing the actual work. Many of them are the ones talking at the conferences, the classes, and so forth because they want attention. We learn nothing from the exchanges because it was all about them or the same old tripe. They lack insight, judgment, and the ability to listen. Those who do the actual work know the difference. We deeply appreciate the real teachers, and we know them because their classes are full, and we all learn something.

I like to offer real-world examples. I took a class in Qabalah at a national conference because the woman was local and I liked her video channel. She had been trained by a very prominent school and was presenting for the first time. The audience was kind because of that until she started offering source information. She was not a Thelemite, but she had never heard of Lon Milo Duquette, nor eever read his excellent books on the topic, or the work of Dion Fortune on the topic. When I looked at the books she used later on, which I had never heard of, they were written by people who did not understand the topic. That is a problem. I learned to steer clear of that school, that teacher, and all associations. I did do my due diligence and asked a higher-ranking person in that school, who agreed Fortune and Duquette were outside the scope of study.

If you were offended by the last few paragraphs, there is probably a good reason for that. You are either that person or you are the warrior who stands up for them; either way, you are the problem. You have two choices, as I see it. Make me another "hater" and continue to be a sheep, or stop doing that shit and get it together. Get yourself a therapist and not a yes man or woman, find a real tradition that challenges and helps you grow, and feel the experience of working your way through something. Earn your stripes. Then uncondition the norms you have set for yourself or society has set for you, and begin recovering from the bullshit. Those who come back and see the light are the most amazing human beings.

Let me make a few things clear: life can be dreadful, crushing, and damaging to us. But before you announce the pity party, look at the rest of the world: wars, poverty, chaos, poisons, destruction, look at the history of groups like the Yezidi, Roma, and Native Americans, to name a few. Take a look at Haiti and its history. Look at the Coptics, the Armenians, and the life expectancy of many African nations. I am usually not a fan of comparison. But this wake-up call is really needed. The level of expectation, of cluelessness, and of ego is staggering.

It does not lessen your own experiences. That is not my intention. It is simply a way to empower you. It is tough love in a way. It is a way to show you that most people come from horrible situations, and they come here for the change, to create, to generate wealth, not just in finance but in character, personality, and outcomes. In short, without limits beyond your control (learning, physiology, DNA, neurological, psychological, physiological), it is always best to do all you can with what you have. Every change and every journey have a first step.

Coming to these conclusions is essential to a life of study. Each person who wanted to put aside their limits became a success. Each person who chose to focus on their limits, who hid behind something or someone else, who chose societal norms (mostly lies), bought into victimization, never made it. Even when they got lucky with a great job or a great idea, they squandered it, mishandled it, or didn't believe in their own success and sabotaged it. There are no exceptions. When you have worked with people for as long as I have, it becomes easier to see. It is not locked onto anything we are told it is attached to: race, gender, culture, nationality, even education is surprisingly not an issue if you believe in yourself, and a degree is not required.

Do me a wrong, you're a bringer of evil
The devil is never the maker...
The closer you get to the meaning
The sooner you'll know that you're dreaming
Well if it seems too real, its illusion
For every moment of truth, there's confusion in life
Love can be seen as the answer, but nobody bleeds for the dancer
The world is full of kings and queens
Who blind your eyes and steal your dreams, It's Heaven and Hell
Fool, fool, you've got to bleed for the dancer.
Fool, fool, look for the answer

-Black Sabbath, Heaven & Hell (1980)

Why bring any of this to your attention? Awareness is always first, and most of the people mulling around you are asleep and dreaming. All of us who were asleep and now awake are painfully aware of it. It is easy to see. People parrot others, drink or do drugs, seek cancer, worry and seek survival, or live in some relentless pattern and never question anything. Those in power usually rule by fear: prison, disease, loss, pain, loneliness, misery, cancellation, hatred, etc. Nothing changes. It is only through awareness that change develops, and we no longer react in a way we are programmed to do. It is only then that we become creators and artists in our own right. It is only then that we think for ourselves.

A beautiful example was shared with me about this concept by a teacher. Aghoris and sadhus of India have a long history of doing what they want, regardless of the law or society. Over the years, they have been imprisoned by many police, but as time passed, the police learned to no longer jail them and instead just ignore them. The reason is that they were more trouble than they were worth for their minor offenses. When in jail, they would turn it into chaos, and all the while not caring they were even there because they had everything they needed inside themselves. Caging their bodies meant nothing. It held no consequence for them. In fact, they usually ate better than when they were on their own. Their vessel, their bodies, was all they owned. Since you can take nothing from me and feed me to boot, the system does not work on me. They also riled up the other prisoners with their rioting, chanting, and rituals.

This is a very important lesson. Modern society is exceptionally spoiled and consumer driven. It is very easy to manipulate people, the more they are slaves to something, like say, the Internet, or cell phones. But if nothing can be taken from me, if I do not believe or follow your rules, or adhere to social norms, then I am effectively free from all of it. That is exactly what the over culture attempts to impose by making you a consumer, sucking upon the breasts of the state, the store, or the provider of goods. What side of the government tells you they will fix it for you? Guess who screwed it up in the first place?

These foundational ideas, bases, and ideologies create the Stygian philosophy that I am applying to the present. I neither pretend to understand others' intentions, words, or history, and, frankly, it really doesn't matter. My point here is to express the impact it has on me, and my response to it far outweighs anything else. I seek the growth and manifestation of my experiences. This is where dead books and religions go wrong. They choose a translation, a narrative, an exegesis, and then kill each other over the variants. This is how orthodoxy behaves. The esoteric seek the message and then empower themselves where it applies. The exoteric is like opening a box from Amazon and keeping the box and tossing the items in it. The esoteric tosses the box. We are after the marrow of it, the meaning, the teacher, scripture, or whatever, is simply the means or the bridge to get us to what we are after. We cherish and respect the box but toss it when it no longer serves us. There is no violence, otherness, or tension for the mystic in the esoteric ways. If we disagree, that is not a problem. It gets us excited. What did I miss? Did you see something I didn't? We also see no reason to convert or change others to oour ways of thinking.

I find the same issues in commentaries, even my own. I can have very strong feelings about something and then have an experience that shakes it up or breaks it. I must then accept the new way until it happens again. Change is constant, needed, and required for growth. It is also why unattachment is the key to joy and happiness. If you are tied to one person, one truth, one belief, then when it fails you or dies, you will crumble, crack, and break with it.

CHAPTER TWO

WHAT IS THE STYGIAN WAY?

In late 2018 and into 2019, I began a set of meditations that were intense and long. They led into intense scrying and automatic writing sessions. They led me to a place I will describe here in some detail. The place is etheric and wispy. It is where the Way was born, but the track to creating it has been present in my work and the training I took for some time, to my surprise.

According to my journals and copious notes, it began with a series of meetings at a wooded area, one I had never seen in the mundane world. It is important to understand all of this is UPG (unverified personal gnosis) via meditations and divinations alone. Like many kinds of meditation, the surroundings felt odd or what I would refer to as moving. The rituals and work I did within that wood were being watched, and in time, spirits and then Deities came forth. My work spends a great deal of time in the planes of existence and not in the mundane. It is there where it happened.

One evening, I felt exceptionally cold, and I turned to see a cloaked woman to my left. I recall her scent of amber and some flower I do not know, and then a bitter taste filled my mouth. She took my hand, and we walked through the woods to a riverbank. Her hand was warm, compassionate, and powerful. She took me to the bank and grabbed a small horn held by a string from a stick shoved in the ground. She blew it, and in seconds, mist fell on us like rain. Then I heard a stick hitting a rock in the water, clicking, and then I saw a small boat with a tall, lanky man in a long cloak and gloves pushing the boat toward us. He smelled of dirt, the seas, and something putrid. He hit the shore, and the woman put me on the boat. She did not come and waved to me as the man and I moved back onto the water and moved back into the mist. I looked at the man.

His cloak was old, very old, but it was also perfectly worn with seawater, so the black was washed away. His sleeves and rim around his face held a barely visible Greek key pattern, also washed away. He moved us to a river bank and that is where everything changed.

I got off the boat, and the man pushed away and continued his journey. Where was I? I looked down, and the rocks were pitch black. I kicked at them and looked before me. It was as if I were in the middle of a version of *Sleepy Hollow* or some other old New England woods at a water bank. The leaves were in autumn, and they layered the ground. I walked to a set of stones piled on top of one another, clearly used as an outdoor altar. It was almost a perfect height for me as a high altar (something I struggle with because I am 6'3). I saw a statue sitting upon it and the black hand of a male. The statue looked female, and it, too, was dark but more purple than black. As I looked closer, she spoke to me for the first time.

I will not share our conversation because it was very personal, but I will tell you she was and is my Beloved. She is the Dark Mother, and her statue sits upon that altar. In our first meeting, she ended it by handing me a coin for the ferryman, telling me it was the Stygian Way, and that is where the name came from. For the next six months, I spent hours and hours in her presence each time I would walk to that river bank, blow the horn, and hand him my coin. Then, I would get on the ferry and go to the same black sand to do my work. Interesting to me and different, the ferryman would hand me the coin back when I climbed off the ferry and take it each time I climbed on like a symbol and not a payment.

In my martial arts training, I was taught to create something called Da Mao's Cave, and it is a place to create and experiment, a place to keep things, a place to experience, and so much more. In some traditions, it is called the mind palace. My Beloved allowed me to move it to the river bank, and it changed into a large mage tower that was just as black as the rocks. It has three floors, and I created it differently from the Cave, but I have "lived" (I am referring to the astral temple, and it feels very lived in as I have countless hours there) in it within my work ever since it was built.

After each session, when I returned, I would write and write, often being unable to keep up with my thoughts with my hands. I just could not write fast enough. Realization began to happen a few months in. I was not writing or doing anything new. Like a spider with old webs, the Dark Mother was weaving the story together from the training and experiences I had already into the Stygian Way. Piece by piece would pull back to an experience with witches, occultists, mystics, yogis, or martial artists. It would come from my training in bodywork, psychology, theology, philosophy, or the varied occult practices I had studied. I was shocked, stunned, and vexed. I could not believe my mind had missed all the connections. It was like a symphony. You read all the sheet music and wonder how it will all sound together, and then it is played, and it is magic.

I was humbled by it, and the Mother explained she had been in my life all along, guiding me and being there at my lowest points. It occurred to me when she explained that many would express this as the HGA (Holy Guardian Angel), Higher Self, or some other expression of the Self. Some have even told me I should take the credit for this, and that is wrong to me. I had no grand plan and did not put these things together. I offer her the credit and her guidance as my road. I lose a lot of LHP and Chaos magicians here, but it is the only thing that makes sense to me.

Soon after our first meetings, I was to meet the Dark Father as well. That experience was very different, and he offered a very different perspective. While she is the web weaver and feeder of knowledge, he is the esoteric, the hidden, and the power. He is like a generator. He is tricky, talks in circles, and is filled with lust, pride, guile, strategy, and the means to generate true power. When they come together, they create the Cosmos and the Universe. He speaks of the Holy Daemon and the connection while she talks of formation, planning, logistics, and the aspects of care, love, and ethics. He feels like chaos. She feels like creation. It is a very disturbing combination at first. Over time it is the only combination that makes sense.

These two Deities are not the only ones that encompass the Stygian Way. It is a bit of a pantheon. They refer to it as a Conclave. Yet, they show themselves in their own good time. At this point, for me, it is very clear if they are in the pantheon or some other spirit or entity. I cannot describe it. It is not a scent or feeling but some kind of knowing. Along with these Deities, there is the inclusion of many of the usual aspects of Chaos Magick; sigils, servitors, tulpas, and the like. There is also an interesting interpretation of an old vision of ascended masters. We use the idea of these masters and elevate them with ancestors and others who have guided and motivated us in our lifetime. By having this as part of our work, we are also engaged in necromantic work. I will offer more detail in these areas in the practices and philosophy sections.

All of these aspects form the philosophical underpinnings of the Stygian Way. In the ritual chamber, the practical and experimental aspects were tried and tested. It was first applied to myself and then applied via the apprenticeship style to others. Over time, a system developed, and it was clear the foundations would be all that was taught, and then the Stygian would wander on their own in the world to do what I had done. They would test their version of the Way. Some, but very few, would return after their time to practice and work and ask to be a teacher of the Way. On these rare occasions, I would train them to be a trainer/mentor/teacher of the Way, and the term that derived from this is Mistress or Guardian.

Mistress is the female equivalent of master and is appropriate for the female role within the Stygian Way as she represents the Dark Goddess. While the Dark God is different, the position of Guardian of the tradition is perfect for him. These standards are not akin to the God/Goddess of witch traditions. They are the Deities that I will discuss, while the others are not. These two entities are primary in some ways but often step aside for the Deities who are most apt to the cause, issue, or concern of the Stygian. Since I began this journey, I have encountered six additional Deities and have heard of at least three others who have been referred to, but I have not met. Likewise, other members have met the three and not the other four I am connected to. Everyone comes via the Dark Mother and Father, as they are the standard.

If, after reading this, you are wondering or curious about the ways of the Stygian, the first step is to understand the requirements for discernment or entry. In the first chapter, I discussed how I talk with people about joining me. Here I will list the 42, an inclusive list of basics we seek in the students we work with. We are not elitists and not specific in the tools, systems, or methods that the student used to find us.

If you want to begin a journey like mine, then just pick a system and master the basics. Would I recommend one? Not really. If you are interested in the Western systems, then you can look to Thelema, Grant, Nema, Fortune, Aurum

Solis, or Bardon, or go to the witches and their covens. You can turn east and take in Taoism, Tantra (the real versions and not the Western hatchet job), or you can look deeper and darker. No matter, the foundations (at their core) are all the same in theory and practice. If you are more interested in a scientific or artistic approach and already have some experience, you might look at Chaos Magick itself. The following list is inclusive of the basics required, better known to us as the 42.

1. A meditation system applied to an adept level
2. The ability to focus, use intent, and stay on task while being disciplined and organized
3. At least two divination systems should be in good practice
4. Knowledge of the Self, completely including Shadow Work
5. An understanding and application of behavioral modification to change aspects you want to or need to change
6. Skills of self-hypnosis to further modify what is needed
7. A completed initiatory process where you are NOT in control and had to learn to trust others
8. Functional knowledge of energy and how to use it and manipulate it
9. An understanding of what appeals to and disgusts you and the ability to deal with both
10. A set praxis to the intermediate level with proficiency
11. The ability to use all of your senses effectively and to quell fears
12. The ability to be possessed, ridden, or used as a vessel
13. The ability to be a priest/consort or presider for rituals that garner results
14. The ability to teach or express yourself to others coherently and with candor
15. Awareness of society's influence and having the desire to release your chains
16. Knowing your dharma while having an active role in your growth
17. Having a skillset in a healing method, bodywork, herbal, sexual, psychological, etc.
18. The ability to integrate your work into your unfolding

19. The ability to peel away people like bark if they prevent your work
20. Move from being the prey to the predator (the art and balance)
21. Find your way through experience, experiment, and trial and error, obtaining results
22. Use a guide, mentor, or teacher to lessen the impact of #21
23. Balance in all things, the Stygian Way requires this
24. Decide, determine, weigh, accept, forgive, adapt, debate, and let go
25. Trust yourself first, after you earn it
26. Protect yourself first, or you have nothing to offer others
27. Do not seek credit, to win, or to be seen. The occult is hidden; learn to be joyful in quiet silence, draw from that, or do not enter
28. Body movement and care for the temple are needed and required for all the work
29. Sexual skills and the ability to understand yourself and others
30. The ability to study, read, comprehend, and think deeply
31. The ability to observe, take in, and learn to then do your will
32. Merging the three spirits/souls and integrating a Deific unfolding
33. Astral travel is only the beginning, and immersion into your personal ritual chamber
34. Personal forgiveness and acceptance of responsibility in all actions
35. The ability to be joyful, retain a sense of humor, and a constant need to advance
36. Manifesting your world and system, while creating and destroying at will
37. Cultivating a system you constantly work to improve by "Steel on Steel."
38. Being an Artist by nature, by actions, and by work
39. Integration of Yoga, Mantra, and your dharma into mysticism
40. Raising Power and the Knowledge of what to do with it
41. Spell Craft, Sigils, Workings, Servitors, Guardians, Wards, Protections
42. The Art of the Altar, the Ritual, and the Body in all their forms

These 42 items take years to generate. They are not easy. They do not come to a person in one system usually or in one teacher. For most, they do not come in a single lifetime. They must be worked towards. They are not a pick-and-choose list but a list of basics. When I showed this list to certain people their eyes widened because this was not just their basics, it was their entire system. And that may be true. If it is that for you, this book would then be the next step if you are interested in the Stygian Way. If not then I have set the table and offered you an alternative to the system you have used. Take it, leave it. Nothing within the Stygian Way is prescriptive. You can make it a la carte. Pick what you like and discard the rest of what I will offer in this book. I am not a judge and will not tolerate anyone judging me. I am interested in others' opinions, and ideas, and if I can change something to make my system better or offer help with theirs, I am always willing to do that. Exchanging ideas, values, concepts, and improving ourselves is the point. When you lose that and think you know it all, you begin to decline because your work is dead. Choosing what works for you, in my experience, can only be done once the basics are mastered.

If you choose for yourself out of the gate, you get watered down and then become (I vomit in my mouth a little) eclectic. This word disgusts me. It isn't anything. It means you go shopping and never really understand what you buy. It also means you pick the stuff you like to do and usually ignore the real work, which is, by definition, watering it down. The opposite of this, Chaos Magick, is the way to do it if you want this kind of feel but wish to do it with results. Chaos magicians are all in when they're doing it and then move on to something else. That means they include the parts they don't like and, in many cases, do a lot more work than the folks who claim it as their religion because they are immersed, and the CM has to do the whole thing. Yet, even if you choose that current, you need the 42, but only if you want to be a Stygian.

Some might struggle with what these items mean or represent. Things like linking to a Current or Egregore might be outside your system of training, or they are in there, but they don't use these terms. Knowledge is not owed by anyone, but it is also not laid out in the open to be easily gathered up. The seeker must reconcile their work to find a method to gather it. If you do have a system capable of that, then I tip my hat to you; you have my respect. If you are not working to be whole, then I cannot help you, and this book will seem inappropriate. It is advanced in terms of what it offers. You must already have a familiarity with these items to benefit fully. If you plunge into this work anyway, you do so at your own risk. You have been warned not to do it.

The Stygian Way is a lifestyle dedicated to the interpretation of my work with the Deities at the Crossroads, and so I am firm in the discipline and daily routines of it. It is dark because I am primal and feral within my sacred space to generate the power to manifest my intentions. Those who embrace and gather in the space are usually dark. It is romantic and filled with beauty and terrors because my heart and style are filled with these things. I seek out the old-world style gentleman to encapsulate myself in who I am, seeking out other ladies and gentlemen. It is not a show or a costume but an intentional mask. The mask is truth to me because I have created it and who is beneath it. My flesh is no more or less the same mask. Some may find it romantic, sexual, and intriguing, and others might be repulsed or find it disturbing, I could care less. It is not on display for others but for my mindset and livelihood. And it is fully supported by the Conclave. The rings, the clothing, the necklaces, the colors, the feel of the materials, and the intention are all on the same layer as Self. This may sound simple to some and a monumental task to others. I would agree with the latter; it is monumental, and it took me decades to align it so all of the parts agree. It is very interesting when you are aligned and you look out. It is very easy to see the unaligned parts of others and when you fall short and become unaligned. However, Stygians don't fix and don't dictate or judge. We help when asked.

Many people in the occult believe they have to hold back information. They need to not tell their secrets, which is a personal flaw that you believe you hold something like that. This is usually based on initiations and loyalty to a system, order, or coven. The beauty of this for me is that I have no such scruples. Why? Because it is a farce. I have the keys to this and that, and you can only get it through me. Where have I heard that before, and what was the result of such a statement? It is a used car salesman approach, one used by many prophets who offered very little to make a profit. In the end, the secret societies all did a lot of the same things because it is simply the nature of metaphysics and the occult. Sure, there are differences, but sitting in a room of this order or that club begins to be a very boring and useless endeavor at the whim of others who say they know. What is always missing is action. Not the pomp and circumstance that is usually present. The action is the only thing that matters. Have we learned nothing from Crowley's history? He ran up the ranks and found the shelves were bare of actual magick. He challenged them outright and their snakes had no venom. Learn from the masters!

The modern proliferation of these stuffy rooms is a ritual chamber. It is for experiments and exploration. It is a workshop and not the mahogany polishing ceremony with a bunch of asses in costumes. That gets you very little. It is also true that it takes years for you to be aware that these systems are the road to nowhere. I sought the masters first, and I cut away the fat through my engagement with their ways. The meat of their work was not worth the time or effort because a Current already had it all without the massive waste of time. Make sure you read this correctly. I am not saying any system, and the basics are a waste of time, they are required. I am saying the methodologies used by many systems you might choose to engage in, eventually, are wasting your time. So, pick wisely. And after you choose, reflect over and over. Know when to leave and when to stay. Chaos Magick was the breaking agent for me and the reasoned answer to why things work without the trappings of Western religions and angels. Even in this last comment, you will find vast disagreements with chaos folks.

You must discover this in your own way. Do not ignore modern technology or the library that is far bigger and grander than any of the geniuses of the occult possessed. But do not fall for the bait. When you have too much at your fingertips, when it is too diverse, then there is no real path and the fool is blessed and cursed at one time with the choices. It creates a paralysis, it makes the practitioner anxious, unable to choose. Do not take that approach. Instead see it as a set of baths. Immerse yourself and fully experience it without reservation. Once you understand it, then, and only then, climb out and move on to the next. It is never to collect but to gain wisdom. Study very hard on these ideas. There is a mystery worth exploring in this paragraph.

I was also very lucky. I admit it. I found teachers who knew the guru principal. They understood that they were not the end-all or be-all. They were spokes on a wheel, they were moments of lucidity, they were very necessary for my remembrance, growth, and wisdom building, and when I had sucked dry the wisdom, I must move on. I offer the same to those on this path. I am well aware that I am not Rome, I am just a port. All roads lead there and not to me. If people choose to come to my port, they get my version and that is all it is, a version. All the rest work as well, some faster some slower but they work. It is a Universal truth. You get to decide or not decide which is also a decision.

How do you decide? Well, I use martial arts as an example. If you were to choose a school before MMA (mixed martial arts), you would see a class or two. You would look to the teacher, but you would spend most of the time viewing the more advanced students. Why? That is what your goal is or why you are there. It tells you if the teacher can teach, how he treats his students, and if you want the result of that teaching. This is all but impossible to do in the occult. You will have to plant your flag somewhere. However, all the systems have a lot of the same basics, so even if you choose a lemon, you can still squeeze out something of an education and then move on with more knowledge. Sometimes, lemons teach you a great deal about what not to do. The more you do this, the more you come into your own and can move on to the second stage of self-discovery. That is done alone. You can maintain a mentor or guide, but you must enter the cave alone when you do the work to look into the mirror of your mind and come out on the other side.

Some will look at the 42 and say that they do not do this or that. I understand that, but on my path of unfoldment, these are my basics. Yours could vary. Perhaps you are an atheist or agnostic or you simply do not buy into deities as a whole. A priesthood, being possessed, or any of these concepts are outside your reference. Or you are not sexual and will not find any use for sexual magick. Perhaps sigils or guardians are not for you. If any of this is the case, it is simple. You can either look past that or you can exclude the whole system for the components. I will say that at some point, we will diverge if you are not a theist. The reasons should be easy to see by now. I am firmly engaged with deities of various kinds and they are neither figments nor psychological archetypes. To dismiss them as such is to miss the point and the advanced nature of my work. Your beliefs are your own. You may come to the work any way you like, assuming it works for you. Otherwise, it is a waste of your time and energy.

Occultists can be odd in this area. You buy a car to drive it. If it does not work, we call it a lemon. Yet many occultists gather their things, never use them, and then grow tired or worse, they then sit in judgment of those of us who do the work. I have found my proof through the years, and my work is reproducible. That, for me, is verification. I have also had my work experienced by others outside my Current, including psychics, mediums, and spiritualists who describe what I see. Again, my goal is not to get anyone to agree. It is simply to express that I am firmly committed based on my experiences. The methods I have used are acceptable for me to feel fully verified, but others are free to disagree and walk their path. I make it my business to travel among others who do not think as I do. I enjoy being challenged, and I endorse all those who work under me or by my side to have the same mindset. I readily take on new mentors and teachers for various reasons, but the primary reason is to always challenge my own beliefs and ideas.

All of those experiences have the foundation in the 42 entries. I would invite those without familiarity with these ideas, topics, or interests to make an adventure to seek them out and educate yourself fully. I would also suggest, if you are embedded or invested in a tradition, ask your teachers or leaders about it. Challenge them to offer you their best. Good teachers love this kind of challenge and relish students who do this kind of thing. Ask brazenly if you have that kind of relationship to show the depth of interest. Remember, your teacher may lack knowledge, and that is not a sin. A good teacher would then do the work with you. A poor one would rebuke you for the questions, tell you these ideas are not valid, and push you to be their very own mini-me. If you plan to be just that, it is far better not to ask and take your place like a good little copy.

CHAPTER THREE

STRUCTURE

Now that we have explained the basis of the Stygian Way and its formation, I will move on to the structural ideal of its apprenticeship and training. It was obvious in all my attention to Deity that they were using the word cult, and I did not particularly like the term in today's atmosphere. Then, as I was meditating one evening and swirling around the idea of a cult, it came to me: . That would be the coven, the lodge, the grotto of the Stygian Way. It separates us from the other traditions and does not share their words or their idea of formation and training, and it keeps the word cult in some form. It was given a k as a tipping of the hat to magick, with a k used originally by Crowley, but also the link to Chaos Magick. There is no getting around my love for all things Gothic, as well as a long history of the merging of all things within the Gothic community that are of interest to the Kultus. The marriage of these ideas seemed well-founded, and those I encountered who drew near seemed to agree.

Within the Kultus is the following apprentice structure currently and what I believe will remain in place at least for the rest of my lifetime, although when you build a system on change, nothing is 100% certain. But it must be said that the Kultus is only the structure and it is not required. The apprenticeship can be taken between two as a dyad or with a teacher and two people training together. The Kultus is helpful for those who want a group structure. For others, they just enter the Seminal Program without the structure of a group.

Grade 0: Thrall

Thrall is an ugly word, and it was chosen because it means slave. It was not chosen because it is the Way to enslave. It was the right word because it informs the person who enters that they are already enslaved. Your awareness is the point of this stage. We seek to remove the shackles you were put in when you were asleep and the ones you have subsequently put on yourself. The first set came from the moral police of your world, the second from religion, the third from your family of origin, and the fourth from the cultural or societal norms around you. The fifth comes from the limitations and additions you stacked on yourself in your current lifetime and former lives. With all this sitting on you, we begin to peel back these aspects one at a time. The more you hold onto them, the more likely you are not to be accepted into the fold. A thrall is not on probation, nor considered even for the question of entry, until they can see their chains. The dialog between them and a Stygian is centered on this. Our goal, at this point, is not to awaken them, it is to see if they are willing to do any of the work they are asked to consider or if they maintain their illusions. This process can take months, years, or end with the thrall choosing their chains over the consideration of freedom.

When the thrall does some of the work and begins to shed some of their illusions, the Stygian will offer behavioral and other changes that they can affect. If they take these cues and begin to see results, the Stygian will decide at some point if they have the worth to take on as an apprentice or if the thrall work should continue for a season or two. The extent to which the Stygian discerns and examines is very personal. The relationship with the Stygian is appraised over time, if they have prior experience with the 42 (listed in the prior chapter), where their willingness is, and how open they are to change and progress are all considered.

Thralls are not wined and dined. They are asked to do tasks and practices, and they are tested while being put under pressure. They are told things to see if they listen. They are sent on errands and not called or contacted to see if they come back or remain away. Books, films, videos, and research are recommended to them. If they do not seek out these resources, they will be sidelined. The Stygian will dedicate their time to others who are doing the work and not to those who are not focused or ready.

The experience can happen even without a direct agreement. A Stygian might consider a friend or a colleague. They might wonder about the person they are having deep talks with or someone they met at the occult event or witches' circle. If the Stygian is not a Guardian or Mistress (G/M) then they must be passed on to a teacher. Only the teacher can discern if they are appropriate for a formal discernment. Until then, Stygians are encouraged to interact and work with potential thralls.

Grade 1: Novice

If the thrall does the work and shows promise and a G/M agrees to their entry, the Stygian will offer an apprenticeship to the thrall. This is the probationer level and the place where the person is tested rigorously. The 42 are applied and it will be discerned what is met and what still needs to be done. The novice is tested relentlessly. It is the most difficult part of the training process and the one where most people crack under pressure. Responsibility and discipline are primary tools. Study is required in both book form (academic), ritual form (theurgy, actions, meditation), and personal development (shadow work and personal growth). Study and personal development come first. Knowing yourself is primary for this, and the student must take the time to determine who they are and what their masks are. Determining who you are and your motivations must be a choice and not some default system. To use the expression "their lot in life" is not appropriate here, we are seeking to be creators and destroyers, and we cannot do that while feeling we are stuck, lost, or limited. This part is painful and arduous for many. Behavioral and personality changes are often required. Add-ons like good communication skills, the ability to be articulate, to speak and debate well, and to understand your thoughts and beliefs can be added if needed. The ability to adapt or change when needed is taught and then encouraged. The ability to know who is for you and who drags you down. The ability to release yourself from personal addictions to people, things, and substances that hurt or destroy you or your passions. The removal of an external locus of control to an internal one where you run your life is essential. No one can go beyond the novice level without this. It is hard to believe, but many people do not want control of their lives or empowerment, they prefer to be enslaved, and they prefer the Thrall. If that is what results from the work, the apprenticeship will end.

The novice takes the first set of vows, known as temporary vows. Vows are made to the teacher, and from the teacher to the student. This is deemed the contract to have the apprenticeship and are foundational for the pair to work together. Some aspects are set by the philosophy and others are very personal to the teacher and student, as to what they both need from one another. The last portion is the breaking of the vows and what that will mean to each one. Vow breakers, from the dawn of agreements, is the lowest form of humanity. Keep to your word. There is a short initiation into the fold as a Novice, and entry into the Seminal Program - the basics. At this time the Novice is not fully accepted, there is no oath yet.

The ability to hear your voice and be able to trust and listen to it over all the noise around you may sound simple, but it is a major change for most people. Most people allow other voices to compel them, and they act and react based on this and not their voice, which is often shunned, discounted, and silenced. The long road of meditation, quieting the mind so you can hear and then listen, is the way to this endeavor. Once you engage this point, then we will continue to ramp up the discipline, including daily meditation, exercise, food, and water intake, and all daily living to enhance your work. Meetings with the Stygian can be weekly or monthly. If there is a group, then group meetings would also be required. If not, the dyad (two people, the Stygian, and the apprentice) would make plans to continue the Seminal Program to make sure all aspects of the curriculum are completed. Results matter on this path, so the student will move towards connection with the Current only after their development and studies are completed.

One must understand the terrain first. Meditation can be added at the same time with the new techniques. Practice is noted and journaled by the student. Questions are expected; if there are none, the Stygian will assume there is no progress and spend less and less time with the apprentice, seeking them to quit. If they do not do so or reengage, they will be severed.

The 42 are required for Thralls to complete. While portions can be incorporated into the apprenticeship as needed for certain areas, the initial teachings that did not happen or were not proficient are required within the apprenticeship. In some instances, the Stygian will explain to the Thrall that they cannot train them in the basics and that they will need the 42 to enter the apprenticeship. Remember, taking an apprentice is a rather high cost of time and resources to the Stygian - they want to only take on serious students.

If the apprentice does succeed and engages throughout their training, they are rewarded with continual materials and projects from experiences to experiments. Their journals will be reviewed, and if they complete them in tandem with the Stygian, on their own, or with an agreed-upon partner, the notes will show the successes or failures. Doing things repeatedly is helpful for success. The apprentice is asked to just do it and, at times, to not ask the questions so they can discover the answers for themselves and build their confidence. This comes up when magick is introduced, as well as divination.

Their practices will evolve, and they will determine their skill sets in these areas. The requirements then of all novices are as follows (beyond/incorporating the 42):

- Know thyself and thy voice
- Know your skills and limits, and seek to push both
- Practice all the methods, study the materials, and learn to journal well
- Reflect daily, monthly, and annually in your journal, and challenge your beliefs
- Study and know the history, myths, and traditions of all study areas/paradigms
- Complete the experiments and experiences as described in your dyad
- Learn the basic magick theory and practice including Chaos Magick basics
- Understand and apply the Stygian Way as a philosophy
- Practice the physical, mental, and spiritual workings
- Practice discipline and responsibility for your meditation and duties
- Explore your interests and bring this back to the mentorship
- Explore your limits, sexuality, and ascetics on your own
- Become well-spoken, versed, and experienced in chosen areas and debate
- Be able to be open-minded and adaptable
- Full sensory work will be completed

- Hypnosis core studies will be completed
- Experiment, understand, and move energy
- Alignment of the Three Soul Bodies & connection to Daemon
- Dreamwork, astral work, and other higher functions will be taught
- Interpersonal aspects of relations to others are discussed and mentored

If all these basics and the specifics of each Stygian are met, then they may move to the next stage/ grade. To enter the second phase of training as an Initiate, the Novice will make formal vows, moving into the Inner Circle. They will also take the Oath of secrecy and that oath is taken to the Gods themselves. Both of these major events must happen to enter the second year.

Grade 2: Initiate

The second year of training is termed the Initiate year. A year is a term of time, but it is never limited to a time frame. Now fully vowed and under oath, the Initiate has been through the initiation ceremony and is within the yard of the Stygian. The initiate is well versed in the basics and can speak the Stygian Way, understands techniques, and is within the lifestyle and discipline. They know of the rites and rituals, especially the ones that have experienced personally. They are full members in training. The Current has accepted them through this rite, and by that admission, they are now full members. They are Stygians. The work, though, has only just begun, and now the Pandora's Box of this Way is even clearer. The Deities become ever present to them as they get closer and feel more supported by the Current and the esoteric understanding is founded in something. The experience of pressure as an apprentice changes to the pressure of the Gods themselves, and that relationship shifts to primary for some. This shift is perceptible, and another time when people crack and run away. Once the deities are seen and experienced, it is too much for some, and they do not take the oath to enter. The oath is part of the initiation and is unavoidable if the member is to be an initiate in the Stygian Way. The initiate rite is somewhat typical within occult circles. The apprentice comes in, strips away what they once were takes on a new identity and name, adheres to a mask they create or buy, and reawakens to their actual dharma in life they were not seeing prior. The ritual is very personal and can change lives forever.

The newly minted initiate now turns to much more advanced work. Knowledge is not enough. Wisdom is now sought. The initiate is highly encouraged to seek out what they are in opposition to, what is taboo, and what they fear, and to face them and conquer them with new power and abandon. They are to be ambivalent to fears and always ready and willing to experience and grow. The initiate is left to their own devices in their sexuality and how they address it. Sex magick is taught by their mentor, and again, experience and practice are encouraged. For us, sex and aspects of pleasure are sacred and not negative. At the same time, they will engage in more advanced meditation techniques to the extent of their ability. The divination systems will need to be fully understood and used to a level of understanding and ease that encourages and fortifies the specific nature of each initiate. The initiate will develop their working model. This model is the daily practice (many parts are included below). The connection to Deity and the direction you feel you are headed often dictates some practices you should add and, on occasion, aspects you should remove from your practices because it is contrary to you. No Stygian is identical to the next for these reasons.

The following is a list of requirements for this stage:

- A complete breakdown of your working model
- A diary of your fears and limits, and how you have conquered them
- The deeper dive into your shadow work and how you have gained balance
- Devise your version of the Stygian Rite with your personal aspects added
- Be able to explain why you have sought and obtained symbols, guardians, and jewelry you obtained and use
- A presentation on your understanding of your personal theology
- The reason you are prepared and ready for the next stage to be a Stygian, and then the Wanderer which would put the majority of the burden of your work solely on you
- Mastery of our system of meditation, as proven by your journal entries
- Discernment of engaging the priest/priestess path
- The ability to ground, banish, and blast
- Knowledge of your key areas determined by your journey

- An Elemental understanding and practical application with your senses, directions, and other correspondences that are reflected in your practices
- Knowledge of Sex Magick, Repulsion, and the nature of Seduction
- An appreciation and understanding of the arts in general and specific areas of interest to you. A presentation of that area as an artist is also required
- Display a working knowledge of the two divination systems
- Display a working knowledge of the tools used and your personal tools
- Articulate an understanding of the concepts of the Kultus and Stygian

With the second portion of the Seminal Program completed, the Initiate becomes the Stygian. The mastery of the basics is done. Now the Stygian will slow down and turn to a priest if they are called to the priesthood of the Conclave, or they will move on to the preparation to move on and become a Wanderer.

Grade 3: Stygian

Attainment of the completion of year two is like a graduation, and grade 3 is the diploma. The equivalent of a Bachelor's degree. A master of the basics with a major has been completed.

The work is either to enter the priesthood, listed below, or to create the Wanderer list and other, more personal aspects in place to take the next steps. The teacher and the Stygian will come together in a releasing ceremony. This is to keep their connection, but it is an act of letting go of the direct mentorship and a shift to something more akin to a resource. The Stygian knows they are supported and always have that resource. It is a family bond and is akin to a child leaving the home. As we take this step (it will differ from person to person), the two will decide on what is needed as far as support. It is always on the Stygian from this point on to be more of the aggressor in terms of asking and seeking. The mentor, as per their role, is to back away. If the Stygian needs more, they need to ask for it.

It should be very clear to the reader here that this is the end of the foundational training created for the development of the Stygian unless they return to a Kultus, or return for teacher training. It is not the goal or the intention of the Stygian Way to keep its members, to seek numbers, or continue to hold people. That is where we differ. We are also not interested in the prowess of our name or the lines or lineages. You represent no one else. You are driving, and you represent yourself. You will have the Current at your back unless you do not do your duty and hold to your oath, and you will know if they walk away from you. The foundation training makes honesty and integrity potent. The Deity will be in every mirror and every action. Displease them and pay the cost. Break the oath, break the bond, and pay the penalty. The next step is the release to your own devices.

- A goal list for your Wanderer journey and checklist, expectations, and plans

THE PRIESTHOOD

Our priesthood does not fall within a grade; it can be undertaken only at the 3rd grade, but can be taken on anytime thereafter. It only has two stages: the Acolyte and the ordination of a priest. I have written an entire chapter on the priesthood, so I will not belabor it here. I will just touch on the steps.

1. If the Stygian feels called to be a priest of any of the Deities or to the Conclave itself, they will go to a priest and discuss the program of study with them. It differs depending on the priest, but is typically a two-year minimum commitment.
2. If the terms are agreed to like the apprenticeship, the priest will accept the Stygian as an Acolyte and train them within our tradition. This includes all the aspects of being a priest, master of ceremonies, commitment work, and the seer/oracle work.
3. If the Acolyte meets the time and work required, they are graduated. The rest is left to the priest and their Deities to figure out on their own.
4. Much like the mentor, the priest can always be called upon for assistance

Grade 4: The Wanderer

The Wanderer is always allowed the connection and the questions that come up. The approach of the mentor changes from the primary source person to the inquiry person. That means they often answer the question with a deeper question and put the responsibility back on the Stygian to further empower them to make their own choices, even to fail if needed. Many outside the occult see this as the "Yoda" or "sage" kind of teaching, but that idea exists for good reason. The student must transition to the practitioner and if they are not empowered, they will return to the source for everything. That is inappropriate and unhelpful to the Stygian. The transition is important, and where the deeper, more functional, and esoteric deep dive is taken. The student is becoming their own teacher, their own resource, and they must now lean on themselves. By doing this they learn to trust themselves completely.

They must rely on the goals they set, their checklist, and their daily practices to reinforce them. Many aspects will arise; loneliness, depression, the Dark Night of the Soul may return over and over, anger, resentment, fear, impostor syndrome, mistakes, laziness, impulse control issues, and much more. This is the time of walking through the Abyss, and the wanderer has the tools to come out the other side, but many will not. All along the way some will fall off the Way. We do not pity them or feel for them in any way, their journey is necessary and purposeful. There is no other way across. Liars sit at the sidelines and tell them about easier paths, shortcuts, and ways to do it better. If the wanderer is taken in by these charlatans and frauds, they will suffer. They are forewarned by the mentors. People want you to fail, they want you to be mediocre like them, and they want to pull you back into their fate. Success is a bull's eye on your back and the knives are drawn.

This is why we stay in the shadows. We stay away from spotlights and social media. We stay away from random advice and keyboard warriors. These infections are a surefire way to poison our path, our minds, and our intentions. Instead, we do the daily work, the praxis, the meditations, and the ritual work to reconnect over and over. We are filled with that in our internal work. Our external work might be a local metaphysical or Pagan store with classes and lectures. It might be an online group or in-person, a coven, a witch's circle, a Chaos Magick group, or the like. It could be a music or rave community; it might be a vampire group or some form of BDSM/Kink group. We have a very different demographic, and it is also expansive into a lot of these communities. Many of them are filled with occultists and like-minded people who share in all these communities, while others might just meet at a local Meadery or coffee shop. Or you may cross-breed religions and seek out the Buddhist Zen groups or monasteries to have people to meditate and grow with; you might go to the Hindu Temple or take up yoga. Nature may be more of your thing. The ideas are endless. All that matters is your goals, your Way, and that you are not distracted from them by mundane time wasters.

I cannot write out what the Wanderer does, as it is as diverse as a color wheel. For each person, it will be entirely different. Their goals, their art, and their investments can be so amazing. Each time I release a person to the journey of the Wanderer, and they return, I am humbled by their progress and beauty. They are the Prodigal Sons and Daughters. They are a rare and precious thing. Remember where we started in these stages? We began with the onion and the peeling away, and we are still doing that until this very moment when they return. It is only here we are sure they have completed the circle. When they return, they are ready to learn to teach others what they do. Teaching others is the gold standard. It means you not only understand the teachings and your path, but you can now teach it several ways to others to further your understanding as well as engage others on their path.

This is not the intention of most occult groups or most covens. They intend to either teach and release or get skills to a certain level and allow them to reproduce through their system. We are probably closer to witches than anything else. The intent here is an esoteric journey of the mystic through the Will of the Daemon, and one's True Will in unison. Within the Stygian Current, the wanderer manifests their individuated awakening. Deity will combine the two, and the person will magnify their Way into the Stygian. If not, they will just fall off, and that is perfectly fine by me. Attrition is the most common aspect of any group, religion, or, for that matter, anything one can join or be a part of. Some stay for a day; others stay for a lifetime. The choice is always yours. The door is always open.

The beauty of the return is a celebration and a time for stories and revelry. It is a time to share the checklist and goals, what adaptations were made, and how the outcome has manifested in the Wanderer. Eventually, the questions are asked:

- Is this it? Is your path over or are you still on a journey you must continue?

- After what you learned, do you now want to learn how to teach?
- Did you find a different way as your path and now you are leaving to further that and the Stygian Way was simply your foundation?
- What is your purpose, your dharma? Are you manifesting it?
- What is your primary mask and how does this transcend all things?
- Do you wish to be a practitioner now, a Stygian in the Kultus, and not teach?
- Define your role and your understanding of the results you have found.

These very difficult questions are walked through. The Way is new, and I have had few returns but they were all amazing. In each situation, I had zero expectations and that helped both the Wanderer and me. They decided on their next moves, and I was a support and a resource. Once the road is determined I must then fall into whatever role is needed. For some, it is to feed them, offer some advice for the road they seem to be on, and send them on their way. For others, it would be to take the next step...

Grade 5: Guardian/Mistress

At this moment, I am the only Guardian of the Stygian Way. There is no Mistress. No one who has returned has sought to be a teacher and take on the next steps, but I hope to see that change in the future. As I grow older, I would like to see many diverse teachers. I would like Guardians and Mistresses to flourish. The female term Mistress is used as the variant of master and tends to be a true master, while the male tends to be the true guard of the tradition. There is a very long history of this in the occult and several religions. I will also say these are less tied to gender than to energy. I have encountered women who could be guardians and men who could very much be mistresses. Again, historically and reincarnation-related, we change genders all the time. This is a long-term journey, not a single-life one. What does matter is the energy and the polarization of that energy is palpable and both sides are required.

This stage is the most esoteric and the most advanced. The Wanderer who returns and seeks to be a teacher is tasked with the training of a teacher. That is done at the side of a current Guardian/Mistress and is done until the teacher determines the Wanderer is ready to be a teacher on their own. They take on two or three students to Wanderer status under supervision. Teachers are somewhat born and somewhat created. The combination is the magick. Teachers must be the most open-minded and filled with patience. They must teach at multiple levels at the same time and be able to effectively have charisma and charm to help people grow. Boring, tepid lecture-makers are not teachers in the Kultus. Our teaching method is dynamic, questioning, and interactive. It encourages the students to gain a passion for teaching and to practice the style for some time so they are driven to do it. It is empowering and hypnotic. It is about feeling, understanding, and practice. Few classes or interactions are without laughter or banter. Our way is alive! It may be dark or gloomy in presence, but in theory and practice it is a carnival of fun. We work with mature adults. No one immature will make it out of Thrall status. They will hate it and split. It is there for a reason. It also kills off the assholes. Yet, we do not do it through anger or just to throw people out. We kill them with kindness and patience. The more they ride nerves, the more work they must do. The harder their stubbornness on their views, the more we challenge them with alternate viewpoints, and the more studies they need to complete that are in direct retort to their stances. We work it out of them, or they go. The more they have political or societal leanings, the more they will be thrown into the deep side of the opposition. They must conclude that these things are illusions, lies, or the other side of the same coin. Once that happens, they are no longer naive or immature. They are no longer slaves to another's point of view. Then we can work with them.

Teachers must learn how to do this through NLP, psychology, charm, patience, and suggestions. It is not to enslave them to what you think or want them to think, quite the opposite. It is deprogramming, not reprogramming. We want the trash out, and then we teach how to adapt and think effectively for ourselves. Once we do that, we challenge everyone to do their work their way. We offer options and viable ways of being open-minded but also finding your own beliefs and understanding. It is a beautiful thing to watch people enter and be around others who they disagree with. While debating appropriately without immature meltdowns and effectively speaking their minds, they are growing. The two can walk away as friends and, more, as people who respect one another. This is a needed aspect because, remember, we are in a world where this is now taboo. You are supposed to hate the person or fear them (phobic/phobia) or make up some idea to call them stupid. We have no interest in these ideas because our goal is to bring people together. Yet, we are very aware that the over-society is broken and will choose other tactics, so we have to be able to swim in those waters. Our pond is very small.

Some people cannot look at facts, consider ideas, or function outside their echo chambers, and so they become enraged, violent, or comical when challenged. That is immature and childish; we are neither, and we cannot have those people in our midst. We deal with them on the outside, but these methods are anti-social and will corrupt any group or system. This includes any discrimination of race, diversity, color, or culture. Racism is the laziest form of prejudice. You just see someone and determine what you believe about them, and this is so oppositional from the Way. We are doing the exact opposite. We are working towards total individuality and destroying all boxes and stereotyping. Make no mistake, it comes out from people who were not even aware they held certain beliefs. When you are very close to other people for long periods, you either see your faults and work on them, or others see you have no idea. You cannot come to an awakened community blind and expect no one to call you out.

These aspects of being a teacher can be difficult. I remember a few years ago a counselor asked me how I address racial issues in a world like this. They were white and felt uncomfortable talking to a black couple about their issues. My reaction shocked him. I told him to stop thinking about race, don't ignore it, and if it comes up, ask them their point of view. If race doesn't come up, stick to the skills you have and do the work. If a problem or issue is around race, face it head-on and ask if they are comfortable with you talking about it with them or if they would prefer a black therapist. If that is what they want, get it for them. Get out of your way. He asked what I do, and I told him I am very comfortable in interfaith and intercultural issues because I am well-versed and very happy to invest with the people and learn from them. We must be able to be effective and not hide when there are topics that are controversial or problematic in society. Teachers must do this all the time. I would prefer a wide arching Stygian community of gender, sexual identity, culture, color, race, and ideas. This brings a deep and healthy soup where we all gain and offer to one another. It is not to compare or step on one another; it is a place to offer each other a step up. Society always gets this wrong. I have seen it done well and want to reproduce the results as a Guardian of a new occult tradition.

The dream is to have different folk traditions and all aspects of the gambit. I would like to sit at a table and look down and feel as if the Kultus has a reply or idea based on any tradition that is offered up. That would be ideal. It is only a dream and highly unlikely, which is why I often go beyond the Kultus and visit many other groups and traditions, seeking information from those elders. I want to understand in case this comes up within my fold or just to increase my knowledge.

Guardians or Mistresses will look past limits and boxes and see the person as esoteric, they will see life. That life is a part of them as well as an individual and both aspects are respected and acknowledged. If the person puts more stock in the boxes, they put themselves in those boxes; it is discouraged as a limitation. Identity is always encouraged but limits are not. If something boxes you in and causes you to look at others or treat others differently then that is a limit. If you carry whatever identity with honor and pride; being gay, African, French, or white Anglo-Saxon, so be it. Identity, in the Chaos Current and the Kultus, is to empower the Stygian, not to cause opposition or division.

It is important to understand the role of the Guardian or Mistress. Their roles are to ensure the training methods continue and that the structure is used. It is not a dead or set religion to pass on some set of rules and systemization to redo things over and over. It is a philosophy and method of teaching to unfold the talents and wisdom within others. This difference is well worth the work. Think of it as the Bonsai tree. The tree will grow in the direction it chooses, and the wires and other methods like trimming and care are used to create beauty and art. So, the student grows with their will, the Guardian or Mistress simply helps them formulate their art and beauty as they guide them through their growth and development.

My goal is for a set of Guardians/Mistresses (G/M) to form a council, not for pomp and circumstances but to invigorate one another and to seek out like-minded people for possible growth. Each will envision their teaching methods in addition to what is taught, and this, too will help each other. Much like a high priest or priestess who will hive off, the G/M can be a way for the Apprentice to get the best person for their process. The more options we have, the better we are. I envision the Technology of a Modern Chaos Reality groups will always be so small, and we will know each other personally. Due to the structure, there is no climbing up over another. It is set up like priories in a monastic sense with no Master General. Each prior is responsible entirely for their priory. It would allow one G/M to ask for help if illness or problems develop but not some form of takeover or power struggle. This method has problems, too; megalomaniacs can be created, even by those considered enlightened. There is no perfect system. We seek to manage this in every way: the elimination of the idea of king-making, no formal head, even the founder is just another Guardian. Since attrition is the most common aspect, it is implausible we would generate crazy gurus, but nothing is guaranteed. There is also no financial gain as we do not deal in money as many traditions do. If we were an organization, we would be a non-profit religion, if we were a club, we would be a private religious club, but we operate more like a mystery school. Donations are primary, and when we do gatherings or rituals, fees are taken for the overall cost and split. We do this for two important reasons: if people pay, they tend to show, and it is unfair to those who set these things up to have to do all the work and pay for it, too.

I am asked by potential members why I would continue the work and why I would not just join a larger organization or order. My answer is not acceptable to many, but it is still my answer. When there are many, it creates a dilution of the product. I want my product to be as pure as possible, as close to Source, to the Deities, and as potent as it can be. When people walk away from my tradition, I am not angry or hurt by it; I feel that it was probably a good decision for them. I remember reading about what shamans endure, what Aghori endure, and the nature of Druid training, and though I am not claiming their traditions or the depth of their commitment, I see the work as similar. I am not those things or those traditions, and we do not have a means to them in this country. There are no funeral grounds, there is no oral tradition of the Druids to follow, only what can be discerned, and many of the methods of the shaman are illegal here. It is also very true that, culturally and socially, this methodology is not accepted at the moment. I believe that these things are a pendulum, and they will return as the New Aeon approaches.

G/M has a great deal of work to do. They must maintain their temples/ritual chambers. They must continue to engage in the Current to the

Gods/ Goddesses as a religion. They must do all the practices to keep sharp and engaged, or the Deities will simply go away. They must teach when asked and serve the Kultus in that way. They must be touched by the spirit, be ridden, and be dedicated priests to their patron and matron. They must be able to evoke and invoke. They must have a vast knowledge and openness to be able to work with the various traditions the Stygians and lower stages bring home. In short, it is a lifestyle of commitment. In addition, they must deal with all their mundane work to care for families, to be parents, or what have you. There is a plus side, and that to me is that they are continually sharpened by their work. They can be cutting-edge because they are challenged often, and it is invigorating work.

All these aspects compose the articulation of the Stygian Way. It speaks to all the steps and the way of training. It does not include initiatory information or hidden gnosis because those things are not for the public. Rites and rituals will also not be included because that would hold no power or reasoning for the public. In the following chapters, I will continue to discuss philosophy and practical approaches. As I peel the onion further and further, you will easily see why this path is not for everyone. It simply would fall apart. It was always made to be for a certain segment. I seek to always speak to and seek that segment, but I also wish to speak to those on similar paths and with like-minded paths who would befriend and understand us and seek us out as friends and colleagues.

****

This is the culmination of my UPG and VPG experiences. It is consistent with what the Deities have asked from me and will continue to be my work until I am no more for this body. I have no intention of seeking out members unless the Deities ask me to do that. I listen to their council as I do to mentors and teachers. I am always willing to change or pivot if needed. This apprenticeship is always available to those who seek it and are prepared for it. The 42 are not a joke and are expected in anticipation of any apprenticeship. If they are not possible based on some form of limitations, there can always be exceptions or guidance given until the student is ready.

CHAPTER FOUR

MEASURING WHY THE STYGIAN IS NEEDED

This chapter is the most important one to me personally. It is the reason behind all that I have been doing my whole life, often without realizing it myself. For me to explain it competently, I must explain the idea of Currents, an oath, and the reason for a cult, any cult, to be needed. I must also describe why now, why Stygian, and why there is a need.

A cult fills a hole. The Christian cult filled the hole for people who wanted to look forward to something in a life not worth living for so many. They wanted forgiveness, and they wanted a code to live by. Modern Wicca, in its way, was a retort to the Christian cult with a stretch to a more organic and nature-based life that was more akin to the old Gods. LaVey's Satanism was a pushback against the Catholic Church more than any other cult, but also Christians in general in the right time and space. Cults do that, they fill gaps and inspire. The same can be said of the Theosophical Society and many other organizations like it, from the Rosicrucian to the Spiritualists. Even movements like the Hippies and the Summer of Love were there to fill a gap and hole in society for those who were misunderstood, hated, abandoned, or thought to be less than. The same is true of the Goths of the 1980s, and it is interesting to watch the trends now are much more positive as that culture returns.

An oath is a commitment by blood, word, and deed. It is an agreement that is not easily broken and always has repercussions if it is. Many occult organizations use oaths or vows as part of their initiatory process, and the Kultus does it too. Our oath is directed to the Deities and held by them, and not a group, medium, or organization. Because of that, the Kultus is not made to be a Daddy shaking a finger at anyone. Each Stygian knows their ethics and rules of order, and if they break them, they must deal with the Deities. No one in a collar is waiting around to "forgive you." This is a human flaw, asking others to hold us accountable is seen by the Stygian Way as a weakness and an inability to discipline yourself. We teach how to do it, but like all practices, it is up to the person in the darkness of their choices to make their own decisions. Keeping to an oath is of high value to Stygians. Breaking them or your word is akin to what it used to mean in days gone by, it is seen as a betrayal and a weak character. Because of the sentiment around oaths and the serious nature in which we take them, it must be said that taking an oath into a Death and Chaos Current without taking it seriously is rather stupid.

But what is the Current? I have given some information on it, explained it as an egregore, and then described that. But what does it mean to the Stygian? When we look at the impact of these Currents on the Stygian, we must understand where this comes from. Our Deities come from the riverbank of the River Styx, including Charon, and all of these regions lead to Hades and the Underworld. There are no coincidences. These Deific beings were not chosen by me. I did not practice necromantic rites before this and had no intention of going in that direction. I was aware of descents in the Underworld through the stories of varied Deities but did not seek to follow or entertain this kind of suicidal progression. The Deities are not aware or cognizant of this, as they simply know better. When you begin to understand them a little better and trust them, things move rapidly.

I was led to the works of Chaos Magick and did not realize I was doing a great deal of it without ever having read a thing. Then, over time, I was pulled to blood magick, which I also had no interest in. It is hard to describe, but it felt as if the puzzle pieces were being put together for me before I could wrap my head around them. I remember thinking when I read about the disciples of Christ as a kid that they were idiots. They got it wrong all the time, and they could not figure it out. What hit me like a shovel is that is exactly the way it works. If you are heartily in control and your ego is leading, you are doing it wrong. I was the vessel, not the driver. The driver, if working beyond their current level of understanding, should not be leading anything. It is folly to follow such leaders, but many do. Let go and become a vessel.

I knew being a vessel was the right answer, but I believe many are given the same message, and then they turn to their neighbors and friends and see if others are doing that. If those people are not doing that, and it is beyond the pale, then they become afraid. Enter another puzzle piece. When I was a child, a teacher asked in my class who was influenced by what others thought. I remember looking down because I couldn't care less. When I looked up, everyone's hands were in the air, and I knew there was something different about me. I thought at the time that something was wrong with me. That puzzle piece was in place, so I didn't care if others let go or what they did. If it worked, I would do it. I recall trends coming and purposely avoiding them, choosing others on purpose. I did not want to lead trends. I just did not want to be a follower.

I seemed to be fit for what was happening. It was not just fitness, though. It seemed I was primed in the right areas. I was trained in Buddhism, and I learned not to fear death. Through many practices, I also leaned into Tantra and again found peace in the idea of death. In my own life, my words often made people uncomfortable that someone so young was not afraid of death and would talk about it openly. I believe this opened me to the Death Current and the Underworld. I also believe this is not an accident. These aspects were thrust into my life so I would learn them.

When the Dark Father came to me at the Crossroads, I was familiar with both the Chaos and Death Currents. I had felt them and experienced them a few times in my life already. What I realized in our dialogue is that the Stygian Deities were ever-present but were never the ones written about or worshipped. They were the peasant deities, the ones who worked with midwives, witches, and sorcerers in the dark alleys. They were the confidants and unknown powers that people feared and did not understand. They were the ones labeled demons or dark spirits. People had enough to fear, and so they looked to Sun Gods and positive deities. They were not interested in the darker sides. There are a ton of examples of this, but one you can find easily is the rites of Hades himself. They would not use his name, referring to him as Pluto or other names, and they would look away if they did dark curses or sought his help because of their fear. He is not alone, but his story speaks volumes. He was one of the three Olympian brothers, and yet he has no high tales, and he has no great temples in his honor. There are some, but they do not match Zeus in any way. These are the Deities of the Stygian.

It is also their time. It is their Aeon; it is the time of chaos and turmoil, a time of great change, and a coming new age. Before that can happen, the world must be prepared, changed, and rightly attuned. For that to happen, there will be upheaval and the changing of the old guard, old religions, and old ideology. That is why the Technology of a Modern Chaos Reality is here. It is to bridge the transition. It is to be an option on the other side. We will need a deep understanding of ourselves and our intention, or we will fall under someone else's machine and be assimilated into their ways, and not into an individualized world with great liberties and reason. The war seems to be over emotions versus reason, and if emotion is to win, as it has for a time now, it will be madness. Do not misunderstand me. Feelings and the ability to flow in a state of lucidity are not the enemy. The idea that what we feel is our reality, no matter how demented or obviously wrong it is, can only be described as illogical nonsense. Yet, in the modern world, it is not only accepted by governments, media, and the medical profession but also by mental health professionals who have all equally lost their minds.

Equally interesting is a large portion of the population who have turned to some form of magick, witchcraft, and the occult. There is also a lot of chatter in left-hand path areas around increasing interest and engagement in many dark aspects, including the Lilith path, Luciferians, and others who are feeling an Underworld Current. I believe this is part of the Chaos Current but is mostly the Death Current. Like any Current, there is no set pattern or path. It does as it likes. The Stygian Deities are present in these Currents, and I see them as having influence, but they are not alone and acknowledge it. I believe the recreating of old religions and Pagan traditions has missed some of the real applications. In recent months, I have viewed a few YouTube channels of Pagans, who I believe are doing it more elegantly and real than what came before. They tend to be young women who have immersed themselves fully into a tradition and live, sleep, and bleed it. It is quite impressive. It is also quite feral and unique from older writings that were made into standards.

The feral nature of this is also present in the works of men like Lee Morgan, Robin Artisson, and Roger Horne. Newer and more compelling versions are also being written and pull me in for different reasons. All these authors are writing from a Trad Craft reference point. Two women, I would add, are Gemma Gary and Shani Oates. All of these writers are exceptional, and their methods draw me much deeper than the works of writers from the 80s or 90s. We needed those writings then, but we have moved on, and ironically, I believe from my experiences, the newer versions are more authentic. I also believe that is due to the Currents. It is bigger than any one author or any one path. It must be this way. That is why we must come together and not be kept apart by some form of limitation, bias, or prejudice from one to the other. The Kultus does not keep to its own long. We do so in our foundational training, but then we are instructed to move out, to wander. That includes experiencing other systems and traditions.

The Chaos Magick world talks a lot about science. That never interested me. I am more interested in the arts. I link the Current to the arts, not the science. It is from art where feelings develop: music, paintings, eroticism, dance, theatre, and so on. Even the written word is an art form. These things create Currents, egregores, and religions. That is what I saw in the Dark God and the Dark Goddess; I saw their art, their beauty, and so much more. If we know it comes from art and we devote ourselves to the arts for this reason, the two merge. They bridge logic and feeling. Emotions (i.e., reactions) are the result but are not the art. We, Stygians, respond; we do not react. We train ourselves to do so. One has poise and skill. It looks at the facts, considers, and with thought, responds. Being reactive is just spewing on others.

All these aspects I have discussed fit into the foundation of the training of the Stygian. Each part is like the instruments of a symphony. Each has its part. Every note, every break, and every pause are left to each player to maximize the feeling and content of whatever we are doing. It is our art. And just like a rock musician or a Gothic band, we color ourselves and dress ourselves to suit. We wear makeup or masks, we put on boots or strip down to nothing to project the art to an audience of one, ten, fifty, or just the Deities.

Why do we do that? For what purpose does the Stygian Way have? You must answer that question yourself. My answer is simple. It makes me alive. It makes me a Stygian and a priest of the temple of the Deities. It is my purpose in this lifetime. It is my art. It is my magick. It is my love. And in the end, it is my thumb in the eye of those who repress, seek to enslave, lie to us, manipulate us, and limit us in all forms. The Underworld is going to have its day soon, and all those Deities will become more and more accessible. I am their vessel, and it is their time. That is why I do it. That is the purpose of the Stygian. It is to ratify and put their work into flesh.

It must happen now because now is the Kali Yuga at its worst. It is the time when a transition must take place. A golden age is to follow. It will not just happen to us. Like all things in life, there must be a spark, a change, and a mission to make things change. I need it like I need to breathe. I need it because I see the unrest, the hatred, and the ability to hurt one another openly. I see the lack of restraint and the willingness to cast off logic, thought, and consideration for the glowing screen of stupidity. It must change, and it will.

CHAPTER FIVE

THE LIBERTINE

As we crest the hill, we look back over our shoulder at the basics and the facilitation of setting ourselves up as individuals, surpassed by a city, society, and the family system we came from. This is the footing, the grounding. Then, we turn back toward the mountain that lies before us. Our next journey is to get to its peak and the peak of the innumerable peaks beyond this one. This work has no end. One rock betrays the one you had before, telling you a deeper tale and giving you a more solid link to what you seek. The art of discarding what you rely on is key. Everything is expendable. At its core, this is a solo journey. No one follows you to the grave, the Abyss, or to the holy ground. We are made to be social creatures but not all animals are social. Lemmings, sheep, and antelopes are social. Yet most apex predators are not when they hunt.

From the 1600s to the 1800s, there are writings and a history of the use of the term Libertine. Like the term pagan, it was a negative. It was used by the elites, the clergy, and others to refer to those who moved away from the church, thought for themselves, denied sin in the way the churches saw it, and became individuals. As always, they added their judgment with terms like licentiousness, perversity, and a lack of ethics and decorum. Many have had this moniker, and some held it with relish while others sought to discard it. Who they were is not relevant to this work as a whole, but I will discuss a few of them. I am more concerned with what the term means and how I would pull it out of relative obscurity and use it as a sort of badge of honor. That may seem strange, but if you think about it, it very much falls in line with what an occultist or witch is and what a rebel is. Both are in the shadows, they are not mainstream, and they are considered other or odd. Their ethics and decorum are not the same as society, and they are often ostracized for it. Often the over society adds all the sins they can muster and projects that onto them as well. Stygians fit firmly within their company.

The sad and lost aspect of the Libertine is we have lost the plot of who they were, why they were, and the impact of them. There are people within all aspects of the occult community who fit too well into modern society. They are in essence, the elite themselves, acting as if they were with the rabble, the peasant, who they do not understand at all. They take political lines, even when those lines never serve the peasants they speak for. They take social and fiscal stances for what their needs are, while the actual peasants suffer. Those are not Libertines, they are false!

My favorite libertine is Uncle Al himself, Aleister Crowley. Here we have a man who gave no shits. He did not care about others' reactions or, more likely, relished in their discomfort. He followed the line that there is no such thing as bad publicity, all of it helps sell your image and doctrine, and it certainly worked for him. Even within Victorian culture, he did not struggle with sex with men, women, or anyone. He did not suffer fools. He did not pull his punches. He was very unlikeable to the average person, but then again, all geniuses have this issue. They are often misunderstood. He was a writing fiend; he poured out more information than is imaginable from the *Equinox* to his books, ceremonies, rituals, and writings about Thelema, he also blurred through the occult organizations of the day in record time. His Gnostic Mass and religious arm, as well as all his formulations, are what make Magick assessable today. Hate him all you like, but give the devil his due. His works were one of the inspirations of Chaos Magick until he fell out of favor. I retain my love for the man because of what he stood for and what he accomplished. I can separate personality from knowledge. As a libertine, he was a gentleman and a scoundrel all wrapped in one. He was an individual, a scholar, a writer, a poet, and a magician. This cannot be discounted or countered. They are simply facts. We have the books to prove it. He held his ethics at a time when they were criminalized. He sought chaos at times, controversy, and power. He did these things with reason and intent. It was not random. He was extremely skilled and is an amazing example of a genius. No one is perfect, and whenever there are amazing feats, there are amazing flaws.

The second man I will refer to is more of a rebel, Dr. Christopher Hyatt. Again, he is very misunderstood by many. His books, ideas, and especially his interviews showed his genius in the understanding of the world around him and the elitism that infected it. Hyatt was sarcastic. He was the rebel, the individual, the psychopath, as he defined it. If you have not read his books, that is a tragedy you should remedy. It is difficult to take in. He was quite different from Crowley, yet somehow owned a similar genius, in my opinion, at times, with even more depth because he was of the modern age and just knew more. A hypnotist and Reichian therapist, he was a fountainhead of information. He formed a great publishing house, and from him came several other great writers. Hyatt referred to much of humanity as "monkeys" in interviews. Unaware and unawakened animals who had no idea what was going on. There is so much insight in his work, and he seeks to awaken people from their slumber. A student of Regardie himself, Hyatt is not far from Crowley either. Yet his own opinion on him is not as high as my own.

For Crowley, the work was academic and deeply esoteric, making it difficult for others to comprehend. He was so thick and heady because of how he spoke and thought, based on interviews and biographies. Hyatt, on the other hand, was sarcastic, a trickster, and sardonic. He was brilliant. Yet, there is room for both of them. I would consider them both libertines and rebels. Both rebelled for different reasons, but both were exceptionally effective in their way and their Current. I am by no means putting them up to some standard of the way to go or the greatest method to follow. What I am saying is more like what A. O. Spare might consider, or R. A. Wilson, that these people had an impact, so I must extract the beauty and wisdom from the parts I do not want to do again. For me, there is less of a breakaway because I have no problem with rebels and libertines. Why? Because I consider myself one.

These two men are not the end. They are simply two of the most well-known figures. When I turn further down the path of the esoteric and the mystical, I run headlong into the Gnostics, the actual Indian Tantrikas, and other visionaries who rebelled against the state, government, society, religions, and methods of enslavement by religion, others' ethics, and a monopoly of elites who decided (while the rest were neither represented nor listened to), what was right. I will not out anyone. Those who know will know who they are. I will partake in the Tantrikas and the Gnostics to further inflame the point.

The Gnostics, who had many different strands, were in opposition to the Church's direction, and over time they lost the battle. A belief that the Earth is a storage facility and in league with the devil for some, a training and testing ground for others, and a difficult hell that must be endured are a series of beliefs from the various sects. Others believed no children should come forth because we want out of this awful place. Some also kept to the belief that priests should be allowed to continue to be married, that reincarnation is factual and should continue to be a church belief, and many other doctrinal variables. The Cathars, being one of the versions, saw the greed and wanton actions of the Church as inconsistent with the Christ they followed, and so they were killed for their troubles when St. Dominic could not preach it out of them. My beliefs and theirs do not coincide, but again, they are the rebels. The variable of thought and beliefs that direct all to look closer at the problems. They put their foot in the wheel of greed and a society that breeds fear, guilt, torture, and menace to those who disagree, creating a Protestant entity that was all too ready to return the favor. Humanity tends to learn little but an eye for an eye. We might have had a revolution and saved ourselves hundreds of years of incestuous institutional perversity, a church that backs slavery and criminals and that markets same-sex relations as sinful while housing much worse practices. Instead, the others were silenced and killed off so they could continue their work. No religion is all bad. There are, of course, amazing people from all the churches who have nothing to do with any of this, and they should not be tarred and feathered by history, but that does not erase it either. Those who stand up have good reason to do so and should be heard as we continue to allow these powers to have more and more power as we have less and less. We are not empowered to have voices but to be silent. Tyrants flourish in this environment.

The Tantrikas were the opposition in India and were based on the books called Tantras, their sacred texts, or, more accurately, their metaphysical occult texts. Americans and Europeans decided to take this oppositional and very powerful system and turn it into a bizarre sex cult. Like most Asian customs, we tend to get them wrong. That is not the Tantra I am referring to. The

Tantrikas of India were esoteric, against the idea of classes and the caste system, and would take women and "untouchables," which was unheard of in India, into their sects. According to some sources, they would also take criminals and anarchists. They were esoteric and very different from the Vedic and the usual religion of the priests in the majority of India. Their work was a way to break from society and the caste system and religion of the time, not to offend or make others fear them. It was not about others; other than the fact they were outcasts with those same others. It was about their path and the need to break from norms, society, and their fears and limits. From the outside, though, these people ate foods they were forbidden, they lived on funeral pyres and burning grounds, and their deities were the darker aspects of the yogic spectrum. These aspects can be very difficult for the Western mind to understand. A large pantheon of deities is difficult enough, but the large number of weapons, heads, blood, and symbols of death is often too much to take in. To make it more complicated, many of the Deities had different aspects, even different colors. For the Tantrikas, it was not intentional as it is for Hyatt or Crowley, but for those looking in, they look like libertines and rebels. Their actions are rebellious, but their hearts differ from those of Western magicians in many key ways.

The reason for this chapter is to provide a backdrop to the philosophy and effectiveness of being an individual and working within a group in the Technology of a Modern Chaos Reality It is an overall philosophy I am introducing to you and a very personal one. The libertine means different things to many people, and some might even call it an outdated term. I am recoining it in the following way:

- A belief that the state and the country hold a method of control over the people, or, most abruptly said, slavery of the mind, body, and spirit
- A belief that the individual is far more important than any box, chosen by the person, or their community, via personal choice and assigned to them
- A knowledge of who you are first, then and only then a determination of your ethics and compass of what morality you adhere to
- The ability to take actions to extricate yourself from society's rules to ensure your trajectory in life, the idea that your life is yours, and you must follow your path

- A philosophy of realism over negative or positive, right and wrong
- A profound intention to move towards your intended "enlightenment."
- An understanding of the physical body, its use, and its beauty
- An understanding of the mind, psyche, and the arts; poetry, literature, art, music, etc.
- Critical thinking skills, strategy, and philosophical cognition of options and reality
- Comprehension and use of the Seven Hermetic Principles
- Belief in self as the experimenter, experiencer, and action-based individual who seeks like-minded individuals to sharpen your skills
- Extremes are sought not for the sake of their effect on others, but for your ability to break your fears, limits, teachings, and embedded philosophies you need to remove, and the effect on you
- The ability to see beauty in the darker aspects of life
- The ability to see death as a stair step on your path and nothing more
- Full knowledge of astrological, psychological, and personality, and a deep reflection on who you are, and then the ability to change and modify
- Cutting away everything that does not serve your path and purpose, including people, ideas, home, job, all of it
- The ability to speak the truth as you see it and modify it if corrected, and you agree, with this the ability to be both humble and sure of yourself, and silencing any need to convert others to your way of thinking
- A style of your design, on purpose and for yourself alone; it may be clothing, jewelry, personality, flair, conviction, charisma, or the like
- An artistic mind in any area where you can derive passion and expression
- A defined presence and way of being

These aspects may appear odd or frivolous to you. They may seem like a lot of work or things you already do. They are, in fact, all congruent with the libertine I am and with the Stygian Way. I would add that compassion trumps all other emotions. The compassion I refer to is volatile and not simple. Compassion may be to allow others to suffer, to experience, to fail, to flounder, or maybe to offer help. Compassion is not sympathy; it is not even empathy. In the world of the

Stygian, compassion is the metaphysical connection and feeling from one person to another (or inward to ourselves) to objectively and honestly do what is best for yourself or others, regardless of its impact on you. This is ratcheted up if that person is considered family by blood or otherwise close.

I would also add that my dynamic has changed over the years and will continue to change with age and wisdom. All things are in movement and should be so. All these characteristics are not in place to annoy or pester others. They are not a means of causing others to be uncomfortable, yet they might cause these results. It is a side effect and not the effect. The effect I am looking for is liberty from groupthink, control by others or societies, and pulling away from what elitists force upon others while not enduring it themselves.

To fully understand this, we must confront a very uncomfortable topic that cannot be ignored. Most of the occultists I have spoken to privately would readily agree with what I am saying and deny it fully in public. That is fair. However, my work does not allow me that coverage. I must unceremoniously expose our society's brokenness. It is beyond the repair of a few window dressings and some pillows. We have misguided people who are running things and wanting to run things. We have violence, war, inciting of wars, corruption, and politicians spending more time in court because everyone is suing everyone. While we live in such incredulous times, it feels more like the Middle Ages, and we are in desperate need of our Renaissance.

In the mundane, some look to anarchy and revolution, but that is just a pipe dream in our current incarnation. Governments could just push some buttons and send drones to do their bidding and never even bloody a soldier. It is just as ridiculous to say we keep our arms for the prevention of tyranny. I must inform you that it didn't work. Tyranny is already here. One of the candidates for president is a convicted felon, and the other one never really ran for president; she was handed it like a door prize at a party. What do people do in such a case? They allow the implosion of a failed government, endure, and try to correct it when we rebuild. Hopefully, other countries will not invade and destroy us in the interim, but they probably will. No one likes any of this, but that is why history is not optional. We must be students of history and understand the outward importance, or we are enslaved by it, and we fall into the same cycles over and over.

We are soaked in ignorance and lies in the meantime. We are inundated with influence and psychological warfare to further separate us, while leaders use derogatory terms for the other team. They also seek to make us inert. They want us drugged out on cannabis and drink. They want us to take our medication, and how else could we deal with them? I am not just saying all this to further people's anxiety and worry but to offer options. We do not look to the source. We look to the outcomes. This mind game is indicative of our society's failures and it is not esoteric or magical at all. Unless we cut out the root and see where the root is, the same rot will infect us.

The mystic, magician, and yogi all look to the source, not to the outcome. As Stygians, we throw our lot with them and do this because we realize if we do not sever the source, then the outcome will just come again. People become distracted by those who tell us how to interpret. We miss the point, and so we endure the same thing over and over. This is our history. We gnash our teeth over the policies of the government we hate because we are told to hate one side and not the other. When the other side screws us, steals more of our money, destroys the economy, and ignores homelessness (or worse, shows it to us and tells us it will be fine), the people just reelect them and don't seem to notice. How immensely insane we have become as a people. We are told we are broke. The country is in a miserable debt we cannot get out of. Both sides of the aisle agree. Then we have a pandemic where many die, many suffer, and the entire economy of the world suffers. On the other side of that pandemic, something changes. Oh, we have billions again, and this time, they are for everyone else. What about our people? Oh, the elites will make their money from the wars we are planning and the other nefarious methods to monopolize. We are not even going to hide the corruption now because what are you couch potatoes going to do about it? Yeah, there are homeless and out-of-control prices, deal with it! We are not going to do anything this time. Hopefully, the increased suicide rate will take care of the problem, and then we can ship in people who had it much worse, kill off the middle class, and go right back to slavery with a whole new set of people. Feudalism worked, right?

If these suggestive comments woke you up, that was their intention, and they are very libertine. If they did not, it might already be too late for you, or you already knew, and it is not shocking anymore, which is shocking if you get my meaning. No one is hiding the playbook anymore, but what they are saying and what they are doing is reversed. Fear the Republicans! They are going to do this terrible thing, then moments later, it is the Democrats who do the same thing they told you to fear? Given the same opportunity, the Republicans do the same thing. They are the same coin with two sides. They all play the same games, and they all get money from the same folks. They are elected actors, nothing more. The problem is they suck at it, and we keep reelecting them because we don't know what else to do.

This is why all these rebellious groups came into being. They saw the problems of governments, religions, and societal norms, and they could not stand by and allow them to continue. They had nothing to lose because it had been all taken from them already, and we are preparing Generation Z for the same outcome. I am by no means and in no way stating we need a revolution of violence or anarchy to cause chaos. At this point, it is the establishment that is the chaos and has been for many years. It needs order. We must find a sane and viable set of people to reverse the chaos so liberty, honesty, compassion, and viability can again prosper and be attractive to the general public. We need leaders who will turn their gaze away from the shiny things they can bomb and destroy and cast their work on the people, domestic issues, and the curbing of spending outside to heal the wounds of what is within, the source of the pain. Why does that matter to a libertine, a rebel? Well, we all do much better when we can all prosper. Violence and dread foster breaking the laws, and more chaos erupts. This is the Aeon of the Kali Yuga, a significant time of devastation, uprising, and what comes after? Re-order always. The Technology of a Modern Chaos Reality vision is to be a darkness that can issue forth the light to bring people together, a small band of people who do not eat at the table of lies and prefer to create and grow from the sidelines, preparing for the light to arrive and making it through the storm.

We see the same dystopias in films where the chaos is just below the surface, or it is the highlight. It is the hero or sometimes the antihero who brings order. The Jedis, *Mad Max,* and Neo characters are in so many different films. There is a struggle, and so many lose the fight. Even in films now, the hero's story has been replaced by chaos, continually leaving us with the feeling that there will be no end, no positive outcome. Leaving us with no hope is now a plot line. When hope is gone, the soul dies, the want ends, the passion evaporates, and the possibilities darken. For the occultists, magicians, and mystics, this is akin to true death without any prospects. Most people who are not occultists don't do this kind of manifestation, so if you take hope from them, they are lost. We must write our myths or generate our paths through the wastelands. For me, that is the new path of the libertine. Also, it must be said that hope is not our way, but it is the way of the masses in general, and very important for them. Hope is an allowance for others to act, it is a way to disempower you. Occultists and witches seek action instead so we can create and manifest. Hope is left to those who are not willing to act. The Stygian does not live on hope and sees hope as a poor vision. We retain the idea, though, in art, stories, myths, and ideas, not for us but for generations to grow and prosper.

In the past, it was French salons. It was art and music, literature, and the pursuits of the gentry. It was the sons and daughters of money who could change course if they had the passion to do so. It was the hippies, the rebels, the Bohemians, and the like who threw caution to the wind and did as they pleased. They also spent a great deal of time in prisons. Now, it could be the tiny home communities who homestead, the witch and pagan communes who join them, and since the mystical and magical are increasing in numbers, this might be a new pattern in the years to come. These people continue to reincarnate and must be led back to their prior lives and their work so we can generate the beauty the world can be and less of the reincarnated dynasties of killers, tyrants, and elitists. Wars will never end. It is simply a fact that we will always have people in different stages of development. Time is not actual. It is not on a line. It is a made-up concept. In the same way, the environment, the planet, and all the Chicken Littles of the world who cause anxiety and worry for themselves and others, need not fear. Just as Mother Earth is not inclined to keep humanity forever, there is no forever, there is no clock.

The Libertine takes their attention to things which matter, to their development, to their experiences, because that is why they are here. They are not politicians, they are not attorneys, even doctors. This imposes the world on them. They seek to impose themselves upon the world. Power, security, art, and the beauty of things. These are their endeavors. Are you a Libertine? Are you a Stygian? Or are you among the mundane?

CHAPTER SIX

EXPERIENCE

The major player in the world of a Chaos Magician is experience. Those experiences are developed through experiments and paradigm shifts. They are found in discussions and in cooperation with others of like mind. That is the foundation of what the Stygian does. Today, there is much more to this discussion. We must talk about what these experiences foster and destroy in ourselves and others.

An author from the 90s wrote a ton of books concerning his UPG. The overarching communities debased him, rejected his work, and told him, in no uncertain terms, that his vision and work were not real. How insane. Yet, he was not alone. Then social media came about, and the lunacy came out in full frontal nudity. Emotions and one's point of view are now all that matters, so people tell of their experiences with deities, and somehow, their audience eats it up. UPG is now like a cookie. It is eaten by everyone. Yet, no one sought to revive or apologize to this author I will not mention.

These rather large jumps also allowed for the dissing of people from the past. We moved to a Presentism perspective where we judge everything through our current position in history. We eliminate the inconvenient truths. But why? It feels like it just strokes the ego and the maniacal narcissism that is so normal now. It is perceivable everywhere if you pay attention. People seem to pay no attention to others, seem clueless about their surroundings, and seem to care less for the most part. The classic example is the coffee shop drive-thru. The person in front of you makes their order and pulls ahead just a little. Not enough for you to make an order. You wait through and then the person gets their stuff and again, pulls up but does not pull off so you have to hit the horn or go around them. The entire time they look down at their phones like trained seals.

The other day, a car stopped in the middle of the road. Both the male who was driving and the woman got out of the car. Both left their doors open. Three cars were behind them. They got their stuff, had a conversation, got stuff out of the trunk, and then kissed goodbye. There were five parking spots within ten feet. Finally, the male walked around the car a few more times, got in the car, and drove away. In another incident on a very busy highway where it is common to wait at lights and not be able to go because there is too much traffic, a man waited as the light turned red. A car behind him, without looking, almost hit me, as the girl who was driving pulled in front of me, upset he did not go. Her boyfriend (I assume they were very young) was screaming at the other car through the entire light, and then the guy threw his drink at the car as he jumped up and down in his seat.

Now, you might be saying that these incidents are random or they do not happen that often. If you live in a major city, you might be saying, oh, that was a Tuesday. What is my point? My point is that these people have no idea that they are not acting out based on these narcissistic tendencies because they believe they are the only ones of importance in the world. These are often the same people who regularly argue and fight for other people they neither know nor understand. It is so incredulous that I am often lost for words.

The reason for this is we no longer have our own experiences. We have experiences through screens. People have jobs where they play video games, and others pay to watch them. Think about that. We watch television around people doing something: cooking, fear, dating, etc., and we live through them. This blunts our experiences and makes everything all about us, so is it any wonder that when we venture into society, we act out? I don't think so. We are also told the sky is falling regularly: wars, weather, violence, and the link. Is it any wonder we have an anxiety epidemic? With these and all screens now used for so much of our work, it is almost comical when a person says, "I think I have ADHD." You think? Let me share a secret with you: we all have ADHD now. It is not because of any other reason but the results of our society. You can still look at manual laborers, the Amish, and others who are not tied to screens for their livelihood and can find people without ADHD. But within the norms of society, good luck finding people who do not meet the DSM-5 criteria.

The reason this matters so much to the Stygian and should matter to everyone is because of the results of the impact of these influences. If people are selfish and self-focused. If people are not looking and are not concerned about what is around them. If we have mountains of corruption and no one is willing to change it or correct any of it as the people suffer, then what eventually happens? This is not a place for growth and stability. This is not a way to raise children and offer them opportunities. The link to trust in our leaders is at an all-time low because they keep lying to us. Who do we turn to? It becomes a situation where things begin to look bleak.

The cold and dark answer is always change. Change is the thing so many fear, yet it is the way out. The Stygian Way is change incarnate. It is the system and philosophy of change. It is also the philosophy of experience and of having experiments. It is a way to test your beliefs, your intentions, and your goals. It is done through UPG and VPG. We do not reject those, but all things must be in balance.

There is a difference between a six-week intensive with a deity where you meditate, journal, and petition the deity, and Lilith showed up at my school auditorium when I was bored. Could that happen? Sure. The problem is when next week happens, and the deity who shows up is Cain, and you just make him into the entity you made up and have no idea where the concept comes from. You also don't research it and are just ready to argue that it is your UPG, and that makes it real. There is a difference between serious occult work and theatrical demonstrations. Now, don't get me wrong, marrying the two can be very powerful. But that can only be done through real experience and not something you are doing to get clicks.

That is the problem. How do you, as the audience, know the difference? You don't, and it doesn't matter. If you watch these things, then watch them for the entertainment value. Time is the arbitrator. Does this person switch deities like swapping underwear? That is a clue. Eventually, it becomes clear who the real thing is, but again, it doesn't matter. The only thing that matters is what influences you let in, what your experiences are, and what you are after. If you balance yourself on these principles, then it is just a difference of opinions.

People who get angry about it, who become keyboard warriors, and who have an axe to grind are simply stuck in their position and are unwilling to allow others to develop or to outright lie. Why? For me, I would platform them and allow them to hang themselves. Show your inconsistencies, show you cannot answer simple questions, that you do not research or know your stuff. Once you have that out in the open, people can judge for themselves. Just remember what I just told you about mental and emotional health: the public is not well, and it is not through any fault of their own.

When I was much younger, it was the norm for people to visit mental health clinics to get their diagnosis. They did that so they could box themselves, name it, and claim it. I thought it was a terrible idea then, and I still do. Consider this:

- It is because of my x diagnosis, and I now have no incentive to change or improve
- I didn't take my medications, so my x made me do that
- I am too old to change now
- That is just the way I do it
- I have diagnosis x and so the prognosis is bad so I am just waiting to die
- I am neurodivergent
- I have ADHD so you can't expect me to do that better

This list could go on and on, and it is by no means everyone. I have worked with hundreds, maybe thousands now, who wanted to change and do the work. But now and again, people who limit themselves settle into their box and even use it as a shield or an emblem of their limits. They are their greatest enemy. Their experience has now limited them, and they cannot get out. Today, we have added to these diagnostic limitations by parading in race and gender to further the limits. It is not sold that way. It is sold as a kind gesture, but the psychology doesn't change. If you tell people they cannot for long enough, then they give up. That is mental slavery. It is psychological warfare. It is wrong. It makes you believe you cannot change your outcomes, and if you do that to people for a generation or more, you break the generations over the knees of the limitations.

Psychology and magick, occultism, and medicine used to be in the same box. Now they have been moved to opponents, and for good reason. We cannot have people thinking for themselves. We cannot have occult-informed therapists who know better than the games endorsed by government-influenced associations who own their licenses and their careers. We cannot have people who see why medications might not be the best course of action. Unfortunately, the majority of the occult community has bought into the same political positions as the rest of society. That always perplexed me because it seems to me if any group should know better and would be able to see outside the box, it would be them.

I have offered you a great deal of information about influence in this chapter. I want to now break it down and offer some options you could take to offset limitations. I also want to empower my readers to think for themselves. Do not take my word for it. Do your research effectively. Why effectively? Where are you going to find a thirty-year occultist with a Master's degree in psychology who did not buy into what was sold to me in graduate school, who took a doctorate in sexology and went to an interfaith seminary? We exist, but in my experience, most of my colleagues drank the Kool-Aid, and their hearts died a long time ago. Their hearts were sold to the profession, higher education, or business. I get it. We have to eat, too. They certainly are not going to lecture or write about it. Someone has to. Yes, I will be canceled, and no one will read my work. I know. Libertine, remember? I don't give a shit. Truth is more important. But what happens to those who stand by their convictions, look up Wilhelm Reich.

Allow others their experiences. Do not silence others. Do not see a need to rip them apart, especially if they are young. If you do not have the same experiences as others in your group, do not doubt yourself. We are supposed to be different. Offer yourself compassion and be patient. If you feel judged or not understood, you are in the wrong place. If you constantly have that experience, seek out an occult-informed therapist. Work out what is happening. Don't give up. If you hate your practices, stop doing them. All occult practice should be an act of art and passion. Use mentors, teachers, gurus, and peers for your growth and development. If they impede you, then they are not a good fit. They need to feed you and not starve you. Remember, we are all human, and we make mistakes. Humanize teachers, do not deify them. Fall in love, write in your journals, make mistakes and learn from them, grow! Be someone other people look forward to seeing. Be kind. Be honest. Be yourself. Don't be your diagnosis or an amalgamation of your family by default - choose, change, and develop as you and your Higher Self deem worthy. Understand and experience lust and passion. Do not limit yourself.

If you allow these experiences while being open, the world is an open book, and you have the stylus to add to the story. Don't just read, write! If others do not like what you wrote, that is an incentive to write more. Remember that most people hate change and are committed to being sheep. If they like what you wrote, it is probably in line with everything else. Break boundaries, fracture limits, destroy aspects of you that you dislike, be disgusted, and ask why. Don't allow cowardice to override your impulses to be fun, childlike, and inquisitive. Learn your ethics by experiencing them and not by taking them from others. If a person tells me they never curse others, I ask why. If they tell me a story of how they did it and what they learned, I am impressed. If they tell me they were told not to do it, or they were warned and scared from doing it by others, or they do not see a need, I feel as if they have limited themselves and growth is needed.

Stygians are not cowards. We do not have that luxury. We are challenged by peers and teachers alike. The very foundation of our work is to push the limits. Because of these factors, we have the benefit of experience. We did not stop at "you shouldn't do that," instead we read it as: why not? Then we went ahead and did it or at least turned to a teacher and worked out why. This is not a case of a child with his hand close to the light switch. It is a case of breaking norms because we have no idea why they are there in the first place. Again, it is looking to source and not to outcomes first. For instance, there is nothing wrong with the Witches Rede and Rules on its face. But why? For the common Chaos Magician, that is not going to work. Stygians follow that same idea, but I will say that some find the Rede to be compelling and keep it. That is not a problem as long as they know why.

These statements are not to be judgmental. Anyone would understand why people would not want to stare a five-hundred-pound behemoth in the face and say, NO! All I would ask is very simple and has been around forever. Look around you. Are you in the group that are judging and violent? Are you in the group that is being judged and receiving the violence? Almost immediately, most people shift to the group, nope! You can't know another's experience, and you certainly cannot believe the narrative of biased media on either side. So, you only get you. You only know your lens. Stay in your lane and do what you know. Honestly, look at your own bias and behavior. Is hate present? Are party lines present like you have a team? When you begin to unravel this, it becomes very clear if you allow for it. The majority set the narrative. The majority is almost always in the wrong. If you are a witch or an occultist, I don't need to explain that to you. The sheep follow the money and the way away from discomfort because that is their goal, not truth. They are always in a place where there is little knowledge and no wisdom. I know this sounds harsh, but it is essential to be honest. Disconnect from this and turn off your devices for a month if you can. Reconnect to nature, to your relationships, and to the music you love. Then, go back and look at it. It is overwhelming and horrific what most people will find, myself included. You will realize how much terrible influence you allow in and how it biases you.

Let me take a moment to break this down further and align it into step form. I am saying a lot of things at once and philosophy can get confusing. This is NOT prescriptive, this is how the Stygian is trained. Do with it what you will.

1. Know yourself and have awareness of yourself. Do your own work and eliminate the habits, behaviors, and ideas you find to be unhelpful, corruptive, or destructive to you.

2. Push your limits then. Do not stay. Achieve, grow, question, and do not rely on your beliefs; make sure they are still true for you. Achieve the goals.

3. Once you know you further, play as a child, challenge and play with others who are like-minded within the Kultus or within other groups.

4. Never assume another's lens or experience. Do not take on their flag, allow them to do that for themselves or you rob them of their journey. Support is positive, taking over is ego.

5. Always stay in your lane, not my monkeys and not my circus, do not assume, do not offer, and do not seek to control another. The only exception to seeking control of another is if they impede you, seek to harm you, or have defined themselves as the enemy to you or yours. Do not offer opinions, judgments, or help unless consulted or asked.

You are not alone. Billionaires, to the best of scholars, are bamboozled by the level of lies they accept as facts. These people have access to the resources and the research, but they never access it or consider it. It is easier just to rely on others. We are pulled on in so many ways and seek to put our experiences in activities we enjoy and in entertainment. What a different world we live in than those who do not work the land, do not eat, and when droughts mean death. Yet somehow, we can judge and castigate another's experience. Let's not do that.

This book is built on my own experiences, and I neither expect you to accept or reject them at first glance. What I would ask is that you consider your own practices and traditions, and you come to your own work with more options. I can only write from my experiences; this book is for that. Write your own experiences into being. And if you know you are lying to yourself and others, stop. If you are unsure, experience impostor syndrome, and are trying, keep going and find supportive people to encourage you.

CHAPTER SEVEN

SAYINGS

Because the Stygian Way is a philosophy, it is important to note how we think. This list of sayings or responses are things I have picked up over the years. I do not claim them as mine, nor do I claim them as rigidly correct. As I said prior, insight changes resolve. If I find something to not be true, I discard it. This list is a way to relate to my journey and, through that, the founding of the Technology of a Modern Chaos Reality and Stygian Way. I share it as a way to assess your own beliefs and thoughts. Discard what does not work for you and keep what does until it does not. Remember, what is foolish today might be wisdom tomorrow and vice versa. I will also say this is a minor list and is not inclusive of all sayings. It is also the ones I still find relevant as of this writing to ring true.

- *Every thought you have either lessens you or increases you*
- *Meditation is a skillset for clarity, balance, and a bridge to gnosis*
- *Time is an illusion, it is not a line, it is manmade, not God made*
- *Society is a set of manmade rules and can change at any time, the powerful make us believe it cannot so they can imprison, control, and have their power*
- *The more advanced a practitioner, the more childlike they become*
- *The more gnosis you experience, the more you lose time, the more difficult it becomes to have mundane relationships*

- *Do not take on the projects of another person, it is not a kindness but your own weakness that is at play, allow them their own experience; failure, or success*
- *Keep people of the highest vibration around you, specifically where you sleep and live*
- *The most difficult journey is the one to joy; it is the most elusive, we tend to like misery*
- *See all things as a part of you, do not divide, enhance*
- *Know that life is not living, it is a death march, so have gratitude each day and joy will be possible. Do not and drudgery ensues*
- *Seekers use their methods not chance or hope, use a method with more success than failures, always experiment and experience*
- *How you see and interpret things is far more important than anything else*
- *Positive words repeated (mantra) quiet and direct the mind and stop the chatter*
- *You were there even in the Darkness, before the Light*
- *So, we are immortal, it takes so many lifetimes to manifest anything, and we are creators and destroyers at our core. People mistake the vessel for reality; it is a simple vehicle for a lifetime.*
- *You must learn your desires and wants, and how you are impulsive to circumvent them; they must be merged with the Daemon to place them in perspective, for balance and wisdom to flourish, expelling and burning away what is not useful*
- *Reactions are an admission to a loss of control; we react because of our interpretation of an incident or encounter, we add intent by others, and reply by allow our emotions to react. We must be aware of this to respond and not react.*
- *In many traditions, attitude is not taught. Here it is, you must be immovable as things happen. The observer, if you are easily corrupted by emotions or*

whim, you will never have peace or balance. You will allow others to determine your attitude and fate.

- *Many believe due to other myths that the astral is external, so they add the word travel, but I say you are the entire cosmos, the Universe, so all is inward, there is nothing outside you*
- *Look to the East and how they see the Dead. The Tantrikas and the Aghori have it well in hand. If you maintain your fear and die, you will struggle with your death. Death must be embraced and acknowledged and not feared.*
- *What you ingest manifests in how the world looks to you. When you fast things become clearer. If you ingest poisons, garbage, and other items, you will not function at your highest frequency or level.*
- *Nothing, by its nature, is positive or negative, it is what you do with them, if you carry them with you, that weighs on you, carry lightly or not at all*
- *Your life externally is the same as it is internally, if you live in chaos, then you are chaotic inside as well. You must clean up one to clean up the other.*
- *Mystics, sages, yogis, and Stygians do not see nations, politics, or wisdom as other people see them, this gives them all a burden that is not understood by most*
- *Understand your dream world, the symbols, ideas, and messages, and ask the deity about them, from them, you can grow*
- *All things weave together and connect, so any energy spent on improvement in one area improves the overall state of the vessel*
- *From Buddhism, we take a lesson. With the bell or ring 3x per day, we settle in stillness, in silence, and just be. Do this for twenty seconds and resume your day.*
- *The Observer is disaffected and detached; this allows for all things without an emotional reaction. The goal becomes the understanding that you are not the mind or its thoughts. Occultists can disagree and see all through the mind, they have not risen to the next level yet.*

- *Stygians are of the Lunar Cycle, so we follow the path of the Moon. Spring and Fall bring our power points because they balance and are essential.*
- *You choose to learn by suffering or through wisdom, the majority choose pain.*
- *You can never know what you have not done yourself, experience is the mother of all teachers. One must destroy thoughts that limit them by exploring and expanding. Without movement, there is only entropy, and eventually, the body dies.*
- *At waking and before sleep, actively speak a positive incantation and allow it to roll over you like a wave, use a mirror to see yourself do it, and never stop doing this*
- *See all people as your teacher, positive or negative, they offer you the opportunity to consider yourself and reevaluate your thoughts and actions, or you can choose to keep old patterns and not grow*
- *Stygians are not evangelical. We do not seek to change others to our way. Fanatics do this because of their deficits, seeing themselves as helpful. Instead, we offer our authentic selves and if others see us and want what we have, then we can offer guidance at the level they request it and not beyond*
- *This plane of existence is a trial of work we are set to undertake*
- *The occult wisdom falls hard on societies. We begin with the mind as the master and not the heart, wisdom comes before emotion and not in reaction to it. Love can bring fools and folly.*
- *Review your life annually, then go to the issues represented and meditate on it, neutralize it by asking for forgiveness and seal it, detach yourself and let go*
- *In the occult, the discussion is often, what is the work? The work is to soften your karma or the energy you carry from life to life, to follow your will or dharma, and to practice walking between worlds so when death comes you are used to the travel and can function there and reincarnate, remain or move on. The views on how this happen are left to the individual and yes, it matters. If you believe you are going to hell, you are. Yogis, meditators,*

occultists, and mystics find all of these practices to be much more comfortable and not jarring.

- *The term Highest Self is aka your Daemon, Holy Guardian Angel, or other such titles, they are all the same. This entity is the bridge from your personal relationships with deities, and spirits, and eventually to cross over.*
- *There is no duality, right and left paths, positive or negative, good guy and bad guy, so I find it easier to separate by words. Duality is couched in emotions which are uncontrolled, reactions, while non-duality, or the observer mind is couched in feelings. Feelings are considered, contemplated, and can be responded to or not because they offer a choice and not a reaction. This is not only a psychological but also a spiritual truth.*
- *Live without expectation, it is difficult to do but allows you not to be rattled. Do not expect the Gods to show up, do not lust for results, do not extend yourself in money or ideas, and expect the result you want. Life is a fountain you throw coins in. Do it with intention and focus and then walk away, never giving it a second thought.*
- *Often people give up too early or stay too long. In one case a person told me they spent seven years waiting for their Goddess to arrive and saw and experienced others- too long. In another case, I would see a person coming to train monthly and they had a new God each time- too short. Balance is the key, half a year is more than enough to ensure the deity is not coming, if they are not, move on but leave the door open.*

Quotes with references:

- *Anyone who has the power to make you believe absurdities has the power to make you commit injustices- Voltaire*
- *The wisest people follow their own direction- Euripides*
- *Those who cannot change their minds cannot change anything- George B. Shaw*
- *There is no exquisite beauty... without some strangeness in the proportion. -Edgar A. Poe*

- *Do you not see how necessary a world of pains and troubles is to school an intelligence and make it a soul? -John Keats*
- *You see things as they are and ask, "Why?" But I dream things that never were and ask, "Why not?"- George B. Shaw*
- *It's frightful that people who are so ignorant should have so much influence- George Orwell*
- *Let everything happen to you: beauty and terror. Just keep going. No feeling is final. -Rainer Maria Rilke*
- *The problem with knowledge...is its exhaustible craving. The more you have it, the less you feel you know. -Olivie Blake*
- *Lock up your libraries if you like; but there is no gate, no lock, no bolt that you can set upon the freedom of the mind. -Viginia Woolf*
- *A person hears only what they understand- Goethe*
- *When you fear something, learn as much about it as you can. Knowledge conquers fear- Edmund Burke*
- *Pain and suffering are always inevitable for a large intelligence and a deep heart. -Fyodor Dostoyevsky*
- *Yes, I am a dreamer. For the dreamer is one who can only find his way by moonlight, and his punishment is that he sees the dawn before the rest of the world. -Oscar Wilde*
- *And those who were seen dancing were thought to be insane by those who could not hear the music. -Friedrich Nietzsche*
- *And once the storm is over, you won't remember how you made it through, how you managed to survive. You won't even be sure, whether the storm is really over. But one thing is certain. When you come out of the storm, you won't be the same person who walked in. That's what this storm's all about. -Haruki Murakami (Kafka on the Shore)*
- *Out of suffering have emerged the strongest souls; the most massive characters are seared with scars. -Kahlil Gibran*

- *Never be afraid to raise your voice for honesty and truth and compassion against injustice and lying and greed- William Faulkner*
- *Life is full of questions. Idiots are full of answers- Socrates*
- *The best answer to anger is silence- Marcus Aurelius*
- *If the truth shall kill them, let them die- Immanuel Kant*
- *When a man cannot find a deep sense of meaning, they distract themselves with pleasure- Viktor Frankl*
- *If a little dreaming is dangerous, the cure for it is not to dream less, but to dream more, to dream all the time. -Marcel Proust (In Search of Lost Time)*
- *A high degree of intellect tends to make a man unsocial- A. Schopenhauer*
- *I love you as certain dark things are to be loved, in secret, between the shadow and the soul. -Pablo Neruda*
- *I am an excitable person who only understands life lyrically, musically, in whom feelings are much stronger as reason. I am so thirsty for the marvelous that only the marvelous has power over me. Anything I can not transform into something marvelous, I let go. Reality doesn't impress me. I only believe in intoxication, in ecstasy, and when ordinary life shackles me, I escape, one way or another. No more walls. -Anais Nin*
- *Man's mind, once stretched by a new idea, never regains its original dimensions- Oliver Wendall Holmes*
- *Courage is resistance to fear, mastery of fear, not the absence of fear- Mark Twain*
- *Self-reliance is the greatest gift a parent can give a child- Virginia Satir*
- *When you judge others, you are revealing your own fears- C. G. Jung*
- *Don't bend; don't water it down; don't try to make it logical; don't edit your own soul according to the fashion. Rather, follow your most intense obsessions mercilessly. -Anne Rice*
- *But better to get hurt by the truth then comforted by a lie. -Khaled Hosseini*

- *There is no experience better for the heart than reaching down and lifting someone up- H. Jackson Browne*
- *Character is what you are; reputation is what others think you are. Reputation is from other people; character is from you- Thomas Jefferson*
- *I gain strength, courage, and confidence by every experience in which I stop and look fear in the face... I say to myself, I've lived through this and can take the next thing that comes along... We must do the thing we think we cannot do- Eleanor Roosevelt*
- *The gods have two ways of dealing harshly with us- the first is to deny us our dreams, and the second is to grant them- Oscar Wilde*
- *Happiness is easy. It is letting go of unhappiness that is hard. We are willing to give up everything but our misery- Hugh Prather*
- *Do not accept what you hear by report, do not accept tradition, do not accept a statement because it is found in your books, nor because it is in accord with your belief, nor because it is the saying of your teacher. Be lamps unto yourselves. Those who, either now or after I am dead, shall rely upon themselves only and not look for assistance to anyone besides themselves, it is they who will reach the topmost heights- the Buddha*
- *Value judgments are destructive to our proper business, which is curiosity and awareness- John Cage*
- *Beyond a certain point, there is no return. This point must be reached- Franz Kafka*

I do not resolve or explain the purpose of these quotes, ideas, or philosophical statements. As in all things Stygian, it is up to the reflection and translation of the person to determine that. It is not important what others think or suggest, this sullies the work. You must do it on your own. You must contemplate it and consider it again and again. I recommend many works to people once I get to know them. Some are to reinforce where they need more support. Some of the references are to vex, challenge, or piss them off because they cannot see aspects where they need to push or are stuck. It could be Shadow Work, it could be defects of character, or it might be that they just need to widen their disposition. I do not do this to judge them. I do it to challenge them. That is very Stygian.

CHAPTER EIGHT

PHILOSOPHICAL BEGINNINGS

This chapter follows the sayings because it is about philosophy and an approach rather than any kind of dogma or explicit teaching. It will not fall into some form of factual right or wrong. It begins a set of meandering tales with introspections and what I would term "scroll-like" ideas instead of solid actualities. There are very good reasons for them, but I will let that play out for you in your readings and your mind. I am offering them because they fit the model of the Stygian Way. It is also a necessity in reading this kind of book, meaning the person reading it is expected to have a certain level of knowledge, experience, and dare I say, wisdom. If not, then you will probably miss a lot. I have read and appreciate these kinds of books. On one occasion I bought a book randomly and it became my "bible" for ten years. I read it twice a year and read all the recommended books in it and the three books that followed by the author, numbering over five hundred volumes and it was worth it. Each time I read it again, I learned more and more as I experienced more. I have followed his tradition, there is a bookstore in the back of the book. In case you are wondering, that book was *Path Notes of an American Ninja Master (1993)* by Dr. Glenn Morris. The other books I am referring to here are the philosophy and esoteric books he recommended, and others I have picked up later on.

In my work, I have founded the Stygian Way through my interactions with Deity, and that is the only system I will be any authority on. All other aspects are my personal experiences, any mistakes or wrong assumptions are my own. In over 35 years in various communities, I have inadvertently or on purpose taken great ideas, and they no doubt sprouted in my dreams, psyche, and gnosis work. That is called living in the world and gaining experience. I neither apologize for being human nor do I expect any different from those who read my work, learned from me, or who have worked beside me. The goal for all of us as humans is to grow and exceed, so by all means, if my way works for you, please take what you need. I realize this is a different tactic from most, and they often seem surprised at my candor. I am sharing it with you now because this is how I write and how I think. I am not a miser or some mystical mind who thinks I have some secret sauce that is quite Universal, and most people who have done enough work are quite aware of it. It is also based on my gnosis with the spirits, guides, and deities who populate my world, and they want the door open, so open it shall be.

My journey, as I have stated prior, is within the Chaos and Death Currents, and I see the Technology of a Modern Chaos Reality as a teaching group that came out of it and the Stygian Way as its philosophy. I tend not to be a joiner and tend to suck the juice out of a system and then make it my own. Having a set paradigm and just sticking to it when it no longer serves a purpose seems rather idiotic to me. My greatest work tends to be solitary, except for two examples I will share later. CM is the realization of modern magick for me, and it is the system I would say that I adhered to the most over the years. There are many methods I have pulled from to create my own, and I freely admit it. I also admit that my methods may not work for you, they are not made for you. You should create your own, but to be creative, you must have a firm foundation to create. Even the greatest artists were taught the basics. The text is practical and goes straight to the more radical. It does not spend time with any basics. It assumes you are already familiar with them. If you are not, you may not understand a lot of the underlying ideas. But you are in luck as a beginner because most of the printed books available in the occult are written for the person new to the occult. Choose one of those books first and form your foundation. If you are a bit braver, and you must be to do any of this, seek out a teacher or group to support your journey.

This is not eclectic. I rather loathe that word. I realize it is readily accepted, but it sticks in my throat. Eclectic means you have no idea what you are doing, and you are throwing things at the wall to see if they stick. That is not at all what I am doing. I am very carefully learning all aspects of each system, culturally, religiously, socially, and practically, looking into all aspects and then, and only then, determining the beauty and the luster to see and behold. At that moment, I may choose to stay for a year or a day, but what is very clear is that I offer respect and credence to the system I am engaging in, or I will not enter. The interesting thing is, I know for a fact some people who call themselves eclectic do all these things too. I just hate the term.

In determining what tradition to enjoy, I check the water first to make sure it is for me, but when I jump, I jump in the deep end. For me, this is akin to what Sri Ramakrishna did with religions to ascertain there is indeed a Universal and understood Godhead from the monolithic religions to determine they are valid. I am not looking for that validity as such; I am looking for something different. As a mystic and a sorcerer, I am looking for other things. I am seeking mastery of the self, the identification with Deity, including gnosis through evocation/ invocation, and a deep dive into the Abyss. The methods, I believe, vary by person. There are no exceptions because we cannot see through another's perspective, and I believe that manipulating people through coercion into following your way is a human error left to those who seek to be herded. Yes, we are taught that we want to be herded, a label, a group, or the in-crowd. We should not follow these ideas for our journeys into the void. Sitting beside one another and doing all the same things without attunement to purpose and individuality is a cult, no matter how many participate, what symbols are on the wall, or what chant is held.

Now, some will say that cults are bad, but not so. A cult is how we created societies, and it is a broken system but one that seems necessary for some to this day. Some are still killing in the name of… (a song made famous by *Rage Against the Machine* pointing out the implications of the results of doing this poorly). The Kultus, by its very name, is a cult, but what kind of cult? The kind of cult matters, as does its intention. Don't get caught up in labels or names, look deeper.

Cults come from tribal culture, and it is very evident we are still very much a tribal culture. From sports teams to politics to just about everything, there are perceived good things and bad things. That very thing can be colors and a flag or team colors, or it can be the difference between life and death when picking sides. Look to the Middle East and the hostilities on both sides. Look to Eastern

Europe. Is it not based on cultic determinism what we do? The establishment leans towards Team A, so if I am with the establishment, then the other country is evil. I pick up their rhetoric, slogans, and mantras. If I oppose, then I see all of what is happening as evil and see the other B team as the real problem. All of these things are cult-like. These are the kind of cults we are not and do not want to be associated with.

The Technology of a Modern Chaos Reality is the manifestation of the Stygian Way and is our working coven, order, or whatever term you prefer. It is created for the benefit of its members first, and by their work and support for one another. The Kultus is not interested in the sheep, the fawns, or the humans who wish to remain asleep. They serve the purpose they were intended to serve and are of no consequence to us. The only exception of this is their mistreatment of their duties and the breakdown of society to make it unsafe, unreasonable, and further broken. The Kultus speaks to those who seek liberty in their minds, bodies, and in their lifestyle to create, destroy, and fall in love. Not some lust-filled action (there is nothing wrong with lust or pleasure), but a deep love beyond what many have experienced. This cult is more of a circus, a place where anything can happen on a stage, in fact, it is your stage. You are the performer and the audience. I am not saying we are performing in terms of theater, although psychodrama is an acceptable idea and bridge in magick, what I mean is we are not boxed in. Much like a circus act, each person masters their work and who they want to be. They are not trying to outdo others or run people against each other. They are all trying to be the best act, the best performer they can be. I want to give you the visual of someone driving themselves to their best.

This book will refer to the "work" but also to various patterns and cycles. We must be experts on how to circumvent some and destroy others. I am a Universalist by nature, I simply see your version as another road to the same place I am going. Assuming you are heading to some form of growth and progress. There is never a need for judgment. If what you are doing is not working for you and you continue to do it, then for me, that is insanity, or you are simply asleep or uninterested in a spiritual life. It is not my place to judge that or for the most part, even be aware of it. If it works for you and the stage you are currently residing in, then you are doing it right. Once you are at a certain stage, you no longer need the nod from a superior. If you are not open to growing or learning, you are limiting yourself. That is entirely your choice. Some want to be knocked out of that paralysis and others do not. This is a book for the former, not the latter. If you are happy where you are I will simply annoy you. If you are interested in change and development, come on in!

I must address the elephant in the room, which is the inclusion of anything mystical and religious engaging with chaos magick. It would seem anathema to many a chaos magician who often sees the mystic and all they represent as religious. While the magician may carry out rituals and engage deities, their belief is engaged in the moment, but often, they do not see the deity as actual. They see it as a psychocosm, a psychological reproduction of the self, or some other method that could make them atheists to most people or at least agnostic. There is so much out there for religion, why bring the mystic and the magician together in this way? For me, it is a natural progression. I had no idea I was a chaos magician other than the language. I had been actively doing it since the 90s. Even more ironically, I had a few books on the subject sitting on a shelf and never read them. It was via the work of Steve Dee and Julian Vayne that I first caught sight of similarity. When Dee wrote *Chaos Monk (2022),* I had put the pieces together by coming at these things through these British writers. I read Humphries & Vayne's *Now That's What I Call Chaos Magick (2004)* first, and it led me to wonder and read the books of Phil Hine and Peter Carroll. There it was, in black and white. There was no getting around it. What got me excited about reading these authors and relating to them became clear. My old teachers either read them, or they too were in their own world and did not know, I will never know as they had already passed on when I came to the understanding.

For me, it is about the experience, and I cannot reject the experiences I have had as a figment of self or imagination, even facilitation or magical manifestation, it is just not right in my head. That is the only place that matters, as there is no set objective reality within a sorcery context. Oh sure, we are not talking about the bus coming at you. We can all see the bus and the impact. That is mundane reality, and the laws of physics, gravity, and others all apply. I am referring to the metaphysical and the cognition from person to person. They are not the same. Many believe they are. I am not here to argue. I am simply expressing my experience and perspective, take it as you will. And just for the sake of clarity. It would be much more in line and easier to promote if I were an agnostic or an atheist. It is far and away more difficult to express to any population of people that there are spirits, entities, and deities. Especially when they are not written in lore, history, or in shared traditions. They would have worked before writing. Now it seems odd to most.

CHAPTER NINE

AN AUTOBIOGRAPHY

It began for me in a small New England city in the late 1970s. It was in the mall at Walden Books- no longer in business. My first books on the occult were the usual- Richard Cavendish's *The Black Arts*, Aleister Crowley's *Magick Without Tears,* and Anton LaVey's *Satanic Bible.* LaVey, more than anyone else, got my attention. Cavendish seemed okay, and I did not understand Crowley, but LaVey made sense, a lot of sense, and that threw me. I still have that Crowley book and the 1972 *Satanic Bible.* It wasn't just the books, though. It came to me in films at fourteen. It came with Roger Corman, with Vincent Price, Alfred Hitchcock, Stephen King's *Salem's Lot, The Lost Boys,* and all the horror and occult films I could find.

It was a great time to be a child, and I took full advantage. My father was a huge horror fan, especially B-movies. It led to films I may have never seen or heard of. I also had the influence of Dominicans, nuns, and Jesuits in a very Catholic community. I knew I loved rituals, robes, incense, candles, and the feel of energy. Something always felt off, but I had no idea what it was until many years later.

At the time, my faith felt like it was steel. I recall that between the ages of 5 and 7, each day I would ask God to simply take me. I would prefer to be with Him. I would prefer paradise because, for the most part, I didn't like other kids. I found them annoying and made my way into the convent as much as I could to be with the nuns. I had strange visions after an eye surgery. They began in dreams and then manifested in visions of Gods with snakes, in blues, and deep black. One particular recurring dream was of my mother turning into the blackest one, with talons, a long red tongue, a belt of heads, and she had this wicked cleaver. She hunted me. I remember letting her catch me and turning to face her. She cut off my head.

This was all very esoteric, and at the time, I was very unaware of what it all meant or why it was happening. I do recall sharing it with my priest and telling him I wanted to go and be with Jesus, and he did not discourage me. He told me to pray about it and offered to keep talking with me. He was an excellent support for me. I wanted to be a priest because of him.

Many years later, I encountered a statue of Shakti-Kali and almost pissed myself. You have to understand, when I grew up, there was one phone line for two floors where families lived in the same house. This cannot be comprehended by many today. We had to go to the library to seek out encyclopedias. There were no other options. I had no idea who any of the Hindu Gods were. Somehow, I dreamed of them anyway.

Finally, at seven, I told a very amazing nun about these prayers and ideas, my experience with the priest, and encountering Kali. She was an excellent confidant. She expressed that I was influenced by martyrs and was seeking to be one. She helped me study them. As I did, I did not want to be a martyr, so I withheld my prayers for death. I turned my interests to history, religion, English, stories, and myths. I had a deep dislike for math and science. I found them to be pointless. Clearly not an alchemist or classic magician.

I liked words, poetry, music, literature; those were magick to me. At fourteen, I met my first witch in Boston, who said he was an Alexandrian. I lied about my age because he was twenty-one. He believed I was older, and since I was six feet tall and never carded at any door, I apparently looked the part. He believed me, and we met at some occult stores in Boston. There were very few then. He had read and understood Crowley and helped me understand it. He also liked LaVey. He understood my interests, and I always looked forward to seeing him. He told me about his coven, but I had a very quick reply. I did not want to join. I gathered more books from my interaction with him, specifically the Farrars, and began to do some of the practices with him and on my own.

Everything I seemed to try with spells worked well. I began to believe I needed to be careful with what I did, and so I sought very little. I was studying martial arts then and noticed that there was a lot in common. The meditation I began so young was helpful for focus and intention. I had studied Buddhism and mindfulness, which also helped. However, just like the coven, I knew I was not a Buddhist, but I did the work and learned a lot. Breathing, relaxation, letting go, releasing attachments, and inner peace were a solid foundation. The series *Kung Fu,* with David Carridine and *Kung Fu Theatre* on the weekend, also showed glimpses of monks and Buddhism. They encouraged me to continue the work.

Life moves on, and I am moved to the Bible Belt in 1991, and it feels like 1982 again. It was a very difficult transition. I had only been to the other states in New England. Trains to NYC, to Jersey, trips to Maine and Vermont, then to Pennsylvania and New Hampshire a few times. Salem was a dream, and I looked forward to going each time we went. Tennessee felt so foreign. It was a different world and taught me to adapt, to be alone at times, to isolate, and I meditated more and more. It forced me to be an adult. I needed money, a career, a direction.

By 1995, I had found my primary teacher. I had encountered several schools and teachers by that time within the occult and witchcraft, but to my surprise, my teacher was within a religious mystical order that had begun in the UK. It used a lot of Celtic Gods and imagery, but kept away from the reconstruction of Druidism that was popular at the time. We stayed away from the masses, the major communities at the time. Interestingly, a lot of the elders I encountered were teachers, professors, professionals, musicians, and some classic hippies. It was musical, ritualistic, and a great deal of fun. Was it right? No idea. It ended in 2015, when the last of my elders passed on, but honestly, it was long dead years before that.

We practiced meditation, yoga, breathing, intention, focus, the arts, magick, spells, astral work, energy work, shadow work (called dealing with your hidden shit), and we did ordeals in the woods, in the water. It was initiatory with ranks, and we were encouraged to read large amounts of information, to experience all we could, and we were taught how to teach. I still use a lot of those skills today, and I use the mentorship methods and visions of that order. I spent ten years with my teacher after the first five years of training with my partner. They believed in a dyad method of duality, male and female energy, and we used this energy a lot. We formed many "magical children," and it increased the egregore, a word we did not use, and it increased our own power, energy, and outcomes.

The order was the only one I encountered that rejected Jewish mysticism, monotheist religions, and, of course, the Cabala and Tree of Life. These usual bases of ceremonial magick and the trove of Thelema incorporate all of this at some level. That means no angels are sought, no four watchtowers, no Elizabethan magic, and no grimoires. We reached back further. It was shamanistic, feral, wild, archaic. It was replaced with Eastern mysticism. Some did use the Norse Tree Yggdrasil to mimic the Tree of Life. I leaned to the East, and when I saw Donald M. Kraig's last book, *Modern Tantra,* I wondered if my mentors/teachers had spoken to him because we used the Sri Yantra. It was a hidden secret, now in print. Perhaps AMOOKOS or the other Tantra/ Magical sects used it? I don't know. I do know it works without angels of any kind. There was no connection to Christian theology or religion, and that is exactly what the order wanted. Because it came from Europe, they were well aware of the impact of Christianity on the Pagans. They did not want any residue from the Judeo-Christian base.

The order saw monotheists as poisons, killers, torturers, zealots, and as seeking totalitarianism. There is no room. The idea of a Christo-Pagan would make my teachers so furious. The conflict was too deep, the bodies stacked too high, for them to see beyond it. That doesn't even touch on how many they killed of their own over different opinions. The mystics can always find common ground in faiths, but their God is full of menace, death, war, jealousy, and violence. Blood thirsty beyond anything else. His angels, demons, and heroes all come with their taint of that history. The order sought aspects of the Aghori, Tantra, folk practitioners, Taoism, the witch, shaman, and archaic. These practitioners, mystics, and natural practices were not out for the same power: nations, cities, or control. We sought an enlightenment path, an artistic path, that had purpose. We looked mostly internally. The external was mostly illusion, but a means to use the flesh to manifest was very different than anything I had experienced at that point. That is how we saw ritual, and for the few of us called by Divinity, now we were priests.

Don't get me wrong. There was no active prejudice or malice towards the monotheists. They are the majority after all. It was simply a recognition of their brainwashing within their customs and teachings, and the results in their followers that we disassociated with. They seek to actively convert and tell you that you are wrong, so there is no real room for dialogue. You cannot blame a person submerged in these customs and teachings from birth to the grave, or expect them to know better. The systems of government and authority help them. But just like I would not go to the farm and seek to reason with a sheep, I have no intention of talking anyone out of their belief system. If you come to me to argue, to convert, and to tell me I am wrong, it won't end well. If you want to debate or chat, please do.

At my core, I am simply a person who enjoys studying and learning. I attended two seminaries. I worked through orders to be ordained within a Catholic tradition outside Rome. I completed an interfaith seminary. I did the work. I am not simply a person sitting in a pew. The second seminary did not work out. I asked questions and fought for answers. I left the second seminary because the professors acknowledged that the theology did not match the dogma, but they taught it anyway. It did not work with their own scriptures, yet they adhered to the hypocrisy. I can't do that. I still have integrity, so I had to go.

I had the same issues with the body. Monasticism and asceticism lean one way, but then the Taoist, Tantra, and witchcraft go the other way. Pleasure versus shame and guilt do not seem like a fair fight. Yet, from the perspective of someone raised Catholic, I did hold a bias. I felt like I did not know enough about the body, so I went to train in bodywork. I failed the A&P exam twice by a very strict nurse, and it reminded me how much I don't like science. It was important to me, and the third time was the charm. Yet, due to life circumstances, I could not finish. I got a lot from it, and I do not regret the time or the people I met. I turned to Reiki later and added it to my skillset.

I went back to college at some point in the 90s, completing a degree in psychology. I moved right on to the Master's, but again, it felt unfinished. I turned to NLP and hypnotism, but without set standards, I took it from three different programs to ensure I understood all of it. I worked with couples and families and felt I needed sex therapy as well to expand my knowledge in that area, eventually getting certified.

I have spent a lot of time and money on education. I will tell you that the best education I got through the years was free. Again, it is through experience. I never stopped the occult/mystical/ magical training and practices. After taking three years to learn the basics within the order, I did the teaching, mentoring, and continued the mentorship of my teacher. In this order, you are asked to go outside and bring back more knowledge. It was for the benefit of the order, but also to refine your path.

I took on an herbal witch teacher, a hedge witch, for two years. We saw to her garden, her cats, did spells and rituals for both years. This confirmed for me that I made the right choice by not joining a coven. I was not made for the wheel of the year or many other aspects of the Craft. The fertility, farming, agrarian, history, and practices feel out of step for me. I simply do not live that way and wouldn't want to if I could. Many Pagan and witch festivals involve camping for this reason. I detest camping. It is just not a good fit. I love nature and ordeals in the woods, but then I want to go home. At my core, I am a city guy.

I respected her and did the work, but when she had to move, I never sought a Wiccan/ BTW again. It's just not for me. I moved on to a few LHP folk magicians for a time. Their work was practical and had an impact. He had a lot of Norse influence, so I was interested in picking up the old books I had from my youth on the runes, sagas, and eddas, and dove into Iceland and my own roots in Normandy, France.

I recall this part of my journey very well, as it was my first out-and-out rejection. I had a few hard encounters with Odin/Woden. It was very clear I was not welcome, and the runes would never be a fit for me. My teacher continued to encourage me, but I felt stifled and that I was being blocked. I loved the runes. I wanted it and worked very hard. I kept going and made a great connection with Freyr. Around two years in, with a pretty big library of very expensive books and a teacher who saw how well I was doing, I had the most disturbing vision. Woden and I were in a hall with many others. He stood with a huff, opened the doors to the hall, and with two words: I knew it was over, "Get out!" I do not know if my teacher, an Odinist, got the message too, but when I came to talk to him, he just let me go.

I gave away my runes, some books, and my teacher, and we parted on good terms. I still have a lot of respect for the Norse tradition and for Freyr, but it is not my path. I remember taking a break after this rejection for a few months. During this time, I met a new friend, a young witch, and she introduced me to

Elemental work, planetary work, and took me to my first Hindu temple. She got me away from where I had failed and moved me closer to my mystical roots. I was so grateful.

I saw her, I felt her, I almost passed out. Kali, oh my Ma, she was a vision. My dreams all came back to me. She had always been there. In the shadows. Then I saw Ganasha and recalled a joke from my childhood. There was a gray plastic elephant whose head could come off. It was my plastic lucky charm. Then I turned and saw him, God of yoga, Shiva. Another memory flooded me, and I never understood until that moment. Perhaps Odin did not want me because it was clear that I needed to be here?

When I was around sixteen, I felt called to Buddhism for a while, but it never felt quite right. I had moved on from Christian beliefs and was doing a long, deep meditation, and a vision of Jesus arrived. He wore white robes and looked peaceful and loving. His hands were crucified. He stood waiting, and I recall shaking my head no, so he tilted his head as if he understood, and he stepped to the side. Behind him sat a barely clothed man on a tiger skin rug or blanket, snakes crawled over him, a trident was there, and a small drum. He seemed to be a shade of blue, and at the time I thought of the *Smurfs*. His hair was long and pitch black, tied up on his head. He raised his palm to me, keeping his eyes closed, but I noticed a smile form on his face. Then it faded. I never understood that dream, but I never forgot it. Standing in that temple and seeing a large version of the same image was astounding.

I must digress here to a tangent. Many people believe, as did C. G. Jung, that we are much better in our psyche if we follow the myths and religions of our forefathers. It is indeed too difficult to break with that tradition from our youth. In the following chapters, I will discuss aspects of reincarnation, cultural, and even gender issues. All of these aspects have the same basis. We can either let society command us, create us, and enslave us, or we can create ourselves. Is it easier to just fall back on what you were taught and what you see around you? Of course. Is that the best for you? That all depends. Ram Dass and others went to India in the 1960s and dove into the Indian culture, into yoga, and the guru traditions. That was vastly outside culture, and what they brought back changed our culture overall. Is that a mistake? Some would say yes, but I believe, looking back, the true answer is no.

In the same vein as the cultural divide, after a year or so, the witch who introduced me to the Hindu temple and I fell off. I began to study Yogananda, his teachers, Babaji, then Ram Dass, Timothy Leary, Rudrananda, Robert W. Wilson, and this drove me to the works of Christopher Hyatt. My understanding opened up even further. During this time, I was well immersed in the religious mystical order, and these concepts were infused together. My second magical partner also arrived in my life, and I began Taoist sex practices and sex magick with the wonders of Kriya and yoga. The results fill six thick journals in my private books. It was the best sex of my life and the best time of growth. We were not in primary relationships at the time, so we also spent casual time together. Once she found a man, he did not approve, and so we ended our experiment. To say I was devastated is an understatement. I loved her and wished her the best, but I sought out another muse, another partner, and sadly, never found the same spark again.

I met my current partner in 2007. More friends than anything. Open and ready for the passions of others, but having a firm foundation was perfect for me and still is.

In 2015, my teacher died. We spoke, and the talk was difficult. He got me to understand the nature of Deity. As a priest, mystic, and occultist, I have been tied to the egregore since 1995, but this work is never about a single lifetime. He reminded me of three readings I had had with a shaman he knew well. These readings explained personal aspects of not just my astral, my birth chart, and past lives, which took me back. The readings were of true events in my life that I had told no one. They included links to dead relatives, detailed descriptions, and even names. In one session, I recall sobbing, feeling the dead relative reaching out. Many past lives were short and quick, showing my deaths, short lives, while another allowed me to see myself as a chieftain. No kings, no queens, but in one life I was the town's apothecary, a witch. I died old and gray after having to save the governor's daughter. He protected me from the townspeople. The visions were potent and marked me. In each life, I felt the tribal blood, no matter the continent, my gender, or race. My failures were laid out before me like a grid. I cannot explain what a blessing this is. It is not possible to describe how impactful this is and the gift given to me by my teacher. In this lifetime, the Gods placed all my puzzle pieces together, from my birth chart in the stars, to my teachers, parents, enemies, and education. Only someone given so much would be so stupid to wait to be so old to put it together. Another fail on my part.

Do not misunderstand. I am not unique at all. I sincerely believe all people are given these boons. They are run through the mud, killed, betrayed, raped, cursed, all of it. We all learn it all. We all experience it all. It is what we do with it that matters. How do we treat those around us? Are we misers and cruel? Do we love and honor? Are we filled with malice and hatred? This is the story of true karma. I see the hands of the Gods in my outcomes. I see their movement and their desires. Why bring this to the forefront so late in my lifetime? It is not for me to figure out this time. Perhaps after a few hundred more, I will be ready for the next stage.

I went on a mission when my teacher passed. I went inside. In a serious attempt at scrying, I dedicated myself to many nights, and slowly things began to shift. It began inside first, but it also merged with the outside. I always liked horror, dark things, but now it was different. A darker Gothic presence arose in me. A dark female deity I did not know before stepped forward with the agreement of my beloved Kali-Ma, and I held on. I was very dedicated to my Tantric and yogic lines and practices, but she kept coming into the mirror. She was fierce, but I could not get words, and she would shift in the mist. I did some of my own divination work as she would not define herself. The closest I could get was an agreement to put a picture of a Fairy Queen on my wall as her picture. She allowed me to have an image to focus on. I found that all to be very interesting because a few years before this, I had taken on a year of Faery Craft, followed by a Trad Craft I really enjoyed.

This Deity seemed to come from that work. I went to my friends who do readings. One suggested she must be Hecate, and I adjusted my work to her. Another suggested Lilith, and the Deity readily rejected that. She seemed okay with Hecate and assented to the name. I dedicated myself to her. She assumed the role of beloved, became my mother deity, and the daily work began. It never stopped. It is the end of 2025, and I still visit her each night. Over the years, I grew darker, and horror became a part of my life again. I return to old films and new ones. I began to decorate the altar. Skulls, death, and all the aspects that never sat on my altar before began to show up. It was almost as if I were unaware, but at the same time knew that it was right, and I went with it.

From 2020 to 2023, I was embraced by the God as well, and he opened the door to the pantheon of deities who come at the crossroads of Chaos and Death Currents. I will discuss this more in future chapters as they are my primary hosts. I learned through those years to let Death in as a friend and natural deity. Their connection is pure, and the Dark Lord, the God of the Crossroads, or the Man in Black, if you like, came forth by night. He has many names, that too will come later.

From these Deities arose my sigils, my servitors, tulpas, guardians, and my priestly duties at the altar of the Lord and Lady, primarily as Patron and Matron, and then their host. These Deities, by evocation, invocation, by scrying, and astral work, have become my Pantheon that they refer to as the Conclave. I discovered my gnosis via scrying and have not looked back.

****

You need to understand that I have no interest in anyone's belief, co-signing, or criticism. I am well aware this work will draw criticism and review, and that is fine. I will not be reading them. I have not written this for review purposes. I have written this for those with personal gnosis who hide it because of the criticism. I wrote it for the Stygians. When I read about personal gnosis, I want to understand who the person is. I have given you what I usually seek. I understand that, being vulnerable in the land of trolls and judgmental people that there will be barbs. I also am aware that my approach and words critique others and question them, so it is natural for the same to return to me. I would say that my intent is for growth and education, and not to be cruel or judgmental, but I know that might not matter to anyone. I believe with forty years of work, I have earned the right to have opinions, and that is all they are.

In my life, I take on mentors who disagree with me on purpose, so I am challenged. I do not like or seek out minions. I like a challenge. Anything in print tends to bring out the trolls, the most ignorant, uninformed critics, and these opinions mean less than nothing. I am very aware that I am no one, so perhaps the trolls will skip me entirely as not worth their time. I love a good debate and conversation, but have little tolerance for those who just waste my time. I simply have better things to do. I have not written a single word for those people. I have written this for other seekers. People who feel alone, weird, and second-guess their experiences, isolated, people who have been judged, or even thought to be insane by society's standards. I also wrote it for the ones who feel they have no home, no real place to be. Lastly, I wrote it for those who have been lied to and sold a system or way that fails them.

I was sitting at a coffee shop the other day, and a man came in and annoyed me by playing his phone at full blast, so I put on headphones to drown him out. He then motioned to me and seemed to want to talk. A lot of people would have dismissed him, but I didn't. I took off the headphones as he went on and on about the hypocrisy of Christianity, the odds he faced personally, and he made sense. He seemed rational, not classically educated, but experienced. He spoke of real concerns and observations. After a while, he got louder, more passionate, and drew attention. I didn't mind, but others seemed to, so I apologized and then expressed that I had to return to my writing to conclude our discussion. I did not want him to get into trouble. He had a large set of papers, a cell phone, but looked homeless. When he left, he took his grocery cart outside and walked away. He had more knowledge than most people around him. He did not use theory. He applied life. He is the experience. Christians judged him. He explained real prejudices and real hypocrisy. Consider that. He has more knowledge than many with advanced degrees, than the usual theologian, than the academic. He listens to the same radio, videos, and input as everyone else. Yet, he has no conditioning to work through, just experience.

CHAPTER TEN

FOUNDATIONS

Within these foundations, you may recognize many universal aspects of occult practices and knowledge, such as pranayama breathing, yoga, and ways of sitting. While others may appear to be completely new to the old guard. This is not some act of rebellion. It is the oddity of current creativity and reflecting on the work with spirits and deities' inspiration. After offering up my short autobiography, I am now moving on to the core training and why it is present. Due to these differences, you may have the experience of feeling like your tradition is in opposition to what I am writing here. My suggestion is that you consider and experiment before discarding it for a very good reason. Modern traditions tend to use the "old ways" because others did, and sometimes, without any reason other than that. They continue to use the old ways in tribute. Other times, the old ways are far superior, and there are very good reasons to keep them, so by all means, do so. My point here is to know the difference and know why you do what you do.

I use what I use because I have experimented and experienced it myself, and for no other reason. I have listened to many arguments from Elders and teachers, both pro and against. That does not mean I heard from the best or the experts. It means I believe they made a reasonable attempt to find out for sure. This practice is reflected in the last chapter concerning the formula of knowing yourself and then seeking out the value of what system, tradition, or guru/teacher works for you. If it failed or did not work for me, then it is discarded, not forever, because I also understand that I might not have been ready for it at the time. Time and further exploration often open things up, offering more pearls of wisdom. Once that happens, something discarded may present value that was not seen before. Nothing is sacred in terms of assessment and discernment. If we limit ourselves, we can miss those pearls. It is also why I have re-bought some books several times. I thought I was done, but someone brings in new pearls I missed, and I buy them again.

In this chapter, I am going to offer statements and then follow up with why they are true for me as core or foundational.

Universalism is a fact that cannot be denied.

Many books, studies, religions, and cultures have reproduced versions of the same ideas and understandings before any kind of written word; the deities and elements of nature, stars, and fertility are all over the world. Each version of Pagan religions and tribal religions holds a fire god, a lightning deity, and a fertility goddess. Each is represented by stars, literally in the Roman religion, and the Zodiac is a very common aspect of Middle Eastern occultism. The elements are found in Taoism, Wicca, and almost all folk traditions and religions that have esoteric leanings. Rituals also came from dancing, prostration, chants, music, drums, and other aspects that are common and universal. Without the penetration of one group influencing another, we must allow for the fact that some things are just universal by nature.

The alternative is to believe the myths of one group of people populating the world, and so it all came from that one source. Even then, the ability to pick up and carry this out to all parts of the globe with cultural distinctions is indicative of the eventual formularies of all tribal and social religions. At a deeper construct, I would agree that all things come from Source, so there is also no problem with all things coming from the same place. Therefore, universality is the common thread. The arguments against it speak to our senses and what we experience, and since we are all humans, we all form similar thoughts. That is more of a stretch for me than a shared idea of deity. The last option, which is the one I hold, is that you are the Universe itself, so, of course, the universals are true, nothing is outside you.

Reincarnation is a cornerstone of life.

Again, because of my Eastern base, nothing works without reincarnation. The more advanced work in past lives, hypnosis, and experiences from advanced deep meditations have fortified this belief for me. We cannot generate or formulate the basis of our highest skills in a lifetime, or two, or ten. The Buddha was keen to answer how long it takes to find enlightenment. He states something like the time it would take for a bird with a silk scarf in its mouth to run that scarf along a mountainside. When it brings down the mountain then we get to enlightenment. That is not a few lifetimes. In meeting those who have not had many lives, it is clear the difference between people. I do not say this from an elitist point of view, but more from "she has red hair, he has darker skin, she is tall," and so on. It is a simple observation. Those who believe and ascribe to atheism or agnosticism are left to their own devices. Cliches tend to hold truth. Some are "old souls." We use this term to indicate people who seem to know way beyond their years. That is what I mean when I refer to the awakening of lives, and the assembly in the current lifetime to advance even further. The frail human body is no match for the work needed. And we must also see death as not an end or a fear-filled incident but a step to the next lifetime. I have also met people who are more than just everyday people; they are real mystics. Their vision is different, their wisdom is beyond. This validates reincarnation for me.

I believe we have all met the "old soul" where wisdom seems to seep out of them. Even as children the truth that comes forth can be devastating to the adults around them. I have had experiences with yogis who could not have gained their wisdom in this lifetime alone. I have seen teachers who literally glow with an uncommon aura and presence that cannot be ignored.

Meditation and yoga are universal truths in practice

All occult systems steal from these two. The foundational aspects of yoga are ever-present for all serious occultists from the East or the West in some form or capacity. Stygians are no different. One cannot manifest anything without focus, intent, and breathwork. The cultivation of flexibility in mind and body is essential to the occultist, as the inside reflects the outside and vice versa. We then add to this seated attunement, self-hypnosis, and mantra to further enhance the work. Lastly, the connection of teacher-student (from the guru tradition).

I believe that those who guide me know more than I do, and that leads to my narrative around not being ready at times for understanding. Because of that, I go back to my work before I was a teen with no understanding of why, but a resolve to do so. I still remember my first encounter with Kali and Shiva, and my response that came up through the practice of yogic philosophy and meditation. When I went to Catholic masses and then encountered Indian deities, I felt I had found my real home. I recall my first Hindu Temple and walking around the shrines. My insides were on fire because, in my workings, I had done this for years before I even saw a temple. This is a yogic as well as a Hermetic principle of what is inward is also outward. Truly a mystic, I had no problem with angels, the dead, and all aspects of the supernatural. I often preferred them to cruel human beings. I could dive into them in my world, in my internal workings. I recall arguments with others around me as to where heaven is and where the Gods are. Something instinctive told me it was all within because that is where I found them, and the yogic philosophies confirmed that for me. The nebulous idea of them being on clouds was ancient and Medieval before airplanes. It seemed like the right idea. Religions cannot move to logic. They are dead and cannot adjust, but wisdom philosophies do not suffer from this problem. Just as the walk between worlds, the planes, or whatever you wish to call them, is not some external thing but an inward journey, so it is with the universe. These are difficult concepts and places where many people have disagreed for millennia.

We all have a purpose in life

The direction and purpose in our lives are a choice. Some people will die with nothing but tons of money they cannot spend and tons of toys they cannot use. Some will die with mountains of debt and problems they pass on to those behind them. Some will never know real love, passion, laughter, fun, joy, or ecstasy. And some will have built on their multi-life process and progress into the next life. Those with mundane goals believe what they see as "reality" is real. Because of that, they fear death, they fear poverty, they fear others, and they seek others' approval. As a result, this cripples them from any true purpose. Some people are on a mission to convert other people to their way of thinking, as if there is a purpose to this. Those who have had events in their lifetime that make them remember past lives and their ongoing purpose do not have time for any of this nonsense. We must keep one foot in this "reality," but it is out of necessity and not out of want or need.

Our real calling is on the spiritual path, our purpose for being here in the first place. It is through that lens that all are viewed and, thereby, experienced. However, if the world indoctrinates us to see it as real and causes fear for us, then we have lost the plot and are forced into the contamination of secular society: a cesspit of lies, stress, broken systems, and corruption. Look at those with the most money or most power. Look closely at them. Do any of them look happy? Healthy? Sane? When you listen to them, they are completely out of touch, paranoid, and live in fear of losing what they have. There are exceptions. Some have a ton of money but hold it gently and follow a different path, and those are the interesting ones. It is not about the money. It is about the intent and path in life. I know homeless people who are much happier and healthier than CEOs, and that is not a coincidence. They may be millionaires or billionaires, but they are also owned by that money, lifestyle, and trajectory. They are slaves who have their keys and refuse to use them. It is the human condition to hate and want to take down those in the spotlight, from Gandhi to presidents, to rock stars, to political or religious leaders. Unfortunately, to get people to wake up and pay attention, these lives are needed. Without them and their sacrifices, society would not make it. What is your role in this lifetime? That knowledge is needed for anything to grow or produce results.

Play, joy, and creation are the work of Deity

The Stygian Way comes from art. Art is playful and joyful. Art is creation. Therefore, they all fit into the work of Deity. The philosophical foundation can be seen in the playfulness of the guru with their student. The professor who knows their subject and plays with their students around it. It is the artist who adds a sigil or item into everything they do. It is the writer who challenges his audience. Do not underestimate this! It falls into the highest order. The best way to tell a bad teacher is that they are always frustrated, they are filled with excuses, they cannot keep their students, and they are never happy, joyful, or playful. There is a time to be serious, but it cannot be all the time. It cannot even be the majority of the time.

Play is art. It is experiment and experience together. If experience is the mother of all teachers, and play is experience and the experiment together, is there anything else more important than this concept? Think about how you learn. Do you want rote and measure, or that warm feeling of being tricked into enjoying the education? I learned this first from my mother, who was a genius. I hated cleaning my room, and we would argue about it. She would then come in and play with me the whole time, and I wanted to clean the room. I remember one day she said to go and clean my room. I went in and started, but she did not join me. I went looking for her.

"You are coming right?" I asked.

I wanted to do the work because of the method. You may say that there was an enabling part of this. That is true. But you have now taught the student how to play. They can now learn to create joy in themselves. The strict method does not allow for creativity, for play, or for unique approaches.

The Chaos Current and Its Use

Chaos is the misunderstood black cat. It is assaulted with innuendo and ignorance. We think of things as chaotic and use the term to represent a lack of cohesion, plan, structure, etc. Yet that is not what we are referring to in Chaos Magick or within the Current of Chaos. Chaos here is a methodology that does have some structure but no limits. We have standards to keep, but an open field in which to play. The Stygian Way is embedded in it because of that. No other system would make sense.

Building a curriculum and a basic elementary foundation of the 42 (a lot of structure), and then adding a 2–4-year Seminal program is also structured. Yet, internally, it is unlimited. You decide your paradigms, your deities outside the Conclave, and even the priesthood is defined more by your relationship and agreement with your Patron/Matron than it is by the seminary-style training under a priest. At the Wanderer level, the entire burden is placed on the shoulders of the Stygian to head their own system. We maintain the mentor/student dynamic as needed, but the Stygian is within the Chaos Current, and it is direct. They are linked directly to the Egregore and the Conclave. There is no intervention or middleman. Chaos is empowering, it is limitless, and it means you must be a creator and destroyer. It means you must rule your Universe. We teach the methods so you do not reproduce the egoic and sophomoric attitude of "my way is right" and open your mind to the Chaos proper. Allow your students the same limitless freedom with guidelines.

Left-hand and right-hand paths

Look down, many of you have a right and left hand, now look to the center, that is you. We need both right and left hands in our work. They cannot be separated any more than you might want to lose one of your hands. The idea that the left is sinister is lost to history with cliches around the concept of handedness when the left was taboo and weird, and those people were thought evil or less-than based on ideas driven by the majority. This follows that, like most things, those societies got it wrong initially and needed to grow and mature as all humanity does. Left-handers tend to be more intelligent and have more potential to be ambidextrous. The idea of handedness in magic in modern times differs from the Tantric version (where it appears to have come from) and is not one I accept as accurate or helpful. One's personal responsibility, ethics, and practices are your own. I do not adhere to the Western mindset (meaning the Christian and monotheistic norms, or the underpinnings of Western society or Wiccan beliefs) other than keeping to laws and required limits. In a different country, I would practice much differently, but there are always limits determined by location, society, and others' limitations. I am not referring to illegal or destructive methods. I am referring to more openness of expression or living within a group of like-minded people who can support and assist one another. People tend to be less and less inclined to do so in the current culture.

The position of the Technology of a Modern Chaos Reality is that we practice a balanced system and not one that leans. However, the truth is that it does lean far more left than right. We are much more akin to the chaos magicians, the LHP workers, and those who would readily assemble for talks on necromancy, the Underworld, and death, than the light and bright crowd.

Fitting into the boxes and not fitting

Here, I will list a set of terms and define what applies and what does not apply to my work, the position of the Kultus, and the majority of the students I have processed through. This seems to be an easy way to associate my system with certain ideas and reject others. It is an easy way to set some definitions down and move forward quickly. I always leave the caveat that your individuality is always paramount and accepted, so you may differ, and that is good.

- Animism: Yes, for me, this is a reality. It is strictly the art of visualization to watch things breathe, have life, and articulate that life. All things carry vibration, and it is by that vibration that we exist. This is articulated in herbology, tree lore, and many of the oldest traditions. It is also validated by science.
- Atheism: No, not my box. I have had too many experiences that are deities. Some may call these experiences delusions, my psyche, projections, or something else that makes them feel better, but I don't believe that.
- Ceremonial Magician: No, I do not use the basis of the Cabala/Qabala, Tree of Life, or any kind of Judeo-Christian-based systemization. I do not use grimoires of any kind, and all the pomp and circumstance engaged in any of these systems. I do not use the tools of the trade as they do, although some may be similar; I do not comply with the systems they represent. I see them as very important to the occult community, just as I do many other professions in the mundane world, but they are not mine. I must also witness the fact that many of those within the Kultus would say yes to this item.
- Chaos: Yes, as stated prior, I have worked and lived within the Chaos Current. In doing so, I can transition and change beliefs, systems, and methods, but the systems I have said no to are consistent for me throughout my work. Using this system is not a form of being eclectic but a form of precision. The Kultus is inside the Chaos Current and is a permanent pylon or pillar that will remain.
- Conjurer: Yes, I conjure often as part of my magick work. I call forth spirits, deities, and other things to learn, grow, develop, and break old patterns and for many other reasons. Conjuration offers many wonderful paths to the Kultus and is one of our key forms of magick.
- Dualism: No, I am not a dualist. Dualism is common in Zoroastrianism, Christianity, and other religions. It is the idea of two opposing deities, God

and Satan, and Ahura Mazda and Ahriman. You can be a monotheist at the same time, and I will cover that here; I am also not a monotheist.

- Folk Magic: Yes and no, some of the work I do could fall under the term folk magic, as it could be called low magick, and it is certainly part of Trad Craft (see below). I have studied a few systems under this heading. In those cases, the answer is yes. However, I do not follow a set tradition of folk magic. Here is another area where individual members will vary. They cannot deny some of the folk work because it is within the foundational teachings of the Stygian.
- Hermeticism: Yes, the use of the Seven Principles is intact within the work I do, and their philosophy is included in what I do because they impact the work and are universal. Inside the Kultus, there is an artistic version of the seven principles, not in opposition but in congress with the scientific aspects.
- Magician: Yes, but only in the sense of being a chaos magician. Many chaos magicians are both, but I am not. I lean more towards the Craft than the other traditions.
- Monastic: Yes, there is a deep monastic level to my work, as you will see in the chapters to come. It is in line with lifestyle and daily practices and is sacramental at times, religious in practice, and my ritual chamber holds my temple. I sleep within it and practice within it. It is sacred to me, not as sacred as my internal self, but it holds a lot of my tools, and my helpers are there. I use mala/Japa, a version of a rosary, and I use mantras instead of prayers, so it is different, but for me, it is very monastic.
- Monism: Yes and no, those who believe it is akin to polytheism, yes. Those who believe all deities are grouped like chords of wood, no. Isis is not Aphrodite, is not Athena, and so all goddesses are not one. This overlapping has been done throughout history. In a modern sense, it is often sloppy and without purpose other than laziness. However, at a deeply mystical level, all is always ONE.
- Nondualism: This concept is close to the last steps of philosophy. Nondual is Eastern and is in a state of Consciousness that allows for Animism,

Monism, Polytheism, and Monasticism to coincide. It is a combination of systems that is not at odds but only opens when the mysteries open. It allows and leads to the concept of the One or the All or, for some, the Tao.

- Pantheist: No. This is not concerned with pantheons (see below) but with the Greek Pan and Theos, meaning everything is God. I lean more towards animism; pantheism takes it a step further for me, and I am not amenable to it. However, I leave room for animal spirit guides, spirits of trees, and various spirits to come forth.

- Polytheism: Yes, there are multiple deities and pantheons, and this is in rhythm with systems like Paganism, Norse, Romans, Greeks, and much of Bronze Age culture. I am a polytheist because I will transition between systems and turn to those sets of deities. I also cross-populate my altars and my systems based on the goal and tradition I am currently invested in. It is based on who my patrons are, who I am called to, and who I seek out. Stygians honor multiple Gods/Goddesses and spirits referred to as the Conclave.

- Sorcerer: Yes, but again, the term is used differently. For me, sorcery is an act of magick that is not colored (black magick) but is feral and wild and comes from dance, mantra, seething, rocking, or ritually trancing out in power work. It is not the mind and only the mind of the ceremonial magician who seeks perfect control. By releasing control and a merging of psychomancy feelings, there is a rising and falling in as in seething or certain breathing techniques that are sorcery to me. This work is not for those who are mentally or emotionally unstable, and can render them much worse than before. There is much preparation for this sorcery through focus, intent, and meditative methods, including initiatory work. Knowledge of how to do feral magick is required learning for the Stygian.

- Traditional Craft: This one is personal for me, and where I have spent a lot of time working through the steps. I did not choose it because it was the soup of the day; I chose it because it came to me. It was the only witchcraft that appealed to me. I transitioned from my work to meet it, and it took me down two different paths within Trad Craft over six years. One had a much harder grasp on me, and has since become a home for me. However, others who are close to me never touch the stuff, seeing it very differently, but usually from the outside looking in.

- Witch: Always, I chose a mentor and a process through Trad Craft, so many would call me a folk practitioner, but the names mean nothing to me. Am I a witch? Yes. By whose definition? The only one that matters is mine. Traditionally, a coven witch? No. Wiccan? No. I would guess that most Wiccans would say I was not a witch because I do not follow the wheel of the year, I am not within a coven structure, or I practice too many aspects outside their traditions. Others would disagree and see me as one of them. I respect our differences and engage in solstices and other holidays, but I do so outside their paradigm. It is not because I see myself as better or even different. It is because I see the differences, and they do not feel right inside me.

As you can see through these words, it is difficult to place me in a single or even a group of subjects. Also, as the founder of the Technology of a Modern Chaos Reality, these ideals are foundational to the work. It doesn't mean you must follow my way. It means these things will flavor the path. I believe if you all look closely at yourselves, you will find similar results in whatever structure you have worked in. Why? Because anyone who can be defined is already on a death spiral into oblivion, following a dead religion and hoping to go to their version of paradise. You can have those institutions (called that for a reason, in my opinion), and equally, you can have all the people who encompass them. New Agers and Wiccans can be great or just annoying. Often, because the over-culture is so powerful, people just take their birth religion and recreate it in their Paganism or Witchcraft. It is the same if you look closely. All good systems gather true outsiders for a good reason. It is by being an outsider that you can see clearly and not become a conformist. Christ was not a Christian. He could not be because that makes no sense. Founders cannot be followers; one cannot be both at once. He could and would not be a conformist. He broke conformity. Forget about the theology and dogma and just look at the writing of the man (assuming, of course, they are his words). The same is true of most of the founders. They were the ones who broke the old system; they did not make a new one, they explored, experimented, and came to understand. Those who came behind them made the systems. Even those who did create systems like the monastics/mendicants, such as St. Francis, St. Dominic, and St. Ignatius, were not followed to the letter when they died. Their systems were broken down, changed, made easier, or had some version of reformation. Why? Because everything must change. Everything must develop and move on. Some of the founders fought that, and some understood it.

The same thing happens when founders in any system die. The specialness is lost, and a new flavor is added or tried. It often dilutes the original. We tend to like the first film in a series and the ones behind it less. When leaders fall, their fracture destroys the organization. The beauty of the Technology of a Modern Chaos Reality is that it is in no one's image. The founder is just another Guardian of many who hold to the Stygian Way. There is an absolute refusal to copy others. That leaves the teaching to enact a new version of the Kultus for each member, each adept, and each temple. The reason for this, if it is not very clear by now, is that it is only through innovation and artistry that one can be a true Stygian. Anything less is not acceptable.

All restrictions and labels are attempts to kill off change and violate individual artistry. It is a way to castrate any movement from individuating effectively by making a set of codes and rules. Then, stating one can only be that thing if they comply. Those who comply are praised and ridiculed if they grow further. One cannot subjugate growth and not endure the death of passion, wisdom, and the individual to the collective. Those who wish to be part of the collective should do so. I am never seeking converts. If you are happy in your collective, please stay there. This book points to the possibilities and ways of those who do not live this way.

There is a puzzle here, however. Even though there is a striving for individuation, it cannot be completely done in isolation. The methodology used most effectively is the sandwich method. A person would first be vetted to ensure their goals and ideals were in line with Stygians. Then, the basics would be taught through an initiatory process of your choice (at this point, outside the Kultus). Then, the person would endure the apprenticeship so the methods of the Stygian Way might be completed. When complete, the wanderer would then be set free to seek out their way with the tools of their basics, other formal initiations, and a link to their tradition by the Guardian/Mistress. For some, this could be months, for others, years. Some never return. I see it as the baby bird leaving the nest. They must go forth and test and experiment on their own. The Wanderer step is the meat of the sandwich. If they return, we can complete the more advanced training when they are ready to become teachers.

CHAPTER ELEVEN

ARTICULATION OF PHILOSOPHIES

A new philosophy must be aware of the modern world and adapt (to some extent) to it. To do this, we now use video conferences and other models to continue conversations and conduct check-ins, facilitating a forum for Stygians to communicate. However, in the past, this was disallowed. It changes with the times. The term from martial arts is "touching hands," and is a way of being sure the student is fully competent in their work. The same is true of the occult in every version where energy and pathworking are present. We must know the energy, potency, power level, control, focus, intent, and ability of the student. That cannot be done online or from a distance, even by the best psychics or on the astral plane. There is just something different about being in the room where it happens. The wisdom of our embodiment is not a mistake. The Gods seek us in the flesh for a reason; do not downplay that, it is quite crucial. We were put in physical form for this function, so ignore this at your peril. I have attended other temples, ritual chambers, and sacred spaces. All have their own feel. Coming to know a person on a very deep level takes time and negotiation. In most traditions, this might read as communication, but for us, it is a negotiation. We are negotiating terms, ideas, willingness, and fit for the Stygian Way. It is not important in my tradition to become friends or carry on personally together (although it is common), but they must be able to get along with others inside and outside our fold. There is a tie to how people treat others and how they handle their spiritual work, so respect and integrity are always present.

Ancestry & Reincarnation

There is a rather large difference in this tradition concerning the conception of the ancestors and what we do with them. It is threaded into reincarnation and our beliefs, or at least experiments around what happens at death, what death is, and so on. Because the Stygian is part of a Death Current, it is necessary to fully discuss this topic thoroughly.

Due to our strong link to reincarnation and all that it means, including our belief that our life offers the same cast of characters over and over, like a theater company. They may play different roles, but they tend to keep showing up as support, our loves, and also our adversaries and those who make us grow. People are also all at different stages in their development, how awake they are, and have their circumstances each go round. With this in mind and within the current society of today, we will have many parents, grandparents, and other family members who are not within the Current, nor would they understand the occult or even an esoteric path of enlightenment. While it is true we could ask family for general assistance (protection, support, love, comfort, etc.), asking them to assist our magical or occult work could not only be counter-productive but could also be rather foolish.

When we seek luck or guidance, seeking support or understanding of mundane ideas, then certainly those who we grew up with and who have passed on can be helpful. They can offer us grace from the other side. It was very common in many cultures over centuries to do this kind of reflection, necromancy, and reaching back. This is why so many excavated homes often have a family shrine or altar in so many civilizations. It is also fairly common for us to return with the same spirits over and over, switching roles, genders, and other attributes or roles, as I mentioned above.

Here is where we differentiate. For our tradition, the ancestors we are interested in are those who are in our Currents. I am referring to the Chaos and the Death Currents, the aspects of the teachers and traditions that formed you personally, in or outside of the Kultus. Even those who you refer to as mentors or the great sages. That is where our power and help are potent. Many will refer to these not as ancestors but as entities we encounter, and for us, this is not so. For us, it is not about blood. That is a mundane and archaic royal methodology of separating people and leads to elitism, racism, and hatred. I am referring to a living legacy of people working towards the same goals. One is based on where you were born, where you have no control. The other is based on your life, choices, direction, and which currents you invest in, join, or are initiated into. Those are true ancestors and the ones who you can gain a great deal of help from that few seek out in this way.

Sadly, some occult groups also grabbed onto the idea of blood, calling it witch blood or vampire blood and claiming that it is more important than anything else. The Kultus stands in opposition to this through its own experimentation, and experiences, and by taking the energy and spirit of Deity to venerate the current blood into the elixir. It is not a generation of a line of succession that creates this and more elitism. It is the actions of the individual and that of the Kultus as a group working as one that generates power and not some ancient made-up this or that. Royalty became such at the end of a sword or a gun and not through some magical blood. If the blood were the source, with the commonality of inbreeding, any modern medical doctor would see the clear deterioration of minds and intellect over time. This makes the entire concept of the bloodline obsolete thinking.

However, the spirits who have passed are a subset of your spiritual guides and those who can assist. The living gurus or teachers are the primary movers, and to fully adjust and find our path, we must find them in the mundane. These are often the reincarnated who have moved further down the path and have either remembered or regenerated their understanding and are ahead of you. In the Kultus, we always push forward. I want someone to teach me who knows more than I do. If you are the smartest one in the room and are not there to teach, you are in the wrong room.

Blood

The culture, gender, or nationality of a person is unimportant for several reasons that will be very unpopular today. You may have been the opposite gender in a prior life, in a different culture, and from a different country. Wasting time and intention on these issues are just constructs that society tells us have importance when they mean nothing. All they tend to do is cause separation when we could opt to simply look at one another as the same species and call it a day. These ideas of bloodline are lost to those who believe they have spiritual bloodlines. My view is in opposition to many folk traditions, tribal traditions, and Pagans. We respect their beliefs and their validation and even worship of those who brought them into the world. However, the long-term beliefs do not bear out over time. Blood dies with the body. The body returns to ash. It is the spirit that lives on, and that has no cultural or blood reference. The blood is not potent due to the line, but due to your incarnation of that vessel and what you do while alive. That is its power and its ambrosia to the Deities. What I am referring to as incarnation speaks to our belief of you being the Universe, deific in that way, so in essence, you are incarnating in the flesh. It is power and ambrosia (immortality in Greek) that is the food of the Gods, and our incarnation is indeed food for the Deity. We feed the deity in terms of ourselves and the deities we seek out. We are a speck of Greater Divinity, yet even the speck is divine.

Due to society's incest in religions with shame and guilt, we cannot accept we are All the Universe, and by that, there is plenty of room for petty differences. Racism is as silly as colors in a coloring book. Do not misunderstand me. I am not telling you what to do or how to do it. I would ask you not to join the mob. Be an individual and think for yourself. Race has nothing to do with character, the ability to love, or the ability to be kind. Neither do creeds, organizations, who you have sex with, or what you see when you look in the mirror. The games created by this are nonproductive and lessen the impact of real discrimination and ongoing assaults on people today.

There was a series on a streaming service called *See* (2019) with Jason Momoa that spoke to occult ideas like what I am referring to. The series is about "the seeing" and "unseeing" people and how people compensate for being blind physically. They use their other senses to a far higher degree but they manage to maintain their prejudice against others who can see or who are different. The other portion of the series offers some insight into esoteric and occult knowledge for some, but ultimately it is all about people manipulating other people (a tale as old as time). Societies want the elites, the royalty, and the others. A middle class is still difficult for any society and much like middle management, they are squeezed and face the most problems overall because they have something to lose and they are always on the cusp, always in distress. The poor are poor, they are not getting poorer, and the rich are rich, they may get richer but they are still rich. The reason I share this is that in the Technology of a Modern Chaos Reality, we eliminate racial, bloodline, and incest of what religions and royals imposed on society and instead look to actions and development of the individual. There can be no remnant of this mindset because it is where violence, separation, and hatred live and thrive. They are not welcome here!

Vitae

The reason the body's blood and vitae are so important in the flesh is due to multiple factors. The use of blood and other vital fluids in magick is a major aspect. The use of the blood in your veins and your incarnation are part of your offering through invocation. It can also be ritualized as a holy substance for those who have infused their blood over time. The Stygian has its methods for this. It is important to note that the use of the body in this lifetime within these Currents energizes and replenishes the blood, and the system circulates all that you put into you. It is also true that our work in the flesh is valuable to spirits, Gods, and to our next steps in the process. It is because that vitality is that of a deity you invoke or evoke and, by that act, have linked your body, mind, and soul through occult means: making your fleshly temple sacred. This is why the shaman was feared, and the priest revered. They were the ones invoking and evoking the spirit and were the vessels, so they caused fear through power.

The subject of blood is a very old one. It is not the plain blood but the infused blood through the work of ritual, ceremonies, and other practices that create what deities of all religions have always craved (leading to terms like soma, amrita, or ambrosia- all used interchangeably depending on the culture and time frame), leading to immortality or as the food of the Gods. All religions sought sacrifice and blood, but it was the Path of Blood that stimulated it, the energy within the blood, and the Current used by the flesh and through the blood that empowered it. It is the connection to Deity through your Daemon that links our spirit to our blood.

Think about how cheap life was for so many years. Some might say it still is. No one cared about that blood. No one was interested in it. The only ones interested in this area were the occult, the archaic use of bleeding someone medically, or in the blood of a royal. Why? Was it prejudice, or did they know something we wanted to ignore? It is the infusion of the blood. Remember, this is entirely wrong and mistaken. Since we are all One, this is ridiculous. However, if you enslave people and must murder them, you have to tell yourself you are superior to them, and that they do not matter. The term Mudblood from *Harry Potter* is an interesting development. Even in a children's story, the bad guys seek pure blood. Nothing changes in reality or fiction. Blood sorcery, blood sacrifice, and the like have been in place for centuries. Some believed it to be our essence, and it is. Some believed it to hold power, and for some of us, it does, while others' blood might hold disease. This topic could be a book in and of itself. The point is that it is often misunderstood or accepted by other members of the Craft, taken from society as is, looked at from a tribal or arcane position, and not fully defined, so it needed attention here.

Societal Impact

If you notice societal trends, it is almost always true that the world is the antithesis of where occultists, yogis, and the esoteric are going. The idea of gender diversity and the controversies are simply regulated hatred for one another and have no basis in a spiritual path. That is not a passive response. It is the same as gay marriage. The burden of marriage was always on the woman historically, with dowries and the words still in use of "giving her away" as if she were oxen, which is a terrible societal norm. Gender and sexuality are determined by the individual. What turns you on may change. What inspires an erection may differ. So what? Society and its opinions mean nothing unless you let it mean something. Marriage is a tool of the state to give benefits to people and to offer deals for multiplying (offering up more chattel). These social mores are traps and tricks and have no real impact on your life unless you allow them to. The trend of allowing domestic partners and other reclassifications to allow people to remain single and still insured, and still get benefits from others, is well overdue. Some people tend to just want to rebel; it is a part of immaturity and adolescence (and that is not a negative, it is a natural break from societal norms). Yet, at some point, we must move on to maturity and release the thought that any state will get it right, any society will be a good one, and any leader will fix the problems, and instead resolve to embrace who we are and damn the judgment.

Acceptance is the only way to truly allow yourself the freedom to be who you are, regardless of those around you. This is why the Stygian Way is only open to those with internal motivation, as external motivations can easily lead to toxicity. If you are judged and ridiculed by those around you, seek out those who will not allow for that behavior and who have higher standards. Occultists have mastered this over the centuries. We are always the group that people fear and hate. We are misunderstood based on the powers that be or, in today's landscape, how Hollywood and society cast us. Some accept this and move on to do amazing things. While others are footnotes and often remain in the shadows on purpose. Those who complain, resent it, and carry all of that around with them are doomed to all the depression and anxiety society offers. Don't get me wrong, the negative treatment of people by societies is entirely wrong, and any change towards a live and let live mentality is better, but not expected. We all have work to do in our lives, and for those who are set in the mundane and set to change society, I tip my hat to you. I do not envy you, and I would not do that work. For me, it is like making a house at low tide on a beach and trying to tell the high tide to stay away and not wash away your home. Good luck with that.

A Monastic Twist

Because I practice what I consider a version of a monastic tradition and religion that does not face outward (meaning it has no public face), I am only concerned with the training of the inner circle. There has never been an outward side whatsoever, which is why writing and opening this tradition was difficult for me. There are no temples people can attend, public offerings, or even classes for the public. The Kultus has never supported these ideas, and there is no intent to change that to some public-facing entity. This book intends to expand the consciousness of people and to throw open the ideas we typically keep to ourselves. There is an undercurrent of practicality in the work. It is through that lens that dead religions seem broken to me. A dead religion is not a religion that is no longer in business or has been lost to time. To the contrary, dead religions have billions of followers. Their tradition is dead because nothing has changed for thousands of years in their religion, so it is dead. It has no future, there is no life, and it is as dead as its books. You cannot bring it back to life.

Nietzsche referenced this in *the Gay Science:* "God is dead. God remains dead. And we have killed him." He was referring to religion, and as an atheist, he saw them as all the same. The pushback is always that it is alive in the people. Have you met the people? If you have, and almost all occultists have, when they speak, they sound like cultists. They are sure to the grave, even though no predictions were kept, and so many "facts" are proven wrong. That sounds like a cult to me. Some of the books with predictions in them even went back and changed the dates multiple times to try to make them correct and continue to cause fear for their sheep.

Religions should continue to grow, and if you constantly engage deities, then they do just that. We cannot have a "book" that is constant because that creates a dead end and a dead religion. A root will always be a root, and a tree will remain a tree, so we can fortify a basis of knowledge and keep that in book form, but that book must remain a living document (a kind of Book of Shadows is a good example), or it is useless. We use the old term grimoire, not in the sense of a Medieval Grimoire, but the phrase living document is a much more feasible term. We can keep the same spells, the same initiations, and many of the same foundations, but if we fail to recognize the changes in the world and not listen to the Deity today, then we die with what is old. Change is a constant, and many of the old religions of oral tradition changed all the time. They developed, they dealt with other tribes and religions, and they sometimes added new Gods to their pantheons. They were tied to the seasons as hunter-gatherers or farmers, and so they kept to the seasons and the fields. The Kultus is not some religious New Age mixture of picking this God and that Goddess and following a wheel of the year. While not having never left your 7th-floor apartment and claiming you work the Craft. Something feels off. Perhaps I am too practical?

The Wheel of the Year

The Stygian views the priesthood very differently from major religions and even Pagan or witchcraft covens. The mimicking of holding the same rituals in the same way year after year does not add anything to the beauty or the vitality of the Kultus. That does not mean that I am against repetition for the intentional use of ritual, but just doing it because it is this date or that date is symbolic of fertility cults that the major religions took on. Since the beginnings of shamanistic and tribal culture had no measure of time, this is indeed a modern pattern, invested even deeper by modern forms of Wicca and other traditions. At best, the wheel of the year is a teaching tool and a way to generate a connection to what was and to keep those same Gods in your heart. Some would argue it is a way to raise power and be in the presence of a deity, but you do not need yearly rites for that. As always, I am not suggesting this to you. I am sharing the Kultus and the Stygian Way, and why we go a different way. If you love the wheel of the year and it keeps you grounded and keeps you practicing, do what is right for you.

The use of puja, of small magical interchanges, can do the same thing. If you study those who were touched by the Gods, they relish in the ecstatic connection. Their practices and actions are small and often childlike. If we opened their consciousness, I suspect we would see a Shakespearean performance, the art of the greats, majestic beauty, the feelings of a true love connection to the Beloved, and other such connections. At worst, the use of a wheel of the year by a priesthood is an outdated method that has little to no connection to modern living unless you are still a farmer or attached in some way to the land, or still working within a fertility cult (which is always encouraged). Some may argue that by utilizing the same systems as other witches and Pagans, we are all wetting our beaks in the same pool of power, and that is valid. My question is a simple one: is that what is important? If it is, then become a Catholic or a Muslim. There are far more of them, and therefore, by that logic, it is far more powerful. We don't because we are not Catholics. I do not dip my beak in that pool because I am not them. The Kultus, rightly, keeps to its Egregore, and that is plenty.

I realize these statements isolate this tradition from the masses of the Pagan, New Age, and others. It even separates us from the tribal and native populations, who may still follow these seasons for survival. I am by no means downplaying their worth or their merit. I am simply stating that it does not serve my tradition. It is through diversity that we find wisdom. We are simply taking a different path that does not need a Wheel or a set methodology for the year. The only method we use is the Moon. We follow the Lunar calendar as a method of waning and waxing. We use this in a watery balance of our time and for deeper esoteric meaning and connection. No other "time" for us exists. Time is an illusion dreamed up, just as the paper was a promissory note we used to suggest we owned the gold we no longer have. We play along with time in the mundane, but in the temple, it is not real.

Flexibility of the Mind

It must be said that the inflexibility of movement, change, or growth is always problematic. Flexible religions do not need to break away from orthodoxy or the core theology or system. There is room to grow and no limitations. Most breakaways are egocentric pulls of running your own show because of a belief: *I know better than anyone else.* Here again, we have the dumbing down of traditions. I learn something for two weeks, and then I am a master. People buy ordinations, initiations, and so on from corrupt individuals who do not understand what they are doing or, worse, they do understand and do it anyway. There is never a need to do this inside the Kultus because the nature of the tradition is already individualized, unless you feel a need to break hard on the foundational basis of our training. It may seem that I am talking at cross purposes, and I do not want to be misunderstood. When people gain wisdom and insight, when they are well prepared and choose to move on, they are readily respected and loved as they walk away. I am not talking about them here. I am referring to the takers. Takers vary, but for the most part, they are the ones who did not stay to go through the gambit but found a quick and dirty way to scam the system and then attempted to sell it to others for money, personal gain, or aggrandizement.

I must digress for a moment. Many years ago, I ran a martial arts school. A person from another style came into my school and asked a lot of questions. The usual: how long for a black belt, what is taught, who was my teacher, etc. Then they told me they were a black belt. They then asked if they could wear and be a black belt in my school. I quickly answered no. When they asked why, I explained we taught the art of combat-oriented martial science in a way that was street-practical, while their system was for sport and a ring. They assured me that they, too, could do all those things and more. I smiled and told them we could get on the mat, and if they could indeed defend themselves, then I would happily allow them their belt in the school. They agreed, and twenty minutes later, sweating, panting, and highly frustrated, they walked out. Why? Because when they tried, their system did not do what they were told. Their "self-defense" was symbolic and not actual. Practicality reigns supreme.

I do not see the person as the problem, but the system as the problem, and the people who lied to them are misguided. That is what we are talking about here. The system is broken, and over time, the only changes that are made are the ones designed to make things more approachable and easier for the public. The public seems to need easy and quick. So much so that martial arts schools have what is known as the green or blue belt level. It has a simple meaning: most do not make it to that level, and if they do, they will probably stay. That is why most schools only teach the basics. Most people do not stick around long enough for anything else. The same thing happens with a black belt. Some come for that prize, feeling it is a milestone, and it is, and then they stop. Ironically, this is like learning to read music and to play the instrument, and now that you know all the basics, you will never play again. Black belt levels or degrees are where the real fun stuff is and where you learn the art. I relate this to the 42, and then I overlaid the Technology of a Modern Chaos Reality on top. The Stygians have the basics and then learn to use their art form.

There are always exceptions, and they stick out. Recently, I have run into several younger teachers who are so well-versed in the Ceremonial Magick world, and they knocked my socks off. They know their shit! Not only that, but they are purists too. They want to do it exactly how it was done when the medieval grimoires were penned. They use wax seals and have advanced much of the math and planetary work through technology. The precise and dedicated time for all the intricate times, astrology, and alignment of all things bores me to actual tears, but my heart overflows with pride that people are still doing this work. They are exceptional people, and I am so happy to be aware of them and know them.

The basics are everywhere in occult books and glut the market of publishers in the space. This is akin to the martial arts discussed above. Most do not stick around for the hard work or the long term. What is not taken into consideration is the validity of the original work. Often, especially in martial arts, the reason a technique or idea was kept in is that the other ones got people killed. Reducing these systems does nothing for the style, practicality, or reality. It might look prettier, but then you could just learn to dance. It is also true that some systems added other katas (forms) or extras to keep people paying for lessons and to get more. It was a business then, and that is part of the world too. It is hard to know the real truth.

I have no problem with the basics or many ways to say the same thing for those just starting, because we need the flexibility of the mind. On the other hand, I do have a problem with the act of dumbing things down. I see it as dishonest, insulting, and a disgrace to the education and work of the occultist. I remember when all the traditional schools went out of business due to mixed martial arts. MMA has a lot to offer, but it is not for everyone. It compounds the systems for use in a ring with rules, and that is a limitation, not flexibility. However, there are some amazing styles I do not see anymore. That is a shame. They offer a great deal to people of all ages, and when they went away, a lot of ethical, moral, and goal-oriented training went with them. The loss of the balance of culture, style, and deeper understanding should not be lost to the practical. They must marry to get the best from both. That idea has a lot of flexibility.

The Oath

The use of the oath is retained in the Kultus as a Stygian Way need. Taking an oath to a way of life, to a tradition, and to the Deities of that tradition is a common aspect of initiatory work. The intent of the oath is outlined and personal to each initiate. The oaths have a lot in common, but the personal aspects are much more important. The forming of the vows is the preliminary step towards the oath and takes time and attention, with a large emphasis on keeping your commitments and your word as an apprentice. The tenets of the Stygian concerning discipline and contemplation are set, but these vows are personal for each member. The oath is made to the Deity/Deities alone. It includes the secrecy oath we all take. It is a deeply spiritual and personal dedication ritual and is written with poetic flair, with the endeavor to express your willingness and dedication to be a Stygian for life.

A secondary or added aspect is added for those who become priests. Most Stygians will not be priests at all. They will be mystics. The priest/priestess becomes a devotee to the Conclave, and a Patron/Matron becomes apparent.

The service of the oath is outlined and expressed in hand- written form by the one taking it. Throughout the time of vow and oath-taking, the member is taught and shown by example the art of discipline, commitment, and the practices of the dedicated. They are also fully immersed in what they are committing to before they are allowed to take the oath. They must know it before they commit to it. We do not spare the timid or the weak as mercy. The Gods are not human and do not consider these limits. When you come into their presence, you must be prepared. If we did not prepare you, then we are culpable. G/M's and Stygians take this role very seriously.

This is not dress-up, it is not a role-playing game, it is not Hollywood, and it is certainly not New Age. It is new in conception, but somehow, it resonates as a time-honored tradition. We are not just walking through the steps as so many priests do. It is not about the rubrics and measures. It is not a ceremony with some songs. It is a dedicated ritual engaged with the deities. They are our allies, and we respect them. Our goals are not to grovel and serve the Deities like serfs. The goal is to discover and work to manifest our Daemon as our bridge to the Divine and, by doing so, to come into our understanding and being as divinity itself. Our beliefs include having the sacred Source within us. We also realize that we are under all the garbage heaped upon us by society that buries and keeps us from the Source. We petition the Gods to burn away all that is unwanted or unneeded through our work and effort. The inner world is the key. We all have them.

The Conclave seeks to lift us out of the morass and debris. It also seeks to burn away our trappings, weaknesses, downfalls, and those who seek to take us down or back to societal norms. The Gods are not only our allies but our protectors, those who ride us, those who enlighten us, and those who rid us of our memory lapses between lifetimes so we might recall who and what we are. They see society as an aspect of initiation, a cesspool of filth we must wash off because the majority is never in the know. Once cleaned, we can create a paradise in the flesh of this world while we do the work. The Oath is not just for the Deities. It is for us. To keep us on track.

Hell

What do I mean by hell? Hell is repetition without reason or ceasing. It is the anxiety of no peace. It is the what if, or I wish, if only, and so on, and is the place to be unsure and ungrounded. To the Buddhist mind, it is called suffering. I am not talking about some place of guilt and sin or some fiery pit. I am referring to a place of your creation. Societies and the world also make them here on earth, too; warzones, places of poverty, violence, torture, slavery, the Killing Fields, the Trail of Tears, the Holocaust, and so many more. Any government or ISM that has starved its people, chosen war over humanity, chosen money over citizens, and chosen resources over prosperity for the people is a country or system that rules by threats of violence, overflowing prisons, and terrible leadership. All countries have parts of this, but the balance and the guidance of nations can lead to hell for their people. These hells are forced on them. The worst hell lives in the mind. That is confirmed by many of the people who have endured the physical ones.

Spiritual traditions cannot turn a blind eye to this. They must be vigilant, keep awareness, and seek ways to sustain life while doing their work. Many members of the systems I cut my teeth on were from the middle class. They do not have the time to seek mundane aspirations. Instead, they do what they can to sustain themselves and, for some, their families. Then they move on. The need for having children tends to be different if it is not about your name and bloodline. Stygians, as a rule, are fine with coming back to a different gender or country, if it rightly takes us to our next steps. Some might even say that we get the choice. Many who have memories of their past lives report this. Others do not believe it, but we must look deeper into this.

We must not make hell for ourselves but seek peace in our minds. Spend the time to create the sacred space, the joy, happiness, and wonder. Do not toil to create anxiety, depression, sadness, limits, and your own personal hell.

Subjective Reality

It is important to look at the idea of subjective reality, or what I would prefer to call it, your lens, and, with it, your personal bias. I have attended classes and training within the occult, witchcraft, and the like for over thirty years. I have seen the dumbing down, the removal of powerful magick because it might offend, I have seen the mysteries corrupted by New Age drivel, and I have seen the new teachers (of no fault of their own) not know what they should know and pass it on to others. I have no authority in those rooms, as my tradition has remained in the shadows. No one is going to listen to me anyway, so I remain silent. Yet I am aware. It is not my reputation, my connection to the deity, or my vision for the future that is at risk. It is those teachers and the students who are not given the full story that are impacted, and the dumbing down is not their fault. It is like watching a car accident you cannot prevent. I try very hard to attend only those whom I believe will not do or act in this way, but sometimes I get it wrong, and it is painful to watch.

Although karma is used incorrectly most of the time, I will use it here to express my concerns. Teachers take on the karma of their students. Some burn some of their karma away. These are the good gurus. Some add to their lot. These teachers are responsible for that. I do not believe ignorance will shield you. It is your duty to know or not to teach it. It is your responsibility to find out before you teach it to anyone. Do not assume your teachers are right. I promise you, many of them have faced the same karma as you.

Subjective understanding impacts a lot of our perceptions. If a person cannot see in their mind's eye (clairvoyance), they may preach that no one can. If someone has never felt a touch, heard a spirit, or been visited by a deity, they might then determine they are all psychological archetypes and not actual beings. If we have never smelled a spirit, touched the astral, and so on, then they might believe there is no such thing. We tend to limit our understanding based on our experiences. This may sound like a contradiction, but it is not. We need the room to experience, and our perception does matter. However, we are trained to explore and expand that perception and not make it definitive and thereby limit it to our senses and personal experiences alone (like unverified personal gnosis UPG, which is often ridiculed). Ironically, currently, we are in an age where UPG, better known as your subjective reality, is all that matters. Reality has moved further away from our own beliefs, which seem wrong when addressed by objective reality. Yet, they seem to mean more and have no restraints, yet at the same time, and in the same period, the occult community has turned to limiting experience and casting off UPG. They are moving further away from UPG and what used to be referred to as "supernatural" experiences.

And if that is not confusing enough, ghost hunters and the like continue to be popular for both the occultist as well as overall society. There is no accounting for taste, congruent thought, or experience when subjectivity and narcissism reign supreme.

The world seeks boxes, limitations, and ways to define things, and not ways to expand and explore them. It prefers to demonize those who disagree. It is a bit of a trip to change our patterns while allowing the mind and its ideas to expand exponentially. It is not only well worth it. It is the Kultus as a whole. If I had to break it down into its most critical aspects, it is this. Believing yourself, trusting the deity link to the Daemon, and then leaning in when people tell you it is just your personal gnosis. That may be true, and that is all anyone has, so their criticism means nothing. See that as their ignorance. It is ONLY by your gnosis that you can advance. Now, this must be balanced by knowing yourself and having the experience to discern. Being a witch for two weeks and telling an elder they are ignorant is not at all what I am suggesting. Knowing better and having experience must go hand in hand.

There are many aspects of philosophy and theology I was exposed to, used, and modified throughout my life. Yet, I find consistency in it, in direct opposition to current trends. I believe we all have the potential to peel the onion back, to allow the flower to blossom, or whatever cliche you like. I deeply love my path, the Deities who are on it and near it, my continued growth and education, and the ability to teach, mentor, and be there for others. Often, a single monk works alone, but when honored to be with others, he also works in groups. The always expansive desire to broaden my horizons and my understanding is a distinct part of my path and reminds me that life can be a pleasure.

Protocols & Working with Others

Because of the nature of the closed-door methods and systems where I developed, all members attended others' training courses, groups, conferences, etc., outside of the Kultus. This experience can be both positive and negative. It means we spend a lot of time on the outside looking in, it means our outside relationships are very important to us, and it means we keep some of who we are to ourselves. It makes us into a bit of a chameleon. We tend to fit in well.

We follow the idea, "When in Rome..." Yet, we are often kept at arm's length because we don't carry a line or tradition we can share openly. I expect this might change with the release of this book. Luckily, with a chaos magick current at our back and it's coming back out more, we do have some concessions. It does still carry some oddity with it and can put us even further outside for some groups. The usual entry point is if you have taken on a teacher within one of the traditions and are currently deep within it, then you have some credibility. During those times, you do have connections and people who will work and talk with you, but sometimes it is only for a season. When you move on, so do they.

There are exceptional examples of people who know how to be friends, and we usually refer to them in our tradition and even outside as family or siblings. Within the tradition, we would use the terms brother or sister for peers and varied titles of magical names for others. We do this because, for us, the Kultus is a family. It is important to understand our progression into social situations, practices, and lifestyles. You cannot be a constant guest and not know how to be a good one.

I am not the medieval Gnostic who is said to hate the body and the world. That would be utterly incorrect. It is not the world that is a cesspool; it is the creation of the cesspool by human hands through greed and avarice. That is what disgusts me and what I refer to throughout these chapters. As you will see in the coming chapters, the body is also a temple of the Gods. The mind and all the attributes of the human can be used for amazing good or amazing evil. The choice is left to us, and so is the discernment as to which is which. The use of personal responsibility and the use of isolation from those who would be violent, steal, kill, or murder so that those who are here to live in peace may do so is the anarchy I seek. Let those who wish to wage war and kill each other do so. Allow those who choose to live in peace, care for one another, and co-exist to also do so. Humanity is corrupted by people who want *other* people to kill one another while they sit behind tall walls and militaries, while the rest of the planet suffers and eventually dies off. It is those people who make up societies' cesspools, with very few exceptions. That is what this chapter refers to. Human life can be a wonderful gift and a path to wonders, beauty, and vast experiences. There is a great difference between the two ideas.

CHAPTER TWELVE

GNOSIS

A word with a history of misuse, abuse, misunderstanding, and for some, a deep drive to make the word synonymous with making shit up, is gnosis. There is a little truth to go around. From the Greek, it means "knowledge of spiritual mysteries." It was a key term from the Nag Hammadi Library, found in Egypt in 1945. It developed resurgences in French and other Gnostic Churches. It also created another cringe ferment that led to a shelf at New Age shops. It means little to most Pagans or occultists. For them, gnosis is very different and much older.

That is the gnosis I am referring to throughout this chapter. It is the link to Deity, to spirit, that brings understanding and knowledge, or wisdom beyond the scope of your own potential. That is not the global or overall definition. As always, everything varies by lens. The method of gnosis also varies based on the divination tools, meditation, diksha, event, or even kundalini rising. Some drag it from the ordeal (I am one of those). All, any, or nothing can generate gnosis. That is its mystery and for some, its frustration.

Two distinct versions have come to be normalized. UPG (unverified personal gnosis) and VPG (verified personal gnosis) are both used and encountered by the Stygian in the course of the work. UPG is the most common and the most doubted by others. Still others respect it, if it is admitted and not some yarn or method to make you special. The methods used to manifest vary.

Substances: mushrooms, cannabis, psychedelics, hashish, peyote, etc.

Sweat lodges, near-death experiences, ordeals, BDSM, etc.

Meditation, hypnosis, psychosis, or a mind break, diksha, etc.

All of these change perception, often violently, are usually fast, and in other cases, in a single moment. For others, it happens after long periods of practice. Fasting, astir practices, deprivation, torture, violence, or absolutely nothing can all achieve the same results. Think about that. For some, it takes terrible conditions, while others can walk past a pool of water and get hit as if by lightning. That is why I am a theist. I have talked to different people about these experiences, and the people differ, but the enlightened mindset is Universal.

Authors and practitioners in the occult with outside-of-the-box practices via gnosis are often questioned or not believed. The point is in the term; it is unverified. No one is asking you to agree. Yet the back-biting and witchy wars are no less present than any other part of society. In some cases, it is actually worse. We are all aware that no one can prove a negative. We are also aware that each lens views things differently. The classic elephant analogy with different people wearing blindfolds and all claiming they are correct. They are all correct but believe very different things.

The Stygian experiences gnosis mainly through the divination of scrying, automatic writing, astral work, and via blood and sex magick. In addition to this work, the Stygian adds the need for VPG in the form of initiation. We verify the experience with Deities in our own way. Without the admission agreement of the Deities, the G/M is not allowed to admit the Initiate to the Inner Circle. Their acceptance is a VPG. There are no exceptions. I have never seen this in another tradition. I have seen it tried and done poorly as some theatrical trick. Yet, I have not formally entered a lodge or a coven in a traditional sense. Perhaps it is in there somewhere? What I do know is that once you experience the Deities of Death and Chaos, you seem less inclined to betray them or lie on them. They show up for betrayers, or they come to scare the ever-loving shit out of certain people so they withdraw. It is for their benefit.

I have read works of people who write in story form, like Marshall the Witch of Southern Light (WSL), who presents an excellent way to express UPG in a beautiful way. You can sit back and appreciate it, or it can be done through experience, as Raven Kaldera does. Because of my own experiences, they both ring true. I do not see a difference as negative. I tend to see those who look down their noses at those who write this way as an indication of their own limits. Religions are made up. Stories are made up. Fairy Tales are made up. Yet the impact of Disney, certain books, or movie series has developed its own egregores. I believe if an ancient shaman were to return and look over the culture as it is, they would see this as Big Magick, as Deities, and they would use it.

In the realm of the Stygian Chaote, self-discovery and the Stygian Way, gnosis is primary. Experience is the mother of all teachers. For us, it is not scriptures, not the guru, and definitely not the dogma. Other people have their own lens, so looking in, this may or may not work for you. Debate and mentorship create balance, and are essential, but never abandon your Daemon and your own way. It is not one over the other. It is a combination of mentoring, challenging, having teachers, and then your own experimentation/experiences. It all comes together like the perfect bite.

I am often asked: *Okay, sure, but how do I know the difference between an actual gnosis and illusions or pipe dreams?* This tells me that you are already diluting your own experience, your lens, and you may be on the wrong track to awareness. It is also why people who are delusional and have severe mental health issues simply cannot do the work. Ironically, the sicker society becomes, the more there will be that will flood in. Once you understand the difference, it is quite simple to see in others and even yourself. We develop impostor syndrome through many influences that want us not to believe in ourselves or create delusions of grandeur. It is one of the many positive outcomes of doing shadow work well. You can see things for what they are, and not how you want them to be.

Those with mental or emotional issues do not know themselves, are unstable, cannot keep things going (work particularly), are indecisive, change Deities as I empty trash cans, and they always seem to seek others to validate them. The opposite is also obvious. They have a balanced ego, they are sure but not arrogant, will listen to alternate views, keep their work secure, are stable and decisive, weigh their options, keep to paradigms/beliefs, especially during the hard times. They are either uninterested in validation, or they check with others they trust only in small circles. It is a night-and-day experience. If you cannot tell by my description, just give it some time, and it will become apparent.

The gung-ho, all in typically burn out because even they didn't believe their initial hype. This can just be immaturity, which, sadly, has become the norm. It is the behaviors that follow that make it clear. Excuses, victimization, anger, irrational behaviors, extremist views, and no move to resolutions are all clear indicators of a lack of responsibility and lack of insight, and maturity. Now, picture engaging the Deities with this mix onboard? No way. These people need other forms of help and are not stable enough for the Stygian Way, or, in my opinion, any form of deep initiatory work or magick. Instead of seeing this as a gatekeeping them out because you are an elitist asshole. See it as a gate, keeping them from the depths of their own madness with Gods of Death and Chaos who will devour them whole. Everything is not for everyone.

If you have been around communities, you have either heard the stories or experienced them with others yourself. The one who signed a pact in blood with a demon, the one who did spells and it backfired, the one who did XYZ too soon and ran back to their religion from youth. These things happen because of immaturity, no or poor training, or you fucked around and found out. No matter, it is a lack that leads to this. Can things backfire? Sure. But did you do the divination first or just acted? One must be adaptable to deal with gnosis. It is not a linear process. It is not simple. It is the most difficult part of working with magick in general. I have seen people leave who did amazing things because they could not take the violent shifts. If you want to be in control, go over and hang out with the ceremonialists and Thelemites. This is a rough ride. The feral nature is not like high magick with a set circle and triangles. Even there it can be dangerous but working without a net... it is just different.

In one instance, with a friend who was an immature witch, he did the divination and kept dropping the Tarot cards. Each time, the Tower, the Devil, the Moon, and the Five of Swords would turn up. When he shuffled and redid, he got the same cards. He ignored it. During the ritual, his robe caught fire three times, and that had never happened before. He kept dropping items, and even his Deity figure fell over for no reason. The results erupted with his spiritual brick to the head. His nose and eyes began to bleed. He freaked out and then ended the ritual. He was sick for weeks. It was clear the person he sought to curse was not having it. The practitioner was beyond him. Yet he would not listen. Eventually, he stopped practicing and returned to believing that magick was evil, and never took responsibility. It is not possible to add wisdom to foolishness. They are incompatible.

Some may argue that schizophrenia and delusions are psychology's misunderstanding of spirituality and visions. That is not entirely incorrect. I have seen incidents of this in person. However, the vast majority are breakdowns and not visions. The interesting point of this is that the majority have Christian delusions; unless you'd like to stretch into Christianity, it can drive you mad. It seems to me this is a break in the psyche and leads to insanity. It can be genetic or induced by stress or trauma.

Gnosis must sit upon balance to be of primary use to the person. In the same way, the kundalini experience must have a body prepared for it, or it is not pretty. That work includes running orbits of energy, breath work, building up energy, and knowing how to alleviate it, while having an understanding of the chakras. In both cases, it can arrive without it, but this has the potential to damage the body and the mind, resulting in madness, extreme pain, or the onset of many problems that Western medicine will be clueless about. This has been maximized and minimized during my time in the occult. Both sides do a disservice to the practitioner. Doing the work of balance and good teaching always has better results. If you are going to play with fire, assume you will get burned, or don't play. Throwing someone in the deep end is cruel, harsh, and foolish.

Tips in general to secure the self and properly align include but are not limited to:

1. Never let anyone touch your crown or brainstem at the neck unless you know their intention, capability, and it is for a good reason
2. Empower a guardian for protection, a talisman to always wear over your heart
3. Flex, attend to, and massage your feet and neck daily, and roll your ankles and neck, and ground yourself
4. Wash your hands and face often, see and feel yourself removing the stressors, dirt, and any corruptions set on you
5. Chant a mantra or seed word at least 108x per day, from a guru is best
6. Stand in a mirror daily and accept yourself fully in the nude

7. Flex your pelvis and neck; your body should stack like dishes
8. Journal daily and review at each juncture: day, week, month, etc.
9. Take 10 minutes without influence alone, engaging a sense each day
10. Meditate daily

These foundational practices allow for the steps to lifestyle shifts and to health and wellness. The Stygian adds the following

- Practice your art form daily
- Divination system and scrying daily
- Meditation at your level
- Pranayama at your level
- No influence allowed in without your conscious consent- always
- Goal setting and putting in that effort daily
- Study a minimum of 1 hour per day
- Praxis for a minimum of 1 hour per day
- If a priest, attend the Conclave
- Energy work praxis daily
- Connect to the Daemon daily in the relative and in the astral

Remember, this is for fully committed members at that level. Their lifestyle is fully in place. For them, for us, gnosis shows up all the time and is the norm.

CHAPTER THIRTEEN

A PRIESTHOOD

Our priesthood differs from any familiar systems currently being used that I am aware of. It will certainly not fall within the normal use of churches or any other kind of modern society. I am not talking about some male-driven system where a man intercedes for God. I am not talking about being a servant of the people. I am not referring to the idea of pastoral care. None of these modern aspects is accurate for my description of a priesthood. These are all classic connections to society and a method of providing service indicative of the modern world and its religions. That is not the purpose or the use of the priesthood within the Kultus or for the Stygian.

For the Stygian and many ancient cultures, the Temple was for the priests alone. It was for them to do their work and where they live. It was dedicated to a God or Gods. It was a sacred place for them to serve Deity, not humanity. People outside their gates and doors were secondary. People viewed them as a needed role within their communities and often sought them out. They were asked for prayers or for help. But these kinds of priests were odd, unsociable, and difficult to associate with. Entirely different from a bishop or priest in a modern context, who are more like chaplains, social workers, or administrators. People feared the Gods in antiquity. Now, God is a party joke. It is something you just agree to, or if it is even vogue to say you don't believe in any God at all. That is something ancient people would never do, out of fear alone. Fear itself was earned. People had a lot to fear.

Ancient temples or even medicine men or witches were the priests of their era. They healed, they counseled, they helped. The villages would come to them knowing they were connected to the magick. Some were advisors to kings and emperors. Their words took root and mattered. They worked with sacrifice and under a certain rule or divine law, and were supported by the people to do their work. Often, the people would pay for the sacrifices of the animals or items to be sacrificed. In some cultures, it was the blood sacrifice or human sacrifice. Their divine law or rules would differ by Deity, pantheon, etc. In the case of farmers, they would seek out a good crop, for example. These are the kinds of priests I am referring to.

There is no context for them in the modern world except for a few Pagan traditions and the Stygian, who do not influence the current world as it is. The nature of the Stygian priesthood is essentially both the invoked representatives of the Gods, while also serving as their priests. It was based on oral traditions at a time without reading or writing, with rare exceptions, like the Egyptian, which was common. That same issue is easy to corrupt and that led to the modern priesthoods. It is not that the old ones did not have corruption too, but the new issue was class oriented.

Unfortunately, illiteracy was and is common in many parts of the world. If people cannot read for themselves, they are subject to the interpretation of others. Allowing people to read and judge for themselves required scholarship and people to train them. These practices have always been discouraged throughout history by both the church and the state. It disempowers people so that the learned and wealthy can maintain control. This offered too much power to the elites, and so, over time, revolutions raged and pushed back the elites. Education increased, and the church and state changed their minds. Priests lost this power, and their roles within societies and theocracies diminished. In modern times, priests are part of social services and often counselors. While clergy continue in a very different role than their predecessors. I am not concerned with their roles and modern interplay with society. We have empowered and enriched elitism so far that they must destroy themselves if there is to be real change.

The Stygian priesthood must turn evermore inward. We must venture out with those who have not been corrupted or cower to the fears of the day. We can then generate a link to Deities who have much to say and offer. The purpose and reason for religions and the state to join arms is to control the people. Whether you refer to Marx in his idea of the opium of the masses, or you see

Constantine for who he was and how he manipulated religion to control people. Whoever weaves the state with religion to control the masses are dictators, tyrants, or kings throughout history. Priesthoods like mine do not seek a link to the state or to control others because we are of the mindset, give unto Caesar what is his, in the Biblical context. The state and religion should always be separated. Power too easily corrupts religion and is not within its political value.

Our priests have no presence in the societal mores. They seek much higher ground and authority to do things society would not readily understand or acknowledge. The only engagement is to seek a peaceful place to do our work, knowing the avarice of mankind and their greed will forever force them to war, violence, and death. The wars or violence that priests like ours engage in are typically for peace when there is no other way to that end. Without the body and the liberty to do the work, we are wrested from our purpose in life and so must take the time to do what we do not wish to do. Butchering and murdering their fellow human beings is left to men like Crusaders (monk-knights), who brought together religion and the state to compel God into war. It accidentally (?) flooded their coffers so high that the King killed them off.

Some priests will claim pacifism, and I would clarify that as a privileged position because others will stand in your stead. If they did not, like in the past, the priest was forced to engage. As a priest, I would take that position as well, but I am very aware that position is not always an option. From a martial position, it is important to always be prepared. You never know when you will need to act. Yet, it is also true that intellect and tact are tools of combat. Strategy and persuasion are tools. In today's environment, everyone sues. Even those who were the aggressors, and all you did was defend yourself. There is a massive difference between someone insulting you and someone trying to take your family and enslave your children.

I neither have the time nor the reductive mind to think war has a purpose other than to lead us into the next war or conflict like dominoes. There is always that moment when you are left with little choice, and valor is the higher calling to cowardice. If you pretend this will never be the case, then you are simply not paying attention to history. No one is exempt from these decisions. But why discuss this in a chapter on the priesthood? Well, it is the ability to see, to understand, and to ascertain the best course of action that makes priests advisors in the first place, and why the leaders sought them. Just because the leadership of many countries is led by money and greed does not mean I have put down my skills as an advisor and strategist. It is simply a part of what the priest is.

Defining it more in detail, here is a list of the skills and duties required to be a competent priest on the Stygian Way. Then, in the following paragraphs, I will expand upon them one at a time.

1. Advisor to humanity
2. Ritual leader and vessel of the Deity or Deities
3. Server and daily worker of the Temple
4. Practiced meditator, diviner, and seeker
5. Educated student of history, folklore, myth, strategy, and the theology of your Deities and others
6. Practiced in interfaith relations, speaker, and keeper of secrets
7. Sorcerer, magician, and artist

I have already written about the principle of being an advisor and why that is important. I will also add that advisors have always held precarious positions in myth and legend as well as in the mundane. Merlin gets his way often, but, in the end, falls into his own pit. The Templars did as they would and gathered wealth and then paid for being the best at what they did. As the fighting monks of France, they gathered more money than the church or the crown and paid for it with their lives and the loss of their order. Gandhi kicked out the British Empire and was then killed for his troubles by one of his own. The list goes on and on. What is always true is that the spotlight often carries a bullet or a knife. Betrayal and savagery seem to be within our DNA. Priests are asked to abstain and cut out these shortcomings, but those who are pulled into the spotlight with their leader often suffer the same fate.

Within our temple, the priest is the sovereign. Gender makes no difference, and neither do any of our physical attributes. The priest holds court and calls to the Gods, is inhabited by the Gods, is one with the Gods, and engages in the work of the priest and the Gods in tandem. When I use the term priest, I mean priest/priestess; some do not like the term priestess and prefer priest, so I use it in that way here. The other expressions of their work cover the numbered items here, but this work is above all others. Within the confines of the sacred space, the priest is also the servant of the Deity or Deities they work with. There are some jobs the priests must do by themselves. Other options are open to acolytes, helpers, and others. No one touches the working items of each priest unless there is a good reason; for example, the use of the chalice or cup is shared. Cleaning, warding, keeping the temple guards happy (these can be dragons, lions, spirits, etc.), and the grounds and the surrounding areas for the Deities you serve are all part of the service.

As if the work within the Temple were not enough, the priest must then maintain their flesh and blood in the current of the tradition. Meditation, contemplation, divination, and following the direction of the Will and Fate are indicative of the priest. This extends from the physical, mental, spiritual, and beyond. The priest in my tradition is asked to constantly seek outside our walls. Due to our isolation, the balance can only happen if we are seeking elsewhere. This wanderer mindset means we must study others' traditions, deities, and practices to ensure we are well-read. We also must continually study and deepen our progression. The work of the priest is inside the Temple and outside. It leads them to learn and grow in our communities and groups. Their deepest commitment is to the Current and, thereby, Deities. But again, we are social animals and cannot neglect that fact. Both can be true at once.

Our priests are tried and tested on keeping their vows and oaths. Keep in mind that the role of the priest, and that is what it is, is not some rank or invested order. It is also not about some form of sainthood or working towards going against your nature. Unless, of course, you are self-destructive by nature. It is the role of the one who is the presider. It is a spiritual link and not a mundane one. But even priests are humans. We know people tend to betray, move on, lie, and write their narrative to be the Grand Poohbah of this or that. We stack the deck magically, and in the blackest of arts, they cast upon themselves their own curse if they break the trust. This happens before any real knowledge is bestowed. The temporary vows and then the oath are taken freely and with the knowledge that Pandora's Box is officially opened. If you were to betray the Kultus and Stygians, you would take all the chaos within it upon you.

You are turning the Gods of Death in your direction. Witches have been known to curse books or items for many generations, as have magical orders. They took oaths and vows of secrecy for good reasons. Their lives were on the line, and torture was often used to get people to tell on others. Crowley himself faced many of these issues through his opening up of the material of the Golden Dawn and throwing caution to the wind. He knew magick, yet he felt that what he was taught had no teeth, and those who might curse him did not have the power he did, so he did it his way and released the information. The results are left to the reader to determine. I have found through my own experiences that writing and taking on these personal vows and an oath is far more predictable than some writ you must read and adhere to. Our methods have done the job as they were intended to do.

The last item on the list will be in opposition to many priesthoods. The very idea of sorcery is the opposite of what most religions endorse. I can only say we are the closest to our friends from New Orleans here. We have no ethical dilemmas in a curse or blast if needed, and we have no problem with helping our people when it is needed. We hold to temples and are not so close to the earth or the ground as the many variations of many African Traditional religions. We respect and love them for their influences and experience. We are closest to them in our spell work and sorcery alone. Many of our other functions draw closer to the Greeks and Romans, but all of it is crafted through Chaos Magick. Sigils abound, paradigms shift, and all is permitted.

This chapter may seem harsh or hard to you. It may seem opposite to the modern Pagan reconstructionists and Neo-Pagans. It may seem that I am negative concerning the human condition. I would offer these examples for what I see as a realistic and practical view. The reason it would seem different to many modern practitioners is that many of their traditions were forged over Christian ones they puzzled together, and the ilk cannot be washed away. It is threaded into the cloth of their work. We have never seen the old Pagans and priests unless we went to the few countries and places where they still have roots. We have sought out feral and wild shamanistic or native tribal traditions. I have seen people become very uncomfortable in the presence of magick and rituals that are wild or passionate.

On some occasions, I imagined missionaries seeing these things, and because it would have been too powerful and too filled with spirits (especially then), it is clear why they would believe devils or evil spirits were there. It would be beyond the vision of a Puritan or a pirate. Their religion was dead even then, and they were just seeking to spread their "good news" and diseases to these people who had lived without it since their tribes first took breath. They would have been appalled. It would inspire fear and misunderstanding of its feral and living nature. From their fear of the unknown, these settlers saw them as possessed and wanted them exorcised from the people. "These savages" needed to have their religions replaced with their holy writ. Do you not think this has an impact on generations? Do you not think the fear held onto the DNA? It is still not difficult in certain communities to find people who call themselves occultists and witches to be run out of town. Thought to be demonic and considered possessed or evil because of a Christian-based community. The over-culture religion still has its power. It stays in the air and in the hearts of people who are trained through the words of men and women who just preach what they were taught, even with the hate. When people step away from this religion, they cannot divorce the entire community, family, and interrelationships all at once. And on many occasions, even excellent occultists return to the fold.

If you are part of a more feral tradition, I would invite you to attend a Pentecostal-style church. If that is too far, perhaps a Spiritualist church. Watch the speaking in tongues. Of course, some of it is fake nonsense. But at other times, is that not exactly what you do in your tradition? Being good humans, they, of course, are the most against witchcraft. Why? Because they are the closest to it. Spiritualists, too, are very interesting but take on English and European trappings. They do psychic work and divination, but hold to rather odd theology. Explore this.

The same is true in occult circles. Sometimes, people leave these religions and go to work on themselves. What develops in the darkness of their meditations and rooms is their dreamed-up evils and demons. They are haunted by them and driven back to their safe spaces. The guilt and shame embedded in them return. They become more religious than ever. Without growth or real insight, they get in line with the rest of the sheep.

We do have the experience now where new generations of witches and occultists are now in their second or even third generation in the family. However, the society still holds the basis of Judeo-Christianity as its major base, closely followed by Islam and other monotheistic religions. All of these are not friendly to the cause of any occult paradigm. Many Pagan, occult, and other traditional witchcraft circles have been unable to form communities. Unable to be seen as a religion and unable to foster community due to the oppressive nature of the over-culture. Even if the temples were to be built, many of these communities are not wealthy and could not support them. It is often a small group of people and not the elites. In the same way, those who are wealthy would want to retain their wealth. Associating with these traditions could certainly change everything for them. That does not even consider those who come and go, who do not take the tradition seriously, or who are flighty and more New Age in their approach. They may say they commit and then never show, even seek vows and claim to want this or that, but have no intention of doing the work. The culture, family, and friends might also work to dissuade them from their path.

There are so many things working against traditions like mine and others that we often remain small. The larger occult organizations and teaching institutions, in my experience, often lose a lot in translation. I have attended some of these schools myself, and I have seen the results of them in teachers, lectures, and leaders, and they often are not well-prepared, well-read, well-informed, or well-adjusted. I admit this is only my own experience and those whom I trust within the community, and of course, there are exceptions. Your mileage will vary based on your needs, your discipline, and the result you are after. I still believe there is nothing superior to the dyad, the small group, and the work of initiation as the basis of great work. Due to the pandemic, things changed. People are more aware that they can do a lot more online. Unfortunately, this always leaves room for the unscrupulous to take advantage of people.

The priesthood is complicated. It means different things to different people. It is the role and structure of continuing an Egregore, a Power, a Tradition, and it has deep meaning to Stygians. You may never see the rites and rituals of my tradition, but that does not matter. What matters is yours. This book is not to teach you to be like me. It is to teach you how to be more like yourself and to acknowledge that other traditions do exist. It is to open the Chaos Current to you so that you might make your mark. And lastly, it is to express that there are many ways to enter the occult that can lead you to where you need to go. Notice I did not say where you want to go or where I want you to go. People often confuse this. One must be one with the Will, one with the Daemon, because the lower self will lead you astray, it will take away your power, it will disorient you, and at the end of your lifetime, it will offer you very little. The lower self is indebted and money-driven. The higher self has many different priorities. Do they need to balance out so you can live in peace and survive? Yes. That balance has a magnification of magick in it.

CHAPTER FOURTEEN

TOPICS OF THE DAY

During the course of writing this book, I felt called to add a chapter on the topics of the day because they impacted my work so much. I recognized my answers differed from many other traditions, and I thought it was very important to mark the Stygian Way's divergence. Or, in some cases, agreement. This chapter will be divided into topics and then short commentaries.

Personal Gnosis

Unverified (UPG) or verified (VPG) personal gnosis is different. Yet, both hold a lot of scrutiny in a world where supernatural things are not in vogue. UPG means that you had an experience, and whether alone or not, only you had the experience, and no one was privy to it. It could have been a dream state, a meditative state, an out-of-body transaction, or several other psychic exchanges. These can manifest in several ways. The problem with UPG is that some people just make it up. The other problem is that some people actually do believe it is actual, and it is really all in their heads. However, it is always in their heads anyway. That is the grounding of it. That does not make it less real or less of a Divinity or spiritual experience. For the Stygian, it is like being told you are a master in this or that. We are not interested in debating it. We sit back and watch. Do you display the character, integrity, and skills? If so, then so be it. If not, then you have shown your true nature, and we believe that. Confronting you will only make you defensive. The Stygian just walks away.

The more controversial experience is VPG. Now, you have had the experience, and others have witnessed it too. This tends to be rare, and many do not believe it can ever happen. They see it as groupthink or the influence of others. They believe it is impossible. Occultists vary on this point. The more egregores and validated new religions and systems that create a group spirit, the more this seems to be getting more common. Yet, it is still at odds with the majority. The Kultus and Stygian were first encountered through UPG and then, through practice, developed a VPG experience via the Deities and spirits. If we did not have this, we would not have a religion, Deities, or a practice. The entire method would not exist. Without these experiences, you are simply repeating dead people and outdated materials and are saying you have had no real new experiences of your own in creativity and a living presence. VPG is the one we lean into in initiatory rites and our work because we are practical. *This thing worked for me; did it work for you? Try it.* We then try it over and over and in concert with another to see if it takes for them or if it is just for us. It is not a requirement, but it is an intentional construct we want to try. This is not practical to the mundane practitioner. It is practical for those working with the Underworld, the Currents we do, and the Chaos Magick focus.

Possession

Many witches and occultists hate this term because it was used by Christians to kill them, and that is more than enough reason for them not to like it. However, it is the proper term. We accept an entity inside us when we invoke it, and therefore, it is a possession. To what extent the entity has control and how much the one being ridden is in control is the question. Even *Harry Potter* lore included this one, referring to it as the "imperius curse" that controlled people's minds. It was easy to see why the author would include this in her storyline. This, too, is possession. It gets a very bad name, but in reality, it has been done in mediumship, by shamans, and within tribal cultures for centuries. It was done to gain wisdom, to find cures, to prevent disease or famine, and so many different things. It was also done to allow higher entities to work through us through a pact or agreement. These entities offer us wisdom and guidance we do not have, and we offer them hands, feet, feelings, and deeds. Talking about possession in this way is not acceptable in most New Age stores or the eclectic or PC circles. Yet, it remains embedded in many of the systems of the occult, although usually other titles or names are used.

The Kultus uses scrying and invocations daily. It is a principal tool for working with our Deities and spirits. Because of this, we are constantly in and out of that consciousness. We would be hypocrites to then say it is not possession. We allow a comingling, and we work on those aspects as a primary feature of our priesthood and our magical work. I can only say that when I commit to a spell with a Deity as part of it or on my own, it is radically different. I am connected through my Daemon to do so, and I have been deterred at times from doing spells or encouraged to go deeper at other times. In these instances, the balance of myself and the Divinity was always a better answer.

Blood

Almost all white and bright systems do not use blood in their rites. Most people in the middle of the road are taught to fear it. That leaves it to the black magicians, left-hand path folks, and some chaos magicians. At least, that is what you are supposed to believe. However, the truth is that it is often done to aid workers and has been done by tribal practitioners for centuries. They don't talk about it; they just do it. Do you have to use it? No. It is an accelerant, just like any fluid: semen, menses, blood, or saliva. It turns up the power. If you don't like it or believe it takes your power or any of the other tales, then don't do it. Leave it to those who know what they are doing and believe in the process to expedite their work. You just might have to wait longer and get less of a result. Safety is more important for some.

In the Kultus, it is just part of the core process. Our deities respond to blood and all fluids for different reasons. Somewhere along the line, occultists and practitioners determined it was all about them. What are they comfortable with? What do they have access to? What Deity appeals to them? It sounds more like shopping. The results also look like shopping. I will bring it back. That didn't work, so I will get a refund. The Kultus has a different framework. We respond to Deity and work through what they need and want. We are less interested in what we want or need. This is fundamentally true if we are priests. There is an expectation that they will move us to places and things that make us uncomfortable. That used to be the point of the occult. We are supposed to overcome it.

That is just us and a few others, it seems. But it doesn't matter. It is our tradition, and I stand behind it. We use blood for many reasons. There is also a vampiric aspect that some of us enable and work towards. Sanguine or energy is always the choice of the practitioner. In the end, it is between them and that Deity.

Shadow Work

Another term, like gnostic, tantra, and mystic, which are way overused, is the term shadow work. Whenever a concept enters the vocabulary of society as a whole and comes from a community outside the norm, it is usually characterized incorrectly. It is then sold to the public in a new, pretty package. This is the case for shadow work. People have written a ton of books on the subject, and most of them are garbage. Shadow work for us is as it was intended. It is a very difficult practice of working through your limits, negative self-talk, traumas, history, and all the things that prevent you from being true and honest with yourself. It is not a weekend class or some self-help book, and then presto, you are done. It is a long-term process like psychoanalysis that is not a quickie. Due to some people's experiences, it can take many years, and sometimes aspects return and need more work in the future. It has been taken to some fluffy place where it never belonged.

In the Kultus, this is a requirement. It runs headlong into mental health issues for some, and they must also be addressed. Often, working alone can be depressing. Rituals can trigger anxiety. A trauma history can be triggered by scary deities or spirits. One must have their wits about them. If they cannot, then they will not make it. The foundational training, the 42, was designed to cull the potential Stygians. At the same time, some of the work can feel almost like versions of schizophrenia or psychosis. We are here to help one another. In doing the work, there are hardships, and they are shared. That is the purpose of an apprenticeship and mentorship. There is a difference between seeking attention and victimizing yourself, and doing the work and reacting to the problems, but pushing on. The latter is good shadow work.

Blending of Traditions

I return you to the world of *Harry Potter* for a moment. There are no true bloods. We are all working with blended traditions, even British Traditionalists and others who believe they are the source or have primary traditions. I believe even the oldest shamans pulled from their neighbors. Yet today, people get all up in arms and use terms like "cultural appropriation" and judge people for blending. There is a place for this term; don't get me wrong, it can be done and is done. But it is often blown out of proportion to encompass well-meaning and excellent magicians who are seeking the best methods and have borrowed to do so. I have also seen it done very poorly by simply pulling a label from a tradition and calling yourself and your work something that it is not. Without calling anyone out, I will use a martial arts example.

Sometime in the 1980s and ever since the *Karate Kid* films were made, many martial arts schools began to create signs that printed "karate" even when they were not selling that. Karate is a Japanese and Okinawan set of martial arts. Taekwondo, Tang Soo Do, Hapkido, and other styles like this are Korean. Yet, I have seen tons of karate signs, and when you walk into the school, they are teaching some Korean style. Or it is Aikido or another martial art that has nothing to do with karate. That is a good example of appropriation of the label and also misleading others. At times, it is done out of ignorance, and at other times, it is intended to mislead. This is another example of people who want exotic titles but do not want to do the work, so they make it up.

I moved to Orlando, Florida, recently and sought a martial arts school to stay in shape. I realized it did not name the style so I called and asked what style they taught. To my surprise the person answering the phone did not know and turned me over to an instructor. When she did not know either I knew there was a problem. It is fine to blend things if you know what they are and you are doing it well. Bruce Lee is an excellent example of this. Another Grandmaster from New England, where I grew up, blended several martial arts into his system, and it was excellent. Not knowing what you are teaching is incompetent.

Chaos magicians do not seek long-term traditions and often switch paradigms and systems, but if they are doing it with integrity, then it is not appropriation by my standards. It is a form of gathering to create the best system for that magician, which is the goal of their entire tradition (and for the record, all excellent martial artists). Being within the Chaos Current it is also the entire goal of the Stygian. We are not taking (again, like shopping), we are seeking to master the self and our own personal system. That is the part of the journey of a magician that makes them whole. I would call that adepthood. After that the artist comes in and tailors as they go. They cut some aspects away and refigure others, as they grow.

Occulture

Here we have the modern selling of all things witchy to current generations, and it worked. In 2018, the identification of Wiccans increased from eight thousand to over a million according to Pew Research. It is thought that Neo-Paganism is included in these numbers and of course, it is fueled not just through culture but through television and film. They have made an industry of horror, the paranormal, fantasy, sci-fi, and all things witchy. It doesn't end there though, it opens to making things (crafting) and all things witchy on eBay, Etsy, and the like. We are also moving to more clothing options, tees, and entire companies that are like what Hot Topic used to be. Dark Candles, a favorite of mine, is one industry set to be occult-driven and carry an excellent product. Zodiac and astrology-based items are very popular. Occult items that used to be seen as dark or spooky and kept to that side of the mall or in a certain section of bookstores are now normalized. Where Tarot was confined to magick shops, it is now made by mainstream companies and used to sell items. Tattoos, piercings, and art seem to follow these trends too.

The Kultus view on this varies. Moving to the mainstream was never the plan. It is off-putting for some to engage with Elder Goths, although I may be considered one myself. I am happy to shop at many of these stores and like knowing who the owners are and that I am giving them my cash and not some company I do not know. I am happy to feed my cash into those who are like me, and that is a part of what these younger generations are doing, too. However, some of it is tepid and showy, and the people using the items they are buying are clueless. But that always happens. Because it is so easy to get, it is difficult to discern who are the real occultists and who are the players. It was simple before. If you took the time to be harassed and treated like a second-class citizen for being a Goth or a witch, you earned your stripes. Now, the "costume" is easy to get, so the person is more difficult to discern. The idea that the box seems to be Wiccan is also problematic. Most people have no idea the world of the occult is so wide or nuanced. They are probably unaware of half of the information in this book alone. People just want to box us up, and we are not the boxable type. The fact more are turning to these arts and the occult is also acceptable to the Kultus because we get to watch better films on streaming services. It would be fair to say some of the best things fall into this genre.

The other day, I was walking by a shop, and out front was a girl and a boy. She was painting his nails black. He wore jeans and a tee. She also showed no signs of any kind of Goth interest. They were listening to rap music, and it broke my head. Her nails were pristine and very mainstream, and she mentioned to him she wanted to change his hair to blonde. I have no problem with any of it, but it does seem not only random and all over the place but feels provocative for the sake of it. Meaning also seems to be lost when I ask questions. Many have no idea what the symbols, ideas, or even the bands they are wearing are. They wear them because they look "cool" or because others they see as cool do. It makes me wonder if *Barbie* will be the alternative soon.

The bottom line then is, if it does mean something, has a purpose, and is intentional (with the understanding of the person wearing it), then I am a very big supporter, as is the Kultus. But, when it is a fraud, when it has no teeth when it is a trend and a grind to be like everyone else, then I am not in favor of it. I still support what we used to call the fakers, but they dilute the pool. I ask questions all the time because so much of the time when I ask what a symbol means or a shirt, the person has no idea. I always ask why they are offering free advertisements for a product they are not aware of, and then we usually go our separate ways.

A Dark Current

I am associated with and work with a lot of people on the LHP. I do not recall when the season of Lilith began, but it was not all that long ago. I recall my first thoughts, which were that it was a trend. It stayed. Boy, did it stay, and it is still very much present. I believe that it was the beginning of the dark current that is very prevalent in the world today. Within the year 2024, I have seen it grow in a different direction. It now seems much more palpable and powerful and has, in some ways, outgrown Lilith. She may have planted the seed, but now her tree seems in full bloom. We are returning to Goth in the mainstream. We are returning to many dark and doom aspects, almost like the modern Middle Ages. Historically, it was a terrible time that opened the doors to the Renaissance. An explosion of art, joy, happiness, and light. The world is a pendulum. It must go to the depths of the darkness to find the brightest light.

I believe the Kultus came from this dark current, and it bleeds into the Stygian. We have come at this time with purpose. It is our defined work to endure these Middle Ages and push towards the Renaissance in many areas. Like all great times, we seek the release of all that kills us, causes harm, and pulls us from our work. We implement this through art, writing, song, magick, speaking, or whatever we are called to do. We do it in our ritual chambers, our temples, and our soapboxes.

Try not to see the darkness that is coming as bad or evil. See it as a cleansing. It is a way to wash away the debris and start anew. I am old enough now to understand it. I am also aware that young and brilliant minds will take it up for the Kultus and others. I leave it in good hands.

CHAPTER FIFTEEN

TOOLS OF THE TRADE

The tools in various occult traditions tend to be the same: the athame, the wand, the robes, the censor, candles, and so on. Not much changes across ceremonial to witchcraft circles. One might claim a sword over a knife or add a shield or staff, but for the most part, they tend to keep to the usual suspects. The Kultus will offer slight differences for good reasons, but the nature and use of the tools are similar. The purposes for some of them are different. Magical tools and their consecration and use are the same across all arts and systems, including ours. We do this because the sacramental use of items must be cleansed and then infused with the energy of the egregore or the person (if it is their tool). It is also true that in many traditions, the tools were supposed to be actual weapons. The Kultus is with them in this approach.

Martial arts and magick again share paths. Okinawan weapons are very common in karate and other systems of martial arts, even though no one is walking around with a kama or katana (sickle and single-edged sword used by samurai). They have a history, and many of them were farm tools or implements. In the same way, the tools of the witch are embedded in fertility cults and a time frame very different than today. Or they use swords and high ceremonies with colors and different altars for their rites. The Stygian is within a modern tradition. We see the reason to keep certain items: knives, wands, and mirrors. Yet, we see no reason to keep swords, shields, or other forms of traditional weapons. Like all areas of the Stygian Way, we do not limit them from our spaces. We seek for the individuality of each person to come forth, but they are not part of our "core toolset."

The Kultus is more practical than flowery. It is more interested in the results than grand rituals. It is instead much more drawn towards art, décor, scents, feelings, and looks at colors and symbols because these things have a significant impact on us. The ritual chamber of the practitioner or temple must excite and stimulate them. It must smell, look, and feel exactly as you need it to. That can open a vast array because some people like to be repulsed, others like to have an inside joke, others are dark, and others may seek a rainbow theme. The options are endless.

I will list the common tools. Like all systems with variants, it will shift from person to person based on the direction, deities, and cultural aspects each person brings into the tradition with them. These are the most common.

- Staff: think of this as the magical item of a sorcerer, the primary tool
- Stang, aka Bident: this is a power item and a centering tool
- Knives: we use a set of knives; each has its own use and meaning
- Wand: these are wooden and created or bought for specific reasons
- Mirrors: Scrying mirror and regular mirror
- Censor: incense and all items for its use
- Mother Goddess Candle: a large candle used to call on the Dark Mother
- Music and Art: to your taste
- Divination Tool: Cards and others (these are typically determined by the specialty area of the member; for example, if they lean Norse, Runes might be the choice, or if they lean Greek, oracle work might be their choice)
- Altar Items: Statues, oils, candles, herbs, pots/cauldrons, chalice/cup, and the skull
- Altar Stone: Wooden and stone
- Clothing or lack thereof: Use of ritual attire in conjunction with Deities/Gods/Spirits
- Books: Grimoire, journals, research notes, spells, ritual books, etc.
- Items/personal items; jewelry, sigils, magical items, familiars, guardians, etc.
- Decor: Surroundings matter, the ritual chamber or sacred space, Gothic

- Specific to the Stygian:
    - Water Bowl: our bowl is specific to us and holds the coin at times, the compass at other times, water at other times, and is more of a vessel
    - The Coin: is our visual representation of what is given to the Ferryman
    - The Compass: is a tool of the direction of wisdom and is included in rites
    - Sand Timer: is specific to us and used to meditate and to generate power

I will not disclose the exact use and operation of the items. The point of this chapter is to express the differences and why these things are used. Specific uses for the Stygian are beyond the scope of any book and are part of the apprentice process. All of this information is for a general understanding.

The first item is the staff. This is wooden and used for multiple reasons. It is also the primary tool of the Stygian. It is the item present in their hands during workings, what they walk with, or by the altar. Some extend this to the Stang or bident. The two, for us, are not the same. The Stang is a function of the God and is the Gate and closing for his presence. That is very different than a tool we work with.

Knives are used for practical and ceremonial reasons. The white-handled knife is our ceremonial knife. It is never used for practical reasons. The black or red-handled knife is used for practical purposes: carving, cutting, chopping, and so on. The burin is also common and used to prick things or to carve on candles or other things. All of these knives work on the altar and are the personal tools of the priest.

The wand is a hidden implement of the Stygian. It is the item we do not show and do not bring up in open spaces. Our wands are private and hold our egregore and other power we immerse into it. The wood and the conjuration on it hold it as our most personal item of power. Our mirrors, one regular and one black are used in scrying and, again, are hidden aspects of our Craft. The wand and mirror could be considered the cornerstone of the Stygian practices. Our wand is held in the left hand regardless of hand preference.

The censor is used in the same way as most occult practitioners. We either use sticks or charcoal burners, depending on the need of the practitioner and the ability to have a lot of smoke or a little. Our choice of incense varies. What is typical is a Greek blend of incense, Red Sandalwood, or an orange/cinnamon variety. Many others are used but these are common.

The Mother Goddess candle is always black and always a pillar. In temples, it sits upon a skull. It is only lit when her presence is asked for, or she makes her presence known. It is a sacred candle and only lit by her priests in a temple. The use of music and art is always left to the individual. Some are musicians and artists themselves, so they play or paint and use that to decorate the air and the place. Others will play music or buy the art they need. What is important is the result. The music or the art must reach your passion and your soul, or they are worthless.

The primary divination tools taught within the Kultus are the Tarot cards and the Pendulum. Those two items are the norm. Oracle cards are often added to spice things up over time. However, each individual would choose their specialty and is asked to take on that area's divination system. These same areas define what is on your altar. What statues or art are on the wall will come from whatever pantheon or culture you find yourself studying and practicing. It can also dictate the pottery, chalice, and many items you will choose for tools.

Our altar stones are always present. One is a wooden circular one that is used to rest power items on. These are bigger, like a serving plate. The other is an actual stone, and it can be small or large, but is ever-present. Much like the act of taking oaths on the River Styx itself, the Stygian sees their vows and oaths bound within that altar stone. If they break their word, the same stone will summon all they most fear to collect them. Being a Stygian is always an act of integrity. We do not like to come from the position of "or else," but it is present in that stone sitting on your altar.

One cannot avoid studying. Books, writing, study materials, journaling, and writing down all of your rites and experiments are required. If you did not write it down, it did not happen, is our motto. Get used to it. Dream journals, food journals, sleep journals, and shadow work journals are all par for the course. In the end, you begin to build your own Book of Shadows, which we refer to as your personal Grimoire. Different from the Craft traditions, it is not a passed-down or copied item. It is always written from the notes and experiences of the practitioner. No two are alike. This is even more true as the adept specializes and adds their own aspects and flair to their work. It does not end there. Stygians are scholars. You must also know your lore, religion, history, culture, language, and whatever else is needed to fully embrace a paradigm. It means a lot of reading and seeking out people. The wise will choose carefully.

The specific items for the Stygian cross the cultural boundaries and are the items we all have in common. They include a water bowl made of red ceramic. The coin is always bought and is the item given symbolically in the mundane and actually in the spiritual realm to the Ferryman. The compass is the item used for direction and is both practical and esoteric. Lastly, there is a sand timer. It is not important how small or large. It is a symbol for the Stygian to know that it is all an illusion, just like time.

You can, of course, add other altars by adding multiple spaces. I have an altar table set to the dead, past teachers, ancestors whom I love and respect, elders, and those I have come to know through astral work. On the bookcases are other statues, pictures, and items that speak to my work, my love, and my practices all the time. In the room beside it is a bedroom that is the ritual chamber and my temple. It is afire with spirits. There is a ritual in there each day, incense lit each night, and it exudes the energy of the Stygian Way. Death and Underworld deities are regularly present. It is rather difficult for people outside the Current to adjust to it unless they are just so unaware that it does not matter. Deities have been there many times. There is a high altar on one wall, and it carries the Egregore. In the Stygian Way, that is where our power sits. To the left of the altar is a small Greek altar where I keep a set of Deific statues for those who are very close to me. Above them sits my first guardian animal spirit, who watches the door.

I meditate in this room. I sleep in this room. It is my chamber, and it is my place of power. It is kept in the dark most of the time. Light is allowed when needed, as is the wind to clear out and clean. Fire burns on that altar each day. It is the Temple to the Deities. Some would not want a bed in a room like this, others would want a ton of light, and still others would want a closed-off place. These personal decisions are up to the individual to determine. For me, the setup is near perfect.

My jewelry and personal items have gems, stones, sigils, symbols, and purpose. It is poor form to wear things you do not understand or simply because someone else told you this or that. Research each item like a pet or a large purchase, and decide only after you are fully aware. The wearer must purify, clean, and then anoint each item, and then do it again at varied intervals. Do not allow others to hold or use these items unless you want their energy incorporated. If that happens, you must do it all over again. There are exceptions. I allowed a person to hold a dagger of mine because I wanted her energy infused with mine. She was quite a powerhouse, and the item has kept this energy within it. I feel her every time I take it up. Other jewelry is used for protection, to hold certain power, or to be used in conjunction with a work or a ritual. Other items, like furniture, can or cannot be crucial. I have used an antique table as an altar for thirty years. It used to be my great-grandparents and I know where it was before that. All the other items I use for furniture have no real value. Items not in use should be encased, folded over, or stored. I do not like to do this for some, so I simply keep the room in darkness. At other times, I am doing a seven-to-nine-day ritual and do not want to unveil and re-veil over and over (again, practical).

Familiars, guardians, and sigils are important for ritual spaces. They include servitors. They are all different and have different purposes. I will not disclose mine, but I will tell you that their presence, assistance, and influence change the work by improving the outcomes. If you care for your guardians and familiar or tulpa, they will see more than you can. The reasoning for this is left to your own experiences. I have had a lot of feedback in this area, and I believe it is all about the relationship you build. They can help you to intensify your outcomes or to stay away from certain things that may bring you harm or folly. They can also ignore you just as much as you ignore them. Trust is earned. It is not given without work or, even sometimes, trials. If you built a house of straw, it would fall apart. Build your structures in stone. Take the time, do the work, and it will be a great foundation and support for your daily journey.

A magician without a scroll, book, journal, and references is not much of a magician. We can do all the high-end esoteric work very well, but at the end of the day, we are researchers, librarians, and collectors of knowledge. What we gather feeds us. It allows us to grow. Good works allow us to come back and gain more over and over. Excellent works become our bibles until we move on to the next one after first sucking the marrow out of the bones of the text or writing out the ritual from the dream. What we write is even more important than what we read. That includes our dreams, experiences, experiments, and how we codify and take in the information we gain from other people. It might be found in tomes, instruction, classes, or three hours at the coffee shop with the witch you just met. The magician is a sponge, and the quill/pen and books are canvases for art. Poetry, stories, quotes, pictures, colors, and anything else you find that speaks to you is collectible. I remember first seeing a film about H.R. Giger and knowing he was a magician. His mind collected, and his art proclaimed. While I am on the subject of art, choose your art and décor with care. Art is a vision board; it is the same art you wear if you have the soul of an artist. The Gothic side within the Technology of a Modern Chaos Reality is important and varied, though most go black and dark, I have had the Victorian, Steampunk, and even a Rainbow Goth. You are not limited! That is the beauty and the goal.

Your clothing or nakedness is a large topic. Both are appropriate at different times. The only hard and fast "rules" are for certain rites. Those who do not want to engage in nakedness are aware and do not attend those rites. In the Kultus, this is acceptable to an extent. There are requirements within initiation that cannot be avoided. I cannot express it enough. The occult is supposed to make you uncomfortable. If you cannot get passed that, then this is not the path for you. We do not make exceptions. It is fine if you don't prefer this and keep to initiations, but even then, the Red Mass will be a problem for you. Over time, you must attend them, or you are not following your oath as a Stygian. The shedding of clothing is spiritual. This is not a debatable area for the Stygian. At other times, the cloak, the robes, are also needed and required for the work. We tend to wear black above and red below. This means if we wear a robe or cloak, it is black, but if there is an under robe, it is always red.

What kind of clothing is usually a rather large debate, also, and should not be. If you love your ritual robes and their feeling and movement, and they bring you to the magick, so be it. If you want the breeze on your naked skin and feel the robes pull at you, then shed them. If you want red because black or white doesn't feel right for you, then dye it or buy it. There is no uniform.

If you all decide to be naked and someone just struggles with it, sit them down and try to help them work through it. If they can't, for the love of the Gods, do not let them dictate the entire group (I share this because I have been there), tell them to find a new group, even help them find one, but do not change the whole group for one person. I promise you the entire group will fall apart. We are no longer trusting the feeling and focus of the group, but allowing one person to dictate. That is a disaster waiting to happen. Covens were not created to make it comfortable for people. This modern spin is incorrect and lost. It is only working through what is uncomfortable and understanding it so you can overcome where there is growth. I join groups to be uncomfortable enough to cause change within me. Otherwise, I might as well stay home. Ordeals are necessary, and being naked is not about sex. It is about something far deeper. If you do engage in sex in rituals, the nakedness is not helpful or hurtful; it is a different aspect altogether. People confuse this all the time. Lingerie is a billion-dollar industry for a reason. We dress up for sex, not go naked. People sleep naked and never have sex. Don't confuse them. It is far more sexual for a man to see a woman half-naked than naked. Even women who love men often do not see a penis in the wind as a sexy thing. For some, I am dead wrong. Do the research; the stats are in my favor in polling and surveys.

Women might fear being naked for a history of ridicule, assault, or being told their body is ugly or worse. A man might have been told the same thing. Breaking this pattern is a part of magick. It is a way to be able to be at home in your skin. Not everyone is ready for that, and without the readiness, they will not be able to endure initiation. Hold your tradition above the individual. It was done this way for many good reasons. It is much more common now to excuse people, to make it comfortable for them, or to ignore tradition. You may find these things to be helpful at the moment, but overall, you take the experience and growth from these initiates and water down the tradition. I realize that to beginners and those who dabble, this sounds archaic and out of touch. Veterans of the occult work know better. If your coven, group, or gatherings constantly fail and you are the accommodating type, consider the alternative. If you just want to do it that way, and that is more important to you than the outcome of the work (yes, I am quite aware of the existence of the crowd who says outcomes don't matter? WTF?) I'm sorry you bought or read this book. We are opposites, and my work is not for you.

If you are alone, this might change for you from ritual to ritual. Do what feels right in that situation and try not to address the mundane of comfort or what you want over what is needed. You must also know the history of the cult or tradition you are engaged in. If it is Roman or Greek, it might look one way; if it is a certain Goddess, it might be very conservative, while another might be insulted if someone wore clothing. Also, know the deity and their predilections concerning males or females. Lilith pops up here, as does Dionysus. Look at what they did historically or in the literature. Find scholarly information on their cults, not just myths or stories. If it simply doesn't exist or it is limited, what gnosis have you had? What have others experienced practically? Can you meet with them, talk with them about their gnosis? A lot of these things can be very limited; for instance, Athens tends to be the only direct source of information for most of the Greek information. That is problematic because there were many cults.

Direct experience with the deities is always preferred for the Stygian but not for the scholars and the reconstructionists. When it is direct experience, does it make sense? Dionysus seems to prefer women, as does Lilith. Did the Deities make an exception for you? Were you a different gender then, and you are still with them, or are you lying to yourself because you just want them? I often make the statement that we are too hard on ourselves. I find this to be the exception. We have to be hard on ourselves here, and often occultists are not and go with whim or want.

It is also important to understand that trends come and go. If you live long enough, they may show up in your lifetime twice. This happened to me with bell-bottoms, skinny jeans, and the Goth culture. This is where the Lilith current comes from. It comes from the same place as everyone being into Baphomet, then Set, then Pan, then Odin, and then whoever. Does this mean the deities are stepping out and calling out? Maybe, but in most cases, it means people are silly and like to mimic and copy others. It is the soup of the day. It happens in every profession and every environment of discovery and journey. The new restaurant has opened, and everyone wants to eat there even if it sucks. Everyone is into Lilith, and you can't miss the bandwagon. Don't allow yourself to follow the crowd. The crowd, rather bluntly, is fucked. Do not follow the lemmings to their absurd conclusions, or you die falling off the mountainside along with them. Just do you. If you have a partner, decide as a duo what the two of you will do. If you have a Kultus or group, determine the focus so that everyone is on the same page, and then do that, or you might consider doing it my way. My way is differentiated, meaning I want a group with several different arms. You have a ritualist, you have a researcher, a Pagan, a witch, even a Satanist. You certainly want a Chaos Magician.

This differentiated group allows for many different people to come together and join forces or share ideas. It allows for many streams of consciousness to come together. This was the principal foundation of the college. It was to be a place where knowledge could be debated, shared, and challenged, and scholarly outcomes might help the greater population. In the case of the Kultus, it is esoteric knowledge, and it is for the benefit of our members and those who associate with us.

If you do choose a group that all get in line and do the same thing, do not read this as conformity. Read this as an intention and a common core that can be changed or swapped if there is diversity or differences in the group. On a side note, there are always trolls or people who must be different. My advice is to eject them very publicly from the group with prejudice. Make an example of them. It may sound hard and harsh, but destroying the bad apples makes for an excellent environment for what you all got together for. It enforces the safety and unwavering loyalty to the group, and not some problem child. We do not suffer through the idea of doing no harm. We suffer with the responsibility of outing someone so they cannot do it again in the next group. The truth is that not one but many groups will ignore your warnings because their entire system is infested with the same people. You cannot help them, and they are not the reason for the outing. It is for other good and well-intentioned groups that you wish to spare misery. Drama and idiots waste time. We are all slowly dying, and there is no time for that.

To be very clear, I am not stating that the trend to Lilith or any other deity is wrong or misinformed. What I am stating is that what is dark or dangerous sounding is often a pull for people to line up to copy, take advantage, and make up some narrative that is not real. Be careful. If the Kultus were to blow up in popularity, I fully expect to see flaming idiots wearing Grim Reaper costumes and claiming to be a part of the Kultus; it will be funny, it will be wrong, and it will go out of style quickly. We must understand the terrain of people and how they think.

In one incident with a friend for whom I did a reading, I saw Persian deities and a form of what I thought was Marduk. He shook his head angrily. He had seen it many times, too. He was trying to avoid it like the plague. He was prejudiced against the culture and the people, and he did not want to do it. He reported other spirits coming at him at times to pull him to this deity. Several months later, I caught him at a coffee shop, and he looked so happy. He was wearing jewelry associated with Persia, had grown out his beard, and reported he had come around, and that same deity was amazing! I was very happy for him in the mundane (to get past the prejudice) and in the spiritual because that God was serious about his attention.

I understand that people might determine that this was all in his head, but I had no idea. He experienced other deities guiding him over to Marduk. He was running up against this form in the mundane and what he was taught here and now, versus his apparent long history in Persia and the Middle East in prior lives. They knew him. Having these experiences recurrently does not allow a person to be agnostic or see deities as some figment. I did not tell my friend, but learned after some meditations when Marduk returned to me and gestured a thank you around the time my friend changed his mind, that I felt my friend at peace. I did not realize he accepted the God and, in time, the Goddess into his life.

This is how deities are discovered. It is not via sitting at a book and flipping pages until you find one. It is not done by copying others. It is certainly not usually done the first time around the block with religions. People need time to develop, experience, and grow into themselves.

It can be comical how much people do not seem to recognize what is right in front of them. It is not funny to them and can be very difficult or frustrating. Teaching requires patience and kindness. It also requires an edge for others. I have seen teachers with too much of one and none of the other be unbalanced and constantly lose students. It is the teacher's job to hold the line. If they are wishy-washy or passive, they are walked on. If they are just hard, few see the beauty they offer.

I had a person I mentored for years. She was getting frustrated and, one day, finally asked what I thought. She had an altar dedicated to a Goddess and had crystal and earthenware items all over the place. They were very delicate, and she never broke one of them. Under her Goddess candle, she had bought four different expensive mounts to raise the candle. All of them had fallen and broken on the floor, even when they fell on the thick carpet, they would roll and break on the floor. It seemed odd. I asked for a picture. When she gave me one, I chuckled. I asked for the name of the Goddess, and she told me, and I knew at once what was happening. The woman wanted the red but did not listen to her Matron, who was telling her she did not like red. Red meant fire and romance for the practitioner but something else to the Matron. I told her to research it. A week later, she returned. Culturally, red meant harlot and the Goddess was offended and destroyed the vessels with her candle. The Goddess also turned up the heat and the negativity. The woman also reported when she put the candle in a porcelain white vessel, as was recommended in her book, she felt less upset and anxious very quickly. The work with her Matron improved greatly. Colors matter, items matter, and the feeling above all matters. Pay attention! There are no coincidences. The gut feeling is important.

The Kultus does a lot of work on the senses and sensitivity. I have never seen this kind of attention to these skills in any other occult system. There is a very good reason for this. Our senses create our reality, so we must maximize their potential, and then we must trust them. The more we do that, the more in touch we are with what happens and why. We see and understand synchronicity better. It aligns more. Don't look for manifestations to happen your way. Deity does as it does, and you are seeking the result. The path to it may not be, and is usually not in your purview or control, of what you envision. I often see this as an ocean. You step into it, and it is in control. You simply feel it, move with it, and if you move against it, it may drown you.

I recently did a hard, long ritual asking for an intervention. Typically, these work out around 90% of the time. I put in the sweat, the fluids, and the passions. All of the signs were there. A blazing flame two feet tall, pictures in the wax, it looked very good. It failed. I was pissed. I left the altar for two days.

Why? How did this happen? I returned to the cards, and it laid it out for me. The Deities saw what I saw differently. They were giving me what I asked for, but not in the way I wanted it. Even though I laid out my way in detail, they discarded that and overlaid their Will. If you are going to work with Deities, you have to accept that it is how it is. As a sorcerer, I want more control over the outcomes. So, for you, is that a failure or a success? I initially read it as a failure, but then marked it as a success because I saw what they were saying, and they were right.

I do not believe you can do occult work without being open and having the ability to listen. How you listen can be very diverse: divinations, automatic writing, astral, meditation, etc. In all instances, you must be able to hear and drown out your own biases or wants. They are not important and are referred to as noise, the monkey brain, and other things. Your will and Daemon, however, should never be drowned out but opened up. The trick is knowing the difference. It is through them that we gain insight and can take the more advanced approaches. Once you are aware of the difference, the Stygian will see you as more advanced. We can say no to the Gods, as the Gods can say no to us. I did not seek out an Indian Current, but those deities sought me out in droves from the entire pantheon. I have had the same experience with the Greeks. Why? Who knows. I do not ask why. I simply do the research and court them as I would any honored guest.

Exactly like the altar, the form of divination can be linked or not linked to the culture or deity. I never liked the idea of scrying because it did not feel like a solid tool like the runes or the cards. That is not what happened. My intent and the outcome are opposites. Scrying and I are bound until the grave. It is primarily not just in the Kultus, but it is where I do my best work. None of the books I read, and I read all the ones I could find (I even spent hundreds of dollars seeking out-of-print and hard-to-find versions, and still nothing close to what my tradition and personal experiences offered.) Those books were all based on the basics and nothing more. This is far too common in the occult world. To make sure I got things right in my work, I also added an oracle deck and other aids. The most important part of divination is that it works for you. If everything you are getting turns out wrong. If all your answers get you going in the wrong direction or confuse you, then it is you. Change it up.

You must understand user errors. If the person is not in line, aligned, and in touch with an actual deity or spirit, then the power is not present, and it is just wishful thinking. This path is simply not for everyone. The reason so many people swap one method for another is that they do not have any connection. This leads to the same comments on social media, telling people no one can do this or that, or that is not real, or some other garbage that is incorrect overall due to that person's limitations. The question also comes up. How can you tell? Anyone who asks this question has not felt the presence. Also, others will leave it at the doorstep of the mind, the psyche, and say it is what is in their heads. This is a double-edged sword because you can say that about anything; if it is not in your head, then the whole idea is irrelevant because you are the creator of your reality. But if they are saying it is not there, that is another thing. That means they believe the spirits are delusions or figments of imagination, making that true for them. Typically, those who believe this have not had an encounter, and it is a way to tell yourself that you are like others.

People influence your outcomes if you let them. Be internally motivated by what you experience. If you are motivated by others to be like them or have their experiences, then you are letting them influence you. Instead, be the one who others follow, and do not be deterred by judgment or criticism. Allow your experiences to dictate, not petty jealousy or envy of others.

Take this a step further. Talk to some psychics who are opening up for the first time and ask them about their experience. In each encounter with these people, it is always the same. Those who have actual experiences know what is happening and are very clear. They often do not express their thoughts or words. Those who are faking are hedging their bets. They are very unclear. I am not talking about being a newbie and struggling. I am talking about being a liar. Everyone struggles in transition. There is a small group in the middle with such low self-esteem or worth that they cannot help but second-guess everything. If they continue that trend, they will not retain their gifts and give them up. Teaching and empowering people to trust and believe in themselves is counter-intuitive to society and a crime against humanity. The Kultus will be a forerunner in changing that in the occult community in small groups. That is one of my goals.

I have been around several people who have experienced other entities. It is not Hollywood fiction. It is not a novel made into reality. It is not fan fiction. The basis of my work is within the realm and guidance from the Deity and the Daemon in a single breath. From the outside, some may say I am talking to myself, my inner self, my Higher Self, or even my HGA (this is usually the tipping point), but does it matter? If the goal is transmission, enlightenment, and merging with deity, how do you merge with something you don't believe in? What are you evoking or invoking? Some of the LHP would say, "Yourself." So, we are calling on ourselves to come before ourselves seems like megalomania to me. It is a narcissist's wet dream. At some point, there is another entity, or it is mindful masturbation. If you choose to believe it is not there, let me walk you through the halls of an asylum with all the religious delusions and schizophrenic psychosis. It might be interesting to note that historically, 80% of psychosis is religion-based (according to statistics from the mid-1990s). It is not a coincidence. People even claim they drove themselves insane. I am not going to try to convince anyone of this. Believe what you like. I am sharing why Stygians are different from most.

The alignment I referred to comes from the aligning of the three souls, aligning the three energies or bodies. I will use the elements to explain it. Because I am speaking to a more advanced audience, I would suspect you already understand. They are the earth & water body, the fire & air body, and the spiritual body. The earth and water bodies indicate the lowest points and many of the most common and needed aspects: the lower chakras, the sexual, belly, grounding, foundational, the legs and feet, the center of the body's energy pool, and the sex and food organs. It is the gut reaction of intuition as well as the center of the body, or Dan Tien, used for the collection of all energy, power, and storage.

The air and fire bodies are the solar plexus, throat, and heart. They are the talker, the emotional intelligence, the knowing the self, and also the intermingling fire of passions, the ability to create and destroy, the breath, the voice (inner and outer), and the mind, meaning will and intellectual mind. This is the focus, intent, driver, and cognition of ideas and events. The spiritual body is called many things: ether, HGA, Higher Self, the Link, the Source, Daemon, and other things. It is the non-corporeal, the place of the Guide, the Whisperer, the High Guru, or whatever term you like. What is it? It looks different to everyone and can have no real description. Here is where the mysteries and the esoteric center meet. Its function is to be connected to Source, power, and direction, to intertwine wills. If you are religious, you might do this with a Deity; if you are not, it might be via a HGA idea or some other version of Source like the Tao. The term Tenchi is valuable here, meaning heaven and earth. Think of it like a lightning rod. Lightning is the power, and if it is faulty, it will fry the building, but if it does its job, then it takes in all forms of energy and drives it into the center. If our aspects are aligned, it works as planned.

The merging of these elements is a basic form of enlightenment. Once it is mastered, then, and only then, can you refine, look deeper, and determine. It can take in energy and power and focus it effectively. Notice I am not using terms "want, would like, might enjoy," or anything regarding a fancy. This is nothing of the kind. This is something you would willingly die for. If it was the choice between being who and what you are and doing what you need to do or facing death, you would raise your hand for death. That is the integrity and depth of the occultist's will. Who among you would raise your hand? Be honest.

You can see that even though this chapter is about tools, the tool I spoke about most is your body and its use. There is a good reason for this. Your body is the ultimate tool and the only one you have to have. The rest are props. It is important to understand that the altar before me is the same one on the astral. There is a reason for the saying that we work between worlds. My guardians, who sit in my Temple, come too. They protect me in both worlds. My servitors or tulpas may vary. Some will accompany me while others are off doing their work.

It is important to differentiate your like or love from what is needed and required for the work or religion. I am a sword guy. I own quite a few, but it did not equate to the work, so I separated my love for the blade from my occult workings. I did not like working altars. I preferred high altars, but again, that was not to be. To the left side of the altar is the working portion. Here sits my working grimoire, a quill or pen, parchment for various things, the scrying mirror, and or regular mirror, depending on the need. I was used to sitting on the floor, but the tradition uses a Blood Throne, and so I was now sitting in a chair.

I share this with you to show you that I work very hard not to get in my way. What is easy or usual is often not right. Sometimes you get lucky, but most of the time, for me anyway, it was a path to growth and stretching. I am quite comfortable with it now. It took time to get there.

CHAPTER SIXTEEN

A DEEPER DIVE INTO THE MUNDANE

Another chapter on philosophy is an even deeper trek into my world. This one may give some a headache because it spins up some conceptions that might cause some angst. I would ask that you consider and not automatically put up a wall. If you have made it this far, I expect that it is very possible.

People often claim they are compassionate. They also suggest it as a reason why people do what they do. As if they knew others' intentions or their hearts and minds. What no one seems to do is allow for personal responsibility. That may sting to some, but it must be explained more thoroughly. For this to be sensible, it means we must up the ante and not lower it. People must, as a society, seek to ratify equality in reality and not in symbolic gestures that make us feel better. They are empty symbols that help no one. To unequivocally ratify equality is possible but difficult. The way it is usually attempted is poor and silly. It is meant to give things away and rectify, which it can never do. Instead, an entire system of education, housing opportunities, and even investments should be made so that people still in poor conditions have all the same opportunities as anyone else. If you leave people in crime-infested streets, do not offer other opportunities, and create markets where they cannot compete, they have no real options. Do you believe it takes decades and decades to change things? It doesn't. It takes intent and the want to do it. Politicians and elitists have neither the want nor the real intent. When they are reelected, they make the same promises over and over and lie through their teeth. What did they learn? We are a team sports country. As long as they wear the right color, you will re-elect them no matter what.

We give people assistance when what they need is an incentive. The assistance can accompany it, but without the incentive, they will be back and ask for more because it is enabling and not empowering. Giving people confidence and experience far outweighs scraps of money or poor jobs. Education and knowledge are priceless if they result in real work and change lives. The usual colleges and universities with agendas of continuing old theories, generating new ones that are useless, and ideas without practicality or real-world investment are debt without purpose. Building self-worth is essential to changing your family tree so the next generations look different. There should always be options to opt out of anything, but it should be an informed decision. That is a program I would be honored to support and work to see implemented.

Let's use an example. The prison system is a privately owned set of institutions where violence, sexual violation, and a massive mental health crisis lives and is not treated. It is fed constantly, but oversight and actual reformation do not seem to do well. Look at the research and the numbers. It exists, and it is terrible. Then people come out to what? They must disclose they are felons and cut themselves out of jobs, loans, and programs they cannot get into. Did they serve their time, or are they labeled forever? If they were criminals, wouldn't crime pay more? What happens to the women who had kids who are in prison? The entire problem just perpetuates into the family tree. Now, their parents went to jail. No one was there for them or to train those children. Where will those kids end up? We must break these cycles. That is the real problem.

Why is this important to an occultist and a Stygian? If we have any children, friends, family, or any of our close ties or even people within the pagan, occult, or witch communities in our lives, we want to see them all succeed. It matters because when you make things too easy, people stop trying. That is the opposite of what we want. As occultists, we want people to thrive. If they are told they do not know, they cannot succeed, or they are from this column, or that one, and are stuck, then this sets limits. By now, you know that limits cause your reality and your mind to limit. Knowing this way is not for everyone is tricky because those who are not awakened may need more help. But do they? I have worked with many different populations over the years. Each time things were given too easily, the person failed to rally to their cause. However, when they were challenged and supported, most of the time, they rallied and did amazing things. Some will never rally, and some will rally with support, but the norm is that the challenge inspires.

Instead, history tends to want us to be dependent. I am being kind. History wants us to be slaves. Religion wants us to be slaves, and so do the state and the elitists who benefit from slavery. You may find this hyperbolic and over the top because no one walks around with a whip and chains unless you head to the BDSM club. However, if you look at the last few paragraphs, there are other ways to enslave. The only thing you need to enslave is the mind, and the body will follow. Those who are asleep are bound by their limits. Yet, to simply look past them is also a mistake. That is why awakening people is part of the job and duty of everyone who is a Stygian, not as evangelists or seeking converts. We do it by planting seeds of doubt in the influence that makes us slaves, causing distress in being a slave, and offering a mirror so we cannot just repeat the same things over and over, convincing ourselves we are right. Allow others to see the joy and beauty that awareness offers, allow them to see the beauty of the darkness even, and when they ask, share what they can hear. Do not overwhelm, support, and seek to clear away a little of their sleep. The more people are awakened to the possibilities, the less they tribalize their mentality of this group versus that group, while allowing the slave masters a pass. Eventually, the better the general population becomes, the better the world around them becomes.

What does this have to do with my tradition or the occult? Nothing lives in isolation. Everything affects everything else, and the system in which it lives influences and modifies it. It is important to understand why there is so much confusion and why it is not accidental. I am going to use Christianity as an example because I live in the US, and it is the most popular religion. It is the most entwined in the culture. I must express that this religion is not the point. All religions of its kind are the same in reference to my argument.

The words of Jesus, if accurate, are quite in line with Buddhism and other articulate writings and speeches of avatars or enlightened beings. It is true that if the words and history are correct, the cult was never to outlast the generation. It was an apocryphal cult. The apostles and the members of their fledgling church were all to follow the Savior to the grave and be with him in paradise. A paradise that never came. It does not take a deep dive into the New Testament to garner this insight, yet I know very few Christians who are aware of it. It is right in their book, yet they are not taught this. I admit I attended a graduate theology seminary. Like many of those who attended (look at how many drop out; it is quite interesting), I dropped out because I could not take the hypocrisy. They all knew the truth, yet they taught otherwise.

Generations later, the same people decided, when they did not perish in some Revelation, that they should compile their religion and systematize it when all the apostles were dead. The reworking led Constantine and others to format state religions just as they had the old Roman one. And in the same fashion, it was a way to get the people or the "mob" to fear, follow, and worship. They did this to create a version of morality, a need for elites (in this case, clergy and the empire) to preach or kill the "savagery" out of the pagan or tribal peoples, as the Christians had been treated at the outset of their cult. Revenge is best served by religion.

When people who came after Jesus became missionaries, they would go out to convert, forcing their ways upon others. This fortified and piggybacked the colonization of the world while also killing those they chose who would not relent on their tribal religions. The sword and the cross traveled together along with disease. As this came to pass, churches were continually built (usually upon the temples, holy places, or altars of the former religions). Puritans and Catholics made their way to the New World, and their priests and pastors came with them. Although the Constitution separates church and state, the stain of history is there. I recall in high school, the teacher commenting, "The Puritans were so puritanical, and yes, that is where the word comes from, the British told them to get out of England!" These are some of the founders of the colonies. The foundational underpinnings are not against any form of slavery, although it caused them discomfort, and some did seek to stop it. The use of people in this way was common all around the world and implicit in their holy writings. When that became problematic and led to uprisings, they simply moved to indentured servants, plantations that needed sharecroppers, or the like. The idea never really changed, just the wording and the extent of the inhumanity.

Today, we have the same thing. People are still kept in poverty by a system that spends trillions on other countries, which it can use to funnel back money through war, crimes, or the stealing of others' resources. The names of political sides are akin to a coin with two sides. Both are part of the same system and out for the same group of players. None of them represent the people in poverty or the middle class. No one is expected to even try to tell the truth. It is all about the spin. The value is no longer present. There are a ton of articles and news reports of teachers, educators, and administrators who see no problem with plagiarism, lies, dumbing down education, and offering slanted messaging because, in their arrogance, they believe they know better. This is not a good direction. It is nothing new, but it is somehow sickeningly distasteful in a world with 24-hour news. It is all so tribal, and that is highly encouraged. People like to hate. I recall films around Rome, especially gladiator films, where people loved the blood and torture. Being eaten by lions or killed off in some fashion, all for entertainment. These people sat in rags, yet they wanted to see others suffer as they suffered. What could that breed? Is it true? Well, the writings of the times indicate it is. But what about now? Have you watched the latest video games or violent films? Versions of pornography? It seems people still like this entertainment.

Talking to people about these issues is like telling a Yankees fan that the Red Sox have a point. It is tribal insanity and feels like the Catholics and Protestants in the time of King Henry VIII. It is no longer just politics, and the people who are aware know it is religion. We have moved to a place where we cannot hear the other side at all. Social media and general media further the divide, but to what end? The end is always the same. It never changes. Those who want control force the people to war against each other, to fear what the other side is doing, and to cause mistrust and doubt. If they do this, the people are not looking at the corruption and destruction of liberty and freedom, which are our real enemies. The undercurrent of modern history is filled with ways to dumb down (I have used this term a lot and for good reason) everything from writing to comprehension to poisoning of our food, livestock, water, and environment, to critical thinking, to the level of education, access to drugs that delude, and quiet us, and not giving us access to medications that help (and has been used by other countries for decades at minimal costs), to massive grabs of money to elitists while the rest of us are never too big to fail. A healthcare and drug company field day on people who now do not trust their leaders or government due to the mountains of lies and still no accountability. There was a break in the people. Even those who might have died from a pandemic they did not see as real, or the people screaming follow the science, who followed a media that quieted the science they did not like. They made it about winners and losers and not what science is, the same as magick. It is an ongoing experiment where the facts change as new data is presented. In the end, almost everyone was wrong.

I could also list the news articles and links to various forums, but again, based on where it comes from, people would either accept it if it followed their narrative or reject it. If they wanted to believe the other side, it would fall on deaf ears. It then becomes a waste of my time and energy, so I leave it to the reader to discern, as always. Spirituality and my tradition kick in right about here. Because society is the cesspool I have written about in this and other chapters, we must further discern ourselves from it and then infect it in a different direction to have our liberties and freedoms in place to do the work we are here to do.

It all began in the Garden of Eden. The first lie is right off the bat. God puts a tree in the middle of the garden and says, "Do anything you like, but don't eat from this." Perhaps human nature was new, perhaps it was a test, or perhaps this was a precursor to Job and his shenanigans. What is clear is who was honest. The serpent arrives and tells the truth, "If you eat from it, you will not die but become like God." Here is where my tradition begins. The first step of the occult is to be conscious. The apple made them aware, but without the whisper of the snake, they would have remained fearful and ignorant. They now knew they were naked. Before, they were playthings, and God called that paradise. Ignorance is, indeed, bliss. Of course, there are consequences to face for the snake and the people. In this act, we removed the fish from their tank, and the experiment (clearly an experiment) was interrupted. With understanding comes hardship. But it was not just understanding they needed, but wisdom.

Is it any wonder that for centuries no one was allowed to read the Bible but the clergy? It takes a hell of a spin to take this story and make God the good guy. He appears like a controlling tyrant from the beginning. He lies yet punishes the one who tells the truth. Humanity, it seems from the scribes of the

Old Testament/Hebrew Scriptures, that this God wanted his toys all to himself. He did not want them to be aware, awake, and preferred to keep them stupid, locked up, and naked. Like all good tyrants, when they did not play his way, and someone told them the truth, they and all their offspring would pay the price. Enter the reality of work, elitism, and power over others, child raising, violence via Cain, and the breaking apart of families. God shows human nature in claiming jealousy, wanting to be the one and only, and very willing to watch his minions commit genocides, as much as he liked to do them in floods, burning, and sending his angels to destroy.

Wisdom traditions take time and work and would show up in the various cultures of Egypt, China, Persia, India, Babylon, Greece, and Sumer/Mesopotamia. Of course, other great empires and civilizations would develop as well. Tribal people would develop through their methods of herbology, shamanism, and even astrology/astronomy to advance their cultures and traditions. Many Gods would come forth.

I cannot help but associate this history with the medical complex. The basis of herbs has been in practice since people ate vegetation, yet somehow the pharmaceutical companies and medical associations often disqualify herbalists and their much older and healthier methods as ineffective or untested, while their drugs list thirty or more side effects (some include death, which seems more like an effect than a side effect) and seem worse than they are worth. Might the cost difference be the reason? Planting a root and healing yourself or having an herbalist help you seems far more desirable than the thirty side effects, but I am not a doctor who prescribes poisonous chemicals regularly, so what do I know? Don't get me wrong, there are miracle drugs for many things, and the research is important. It just seems to me that if you tell a population all these things are cancer-causing and they eat them anyway, we are not dealing with the root issue. If you poisoned a field and then led the sheep there, they would most likely eat the food. How do we prevent suicide but are fine with cancer-causing agents slowly killing people? Is there a difference? If it is all a choice, then shouldn't it all be a choice? That is too much liberty, I suppose.

The difference, and this is a very important factor, is that modern religions are set up to be parasites, moral authority, and indoctrinators. The tribal traditions and many of the historical religions were set up to maximize the individual within the community, satisfy a role, and fulfill their personal responsibility. They would often die or survive based on the wisdom and guidance of their leaders and shamans. They were in it together, but the goals were initiatory and individualized. They were to seek guidance and enlightenment from the deity. This is not the same for the megachurch, which makes millions while its congregations barely get by. They are not in it together. Our government is supposed to be run by the people, yet the polls indicate we never get what we want: universal healthcare, relief of student debt, homelessness problem, security for our people, infrastructure, not adding to the national debt, term limits, clean food and water, and so on. These might not be your issues. Add them in or remove the ones you don't like. It doesn't change the point. We do not get what we voted for.

The truth is, and has been since the Garden, we have the potential to be like a deity, we have the potential to create and destroy, and we can move the mountain if we say the mountain shall move. We have many ways to get there, but it is all hidden, nullified, dramatized, or made fun of by popular media and Hollywood. It is not taken seriously by religion. We have endured the overwriting of history, religion, and our potential for so long that we now make fun of it in cliches: the world will break you after adolescence, it is all downhill, and the two things you can count on are death and taxes. These things strip us of life, identity, and our ability to have autonomy. Is it any wonder that we are having an identity crisis? Is it any wonder people mindlessly go to church to punch their cards, listen to what they have to do, and just try to get by?

At some point, when we began to lose more and more compassion, this changed in my perception. Other people would say it did not change, and they could be right. For me, people seemingly returned to the mob mentality. They wanted to see others suffer, and that changed how things looked to me. The problem for people of the Kultus, the occult, and similar spiritual paths is that we cannot work to cross purposes. If we are to do the work in the mundane world and work our path, there is only so much time. The mundane is so significantly broken that it will take generations to un-fuck. Yet, the work of the Stygian must be done if that is our calling. That work is primary.

It is akin to having to meditate, and the house is on fire. You could burn up in the fire and return in a new life, but that is the long way around. It is more sensible to rise and leave the house. In our current state, the proverbial house is on fire. So, we are forced to split our attention or lose the liberty that is so needed for our freedom to do the work. We all have certain skills, and mine are often to teach, speak, or write about these issues to try to bring people together beyond their limits. Every encounter, when I do that, I deem it as a help to the world around me. I am not trying to change minds, coerce, or get people to think as I do. I am trying to awaken them, to make them see the real enemy at the gate, and to admonish them not to be like sheep to slaughter. When I do this, I am often asked if I am on the blue or red side of politics. My answer is simple: the blue holds a large butcher knife, and the red a pistol. Both are intent on killing me or enslaving me. They are the same. Picking one death or enslavement over the other is nonsensical. If you allow people to box you, they will happily do it to your detriment. Nothing has changed since the Garden.

Instead, gain wisdom and seek out mentors, teachers, and traditions that inspire and separate you from the fold that bays at the moon and follows others. Seek your own path. Be your own person. Be aware of the influences but not subject to them. Be aware of your ethics above those of the state or religion. Seek your divinity, the inner path, and do not allow others to dissuade you from it. Keep to discipline, as laziness can sneak in. Remain awake and not lulled asleep by the drum of others. The compassion you often hear about is fake. True compassion is often discussed in Buddhism and is about the understanding of the Oneness of Being. A true occult master of the self will also understand the remarks from the Bible concerning casting off a leg or plucking out an eye (Matt 18:8-9). These aspects are also true. Compassion is for others because they are part of us, and we are them; however, if the appendage "sins," then we cast it off. Sin for you may be very different than it is for me. I would refer to sin as an atrocity. This is why I can readily cast away politicians, tyrants, and elitists who seek harm for their own gain. Their sin allows them to be cast off. Yet, I still hold an understanding that their system, their training, the government, the society, and their sickness are the root causes. In that, I keep my compassion but still must hold them accountable for their compliance with the sickness. The compassion also must turn inward on you. You must give yourself grace and compassion. Many struggle with this concept.

These are external philosophies. The internal work is far different. You will recall that the Stygian is internally motivated by training and personality. It is the reason death is not feared, and death is preferred over the loss of freedom. I can relate to martyrs and libertines who preferred death to lies or prison. I can relate to people who choose to die over staying alive on machines. I am not judging cowards or people who want to stay alive and who fear death. My role is never to judge. That may seem like an odd statement for someone who is constantly referring to my system and offering my perspective. However, do not forget the instructions over and over throughout; the choice is yours. I am a writer, and this book holds my preferences and experiences. I do not see my perspective as a judgment at all. I see it as the Stygian Way lens as opposed to your lens, unless, of course, they align. It is not via judgment that I determine my surroundings. It is by my foundational training and greater skills sought that I determine my fate with the consultation and wisdom of my Daemon. Through that Daemon, it is further edified by Deities.

It is my spiritual need for higher vibrations that I must attend to. The concept of this is much more advanced but fundamental to enlightenment. I must disassociate from those who are fundamentally asleep in that spiritual work. Fear is the killer of the occult work, and it can be catchy, like a cold. It doesn't matter if it is external or internal. It is a problem when dealing with deities or spirits. The same is true for second-guessing or doubting. These things kill spells, success, and entropy one's skills from improving. If you use the Stygian methods well, you are forced to isolate in a world of fear-mongering and warmongering. Negativity is everywhere. Isolating from it is essential. At the same time, you must engage others and balance yourself by doing so. The isolation happens in sets, regrouping, settling down, grounding, and then you must return to the action.

One of the things I detest in modern times is the Chicken Little idea of screaming the sky is falling all the time, but having no solutions. With that in mind, I am going to put forth solutions. My reasoning and ideas are not for the general public. I have no sway over them and do not seek office to change that. I am not interested enough in the mundane. I am offering options for what I would refer to as "like-minded people." I am staying in my lane.

The problem with isolation is that it allows us to believe our own press. That is why people in my tradition must seek out others. I just read a bio today of a woman who says she has been a solitary practitioner of eclectic witchcraft for 20 years, and my first thought was, Why would you say that? What are you trying to tell others? I read this as antisocial behavior and the inability to work with others. I read this as an untested and unsure methodology of not wanting others to mentor or teach you because you think you know better. And lastly, I read it as a person who can only see through their lens, a massive limitation. She was offering tarot readings. Is she a bad marketing person? Am I reading this differently than you would read it? I found her at an occult gathering. The three people with me did not choose her. I was there for a little over two hours, and she sat alone. I was not surprised. When I went by later, she was sitting with people who looked different than the normal crowd. The unaware? I heard part of her reading. I have read cards for many years. She did not know the meaning of her cards.

I have sought solutions for many years for the many problems I have described in this chapter. I have also been a part of the solution by working directly with many groups and communities to assist them as a professional, and even before. I have a long history of working inside the mental health and addiction communities and treatment programs. I have been part of education concerning sex and AIDS/HIV. And many other community projects to help people change their outcomes. I also grew up in the lower middle class and had my own experiences around all these issues firsthand.

I would like to see any of these options become a reality:

- A cooperative of yurts, tiny houses, cabins, and the like, all built on land for and by the group, with bigger buildings for kitchens, training halls, and a temple. Communal spaces or individual spaces with general areas that we can add to by people who are of similar minds. Ideally, in a place where we could grow and a place where we might have a farm and gardens.
- An urban cooperative where the group buys an industrial building and uses the roof and top floors for the gardens and apartment living, and the lower floor as a shopping and selling space for our wares and skills. We share the

work, and the system feeds us income and support through our trades and wares.

- A pagan monastic community where we come together for the rituals, ceremonies, instruction, and ongoing work towards our personal and joined ventures. I always see a place of varied altars in a large, round tower centered in a village of sorts on the outskirts of a city or town.
- A Renaissance village of sorts with built-in land to live on all year long. A community that uses crafts, seances, witches, wizards, music, and all aspects of food and entertainment. It is run by the artists and the owners of the land, and not some wealthy person who dictates to the players who make little to no money from their sweat and tears. These fairs have been around for a long time in the US, and it is clear that many kinds of people attend for many reasons. An authentic witch and pagan community offering their wares, skills, talents, and being able to live authentically in their ways would be an excellent idea in a time where sexuality, occultism, polyamory, and other ideas are in large flux and change in the mundane. This would allow people to be raised in an open community that supports them and offers them liberty.

All of these have been proposed in the past and, for one reason or the other, never made it off the ground. Usually, it was due to the out-of-pocket costs to go into the land or building. This is made worse in our current state of affairs. I still believe this is the best method to prevent society from fully infiltrating the work. I dream of it a lot. I want to pass on knowledge and wisdom traditions, my library, notebooks over the years, and so much more. In quiet discussions with elders and those over forty-five, I have heard a lot of similar feelings. I also want to pass on my tools and items to people who would appreciate them and use them appropriately.

These solutions are all small. They are all communal. That is not an accident. To prove the truth, you must experiment. Systems like this have been in play for generations now. Some stem from the 60s or 70s and offer very successful people. The catch-22 is that the communities do not promote it. They are probably afraid of publicity or some frame of a "cult" and drawing the attention of the government or media. Larger institutions also do not seem to want to know about them and their results. Do they work? In my experience looking at them, yes, many of them are very successful. Some did exceedingly well during the pandemic because they were already isolated and gathering their own food. The fear is also that they can never be the general population because it is not scalable. All true. However, if we saw the beauty, perhaps we could make changes to move towards these positive outcomes. They just do not fit the outcome of greed and control.

The merging of reality and the occult is always an act of magick. The people who spend their lives in this work has increased in my experience. When gender and other constructs of limitation are broken, it allows us to further benefit from openness, the Chaos Current, and the ability to get closer to the individual, the self. The further we are from that, the more likely we are to be involved in society and the less we do our work. Abraham Maslow, MD, was a genius around the idea of when we are ready to advance and when it is impossible. If you look closer at this, we can see that sometimes the part of society that bucks the system does so during chaos. The 1960s are a great example of this in the hippy movement. It was a time of war and a time of dissonance at war with authority. We are in great need of that again, and it is coming, but it looks very different. I am hopeful it will lead to a deeper identity and bleed into the occult current.

CHAPTER SEVENTEEN

MASKS OF THE RITUAL

Drama, psychopomp, psychodrama, ritual, rites, initiation, theatrical aspects, and the masks we choose to wear each day of our lives are all part of our person. This chapter is all about art. It includes all the ideas and uses of drama, music, dance, actual physical art, the work of the muse, the sexual and romantic aspects of ritual, and so much more. If philosophy helps to define purpose and reason, art defines why we do it and how it feeds us. It is the action and movement that puts the purpose into play.

The masks are not just for ritual. In fact, there are two aspects of using the mask. The first is what we show others, what we see in our mirrors, and what we seek to portray. Masks are useful and necessary to live in the mundane. We could not show up to the office naked with a horned deity mask on our head, and blades bared with an erection or bared breasts, yet if we do this at our altar, it may not only be common but expected by the deity who seeks to mount us. This second set of masks is purely for the spiritual. That means most of the population only has one set. That is important to note.

Masks are part of our societies, but they are not as black and white as we might think. Sometimes, it is very subtle. It is a matter of not telling the whole story to someone who would not understand. It might be that our audience is children, and so we change the narrative of what we are and who we are. It may be that we are working with other people, and they use robes, so we wear robes (when in Rome, remember?). It could be that we are around Wiccans or Pagans, and so we follow them in their patterns. This does not mean that we abandon our identity. If we utter words, recitations, or mantras, we might change them, focus on different aspects, or direct our energies differently. Groups may say this could hurt the overall intent of the rite or ritual, and if they feel this way, we (Stygians) might have to sit out.

The variations of what masks are and how they are used are so wide that they could fill the entire book alone. The Kultus tends to generate a great power surge in our invocations by using actual masks. We also tend to play with masks (not literal) in our everyday lives to fit in or stand our ground. Some use it as a way to awaken people. Others use masks to generate better careers, to market themselves, or to get a date. For Stygians, working in the spiritual is primarily for power generation. I have done bodywork, and it took me a long time to learn how to lessen the flow or, in Taoist terms, use the yin and yang to balance one another. When I began, my scalp rained down in sweat because I ran exceedingly hot. Stygians are trained in energy work and balancing it.

Our masks hold energy. The positions we take, beliefs we keep, and words we choose say a great deal about who we are. These are masks. The question is, did you develop your own mask, or are you a mimic? Do you sound like your parents, your priest, your teacher, or the people you listen to on social media? Or do you take in influence and information and choose? These responses show a night-and-day difference. One has insight and wisdom, the other is just shopping and taking it on as their own, or allowed in influence. Those people have no real mask of their own. That is much more common than someone insightful. It is why when you ask someone about a news item of the day, they either quote someone else or discern their understanding. These are not the same.

We cannot have this discussion without looking at limitations. Anyone who has seen shows like *American Idol* in the early years is very much aware that people who think they can sing often cannot. We must know ourselves, who we are, and our limitations, and accept some of them with some exceptions. There are also times when we must expand beyond our limitations, as arduous as it may be, to stretch and grow and not accept our perceived fate. The other method for this is forging your own mask.

Knowing the difference is the trick. If you are tone deaf, you can try singing for a few decades, and you will still sound tone deaf. That is a fate you might just accept. However, maybe your entire family never got anywhere, and they are used to poverty. They carry a narrative around their last name that it is a curse, and everyone busts their back for a living in this family. That was the narrative I was sold. I was the first to attain not just college but also to complete a doctorate. I refused the narrative in total. I enjoy learning and growing. I read more books in weeks than my parents had in a lifetime. I wanted to go a different way. It is always difficult to do that because you have no role model and you have no guide or mentor. So, I went to find one outside my sphere. I saw the direction, and I pushed. Anyone can do that if they have the aspects of possibility and realism. If they have these attributes and plans. They need to put it into action. Then success is just waiting for them. In case you are saying to yourself, not me became ABC, do a little research, and you will find that the most wealthy and prosperous people living in this country are not even from here initially. They are immigrants who are from the Caribbean islands and India. They lived in utter poverty and now thrive. They did this through a language and culture barrier, and they pushed. There is simply no excuse for anyone not to manifest if they are physically and mentally able. Is it easy? No. Does it suck at times? Yes. Is it worth it? Only you can answer that question.

One of the masks we can work so hard on is that of the victim. We can also mask our pains, hurts, and traumas, and be a disgruntled and hard-edged person that people prefer not to be around. Many people wear this mask with pride. They are proud to be difficult, aggressive, and what those around them might call an asshole. There are many choices for masks, like stores at Halloween. Just like we can walk in and put on any of those masks, putting on this mask is a choice. If you see it as a choice, you can exchange your role, your mask, and your identity through correction or change. *The Joker (2019)* film was very difficult for me to watch. I have worked in the mental health field for many years, and some of what they did was so realistic and close to home it was painful for me. I have watched so many people suffer needlessly and have struggled to advocate for them, often to deaf or prejudiced ears. The film showed the masks of insanity. It also showed the face of abuse and neglect and how insanity is created. People often do not understand this, and so they impact other people in a very negative way. They might see their mental illness and reject or limit them. They might form prejudices around them and add sinister intent.

Recently, I was on a plane where the airline made everything late, causing significant distress to all the passengers and to the attendants working. I remember seeing in the news that people get into fights on planes and hit people and become violent. I wondered how this could happen. I now know why. I watched people being lied to. I watched the attendants hide out and not deal with the customers. I watched them make people wait in lines for literally hours and then walk away from the podium. It does not take a mental health expert to see and understand that the incompetence level of these people is clear. They have no idea how to deal with customers. In one incident, the people waiting in line for an hour were all there because the flights were delayed, and everyone in line was trying to figure out what to do. Instead of addressing the crowd, one of the attendants got the mic and told everyone they could no longer see anyone in line because they had to board the plane. Knowing everyone in line was the same passengers looking for answers. That line never moved.

The people were all on edge and angry. Other airlines I prefer make you feel heard, welcomed, and happy to be there. This airline chose the face of anger, controlling, aggressive, and actively chose to agitate the customer. I do not think this is going to turn out well for them. However, what they put out is exactly what they got. It is easy to see why someone would fight back at the way they were treated. On one connection flight, there was a man in the back of the plane who looked like Nathan Lane from *The Birdcage (1996);* he had the glasses, the swoosh, the smile, the hair, and even the sweater that reminded me of Lane's character. At once, with that mask on, all the customers were calm. We had the worst turbulence on that flight, and it did not matter. Masks matter and have their intended or unintended (if you are not aware) consequences.

Many masks are worn to scare others off. The punk and goth cultures were very much using that as a theme. It was a way to have a subculture of like minds, you could tell by clothing and makeup. The tattoo culture, when it first started up as a culture in modern times, was again a physical sign of difference and a way of life. Before that generation, the tattoo culture was the product of working-class men, criminals, the military, and the like. Initially, it was tribal in various cultures like the samurai, Vikings, or African tribes. Masks do not just cover the face, but they often do because it is where people look first. The monster masks of horror films and suspense are used to create feelings.

Helmets are used in science fiction for the same reasons. Masks used in rituals are often taken on as part of the invocation of a spirit or deity that the mask represents. When the mask is on and present, so is that deity or spirit. Those who do experience this can smell different, mannerisms can change, and other attributes can very much change. I have seen people fake this, and it is painful to watch. It would have been better to just act as a player and not state you are the deity when it is clear you are not.

Acting itself can be referred to as a form of invocation of the character. Adding or losing a lot of weight, eating like the person you are becoming, doing what they do, and thinking like they think are all aspects of the same work we do in magick and the occult, especially Chaos Magick. Coming from the Greeks and falling under Dionysus, the theatre has been around for a long time. The only difference is the eventual intent. The actor will do the portrayal of their role and then remove the role and return to their own mask. Yet, some actors will say that some of the roles or personas may come with them, or they were so freaked out by playing them that they utterly got away as fast as they could.

The invocation and taking on of roles, taking a deity or spirit within you, and sharing the body, is known as riding or possession. I am not talking about Hollywood examples of exorcist films or anything like that. I am also not referring to stories about demonic possessions. The metaphor for this is simple. If you are ninety pounds and you go to the gym and try to lift three hundred pounds, you will break yourself. In the same way, if you enter invocation and seek a great demon lord to possess you, then you are asking to be broken. If you are mentally and emotionally unstable and you seek out powers from within that are beyond you, you will be broken unless it sees the weakness in you and doesn't even bother. Just like you must pace yourself in all things, you must do the same to build up your skills in anything before you can take on higher levels. Not doing so is written universally in folklore, fairy tales, and the like. Invocation is not shopping. It is a later stage of good magick.

There is virtually no pursuit that does not involve going slow until you gain skill, or starting small and slowly gaining speed and accuracy. It doesn't matter if it is the rising energy of Kundalini, running, mountain climbing, biking, weightlifting, or singing. You must have the basics and the foundations to do the work, and then add slowly. The biggest problem is that many people want to skip the line. They want it now. They push for the front of the line. I have watched as teachers, very elderly and wise teachers, seek to tell the person they are not ready. The person does not listen and circumvents them, finding someone who is unethical and who will give them what they want for the right price. What they do not understand is that it has no foundation. Therefore, they get in front of the line, but all those who worked hard to get there do not respect them and know their time is short. Because of their quickness, they lack skill and the ability to be humble and disciplined, and they are a shell and an empty mask of the real thing. That puts a black mark on their tradition, and they are a poison. Yet, worst of all, because of their cluelessness, they have no idea and often blame others for their lack of knowledge and skill. They did not learn responsibility because they have never taken any. They then become jumpers. They go from one group to another seeking what they will never let in, which is a legitimate process to the goal. They just continue to do the quicky, and every time they encounter the real teacher, they see them as the problem and not their antics.

In the series *Game of Thrones,* there is a storyline around a group of people who are "no one." The character Arya enters their domain and seeks to become one of them. This is a very occult-driven storyline, and one most people might find entertaining but not understand. It is an assassin group, but it is far deeper than that. They are displaying the very idea of masks, the occult, and the hidden. They are referring to the drive of self-determination, and there can be a loss of who you are while you play your roles. You can actually lose yourself and become no one. This is not a side effect. It is the effect they are after. Their masks are not simple face coverings but transform them into another person. This is more akin to the Skinwalkers, shapeshifters, and chameleon-like aspects of certain systems of magick, speaking to the idea of full transformation or aspects of initiation. It is also akin to shadow work and advanced concepts of the occult concerning the breath of others. The rituals of my tradition are from the shadow side to keep away from those who might see us for who we are or for the power we might generate. It is also to keep our initiatory tradition to ourselves. It is not for trickery or contempt of others but a matter of self-preservation.

We are cordial and study a wide range of materials so we can fit in with others. We take courses and classes. We attend the local shop's meetings, festivals, or engagements. We seek to know and be known by our community. We may identify (again mask) differently, but we are very genuine in our want to grow, learn, and discover. We are often different from the New Age crowd in general, unless we must fit in and have no other option. We also tend to lean in the direction of the most open-minded option because of our Current. What I have learned over the years is that many of the organizations and systems, though they may be in opposition to the major religions, follow their outline. They use the same form of hierarchy, they keep out those who do not think as they do, they consider themselves superior, and they see their systems as untouchable. As you might expect, this creates a lot of headaches for outsiders. Some, thankfully, are quite the opposite. Those people are very inviting, usually have a universalist mindset, and are agreeable, humble, and open. We all get burned from time to time by the people I indicated earlier, looking for the quicky, and some develop walls to keep these people out. Sometimes, it is fees and costs. Other times, it is evaluations and time in service. In certain groups, only the persistent get in and get the goods.

Consider all the masks you employ: one for work, one for people in charge, one for your friends, one for family, one for the ritual chamber, one for the person you date, and so on. Do you use them to keep people away or draw them in? Are you aware of your masks? If not, you probably have some questions to ask of the people closest to you and for yourself. We all have them. I have been told by several people I would deem as elders that, below all the masks, there is nothing. These masks or roles are simply all we have in life. What lies beneath is complete consciousness if we ever get there. Our work in life is to look further and further down until we come to this nondual hub of nothingness. This is why we are no one. These personalities are furniture. They decorate our world. The true essence of Being is far deeper, and it is very much attached to the One.

Individuality is how we manifest these masks. That is on us, our will and intent in life. When we merge that will with Divine Will, we are aware we are the Universe. The visual I like is that we are at the edge of the great river. It is moving very quickly, and it is sweeping people into the current. This river, let's call it the Ganges or the Nile, flows through consciousness, and the people around it are unaware that they are just existing. Those who are aware use the river as a superhighway. They exchange and experience it by flowing on it for a time. Then they get off (read this as reincarnation) and begin again until they encounter that all of this is part of the same system, the One. The real understanding begins, and the simple aspects of real compassion and love are active. They also realize they are part of the river until they coexist with the river and become it, or more correctly, it is morphed into them as the Universe.

A decision is then made, the awakened one can then come back and teach others to come to the way (bodhisattvas, gurus, enlightened sages, etc.), or they can take the ride to the next stop of existence and move beyond the body. Some leave these choices to the Fates, the sisters, or God, while others see their divinity and come to understand they, themselves, decide. Some would see all these entities as the same. All these masks can confuse and limit us, or we can use them as parts of our personality and discard them when unneeded. We have as much power and as much faculty as we believe we do. We create our reality and our limitations both mentally and emotionally. Like all machines and creations, some have their glitches. Some can be overcome, and others are beyond our control. Sometimes the goal of this lifetime is different. I sincerely believe that people with certain intellectual or physical limitations are mastering other skills in this lifetime. They are often very beautiful souls able to touch real joy, real love, real compassion, and the real vision of what life can be. Other times, it is an utter tragedy, and what the person endures can look cruel and unusual. The reasons for this vary by individual.

It is a miracle any of us survives a single day or moment. We are all walking some tightrope. The real trick is living through this, and we do it through masks, through the animal nature of people seeking to control, destroy, fuck, or enslave us at every turn. It is a wonder we make any form of civilization work. Most do not work well, and most people also do not work well. Yet, it is what it is. I won't make a lot of friends here, but it is why policies on guns, weapons, or other things often backfire. Forget what you believe and seriously look at the facts. Research them. Most of the cities with the highest regulations on guns have the highest violence with guns, why? They are the same communities where other forms of violence often happen anyway. The person is the real weapon, not the tool. If people are violent, we must ask what fuels the violence and not what item they use. Believe me, if it were as simple as disarming, I would be one of the first to say we should disarm. The worst part of society is that even when we do know, there is a lobby, and money overrides humanity or compassion. Today is a great example. We know the economy is terribly out of order and that the middle class, as usual, is being hammered with the same wages and crazy increases in everything. The media and government even tell us we are being gouged, but do nothing to change it. What does this lead to? Increased use of retirement, nest eggs, and savings used to survive. Then the real problems hit, and homelessness increases, then stealing and suicide increase, and violence is sure to follow. If we continue to have terrible leaders, it all leads back to the same things, and unfortunately, criminals tend to find ways to get their weapons, so the problems continue.

It doesn't take a genius, and that's good because it is very rare to find one who can stomach working in the government. The underlying problem is what happens to those who were in the margin in the first place. What happens to the severe mental health clients who work in food service and in the jobs that are lost first? What happens when restaurants, small businesses, and other endeavors fail, and all these people are out of work? What happens when tragedy hits, and insurance does not pay when that is what you pay them for? What happens when you cannot afford your medication or food? Violence, anger, suffering, and disillusion. The next generation is afraid, and for good reason. The last few generations have been left a mess, but the one coming is being left with a catastrophic mess. The system now adds its masks to cover its incompetence and makes the problem someone else's fault. It goes to war, destroys, and does not create. It gives to others and not its own. The system is as broken as the unaware who dictate it. Those masks are manipulative.

Some might say the masks the Kultus use are manipulation, too, and to some extent, that is true. For us, it is not to hide the facts, to seek to kill others, or to gain massive money or stuff. For us, it is for survival and to achieve cohesion with others of similar mindsets. It is a way to share the things we can and keep the things we cannot. Much like martial arts, where people come to fight, spar, or touch hands to determine how good they are personally. It is also a space to learn new things and adjust your style based on your encounters. One of my teachers from many years ago won a lot of tournaments and would often say most people will beat him once or twice, but once he learns your system, you are finished. That was true, and that wisdom ricochets through the occult as well. There were good reasons people first had to fight a high-level student before the master engaged in the challenge. They would figure out the attacker and then determine how to best deal with them. It is the same in occult circles, not that there is a fight, but in terms of keeping wisdom traditions alive. If we simply expose everything, then it will slip into the wrong minds and hands (remember the ones who want the quick ticket or who are mentally or emotionally unstable?) and can hurt people or allow them to hurt others, usually themselves, through delusions of grandeur. It is a poor idea.

It would be like the idea that everyone is a priest. If we said that, then there are no priests because the very idea has been vacated by making it universal. If we say that instruction and training are needed to be a priest and then someone makes priests by payment and certificates, there is public and private confusion. No one knows who is who or what is real. Yet this is exactly where the occult, many Pagan traditions, witches, and even the Kultus find themselves. Then, we must transition to tribal and closed systems to retain a standard. All we have, then, is our word and reputation. We all know who the good teachers are, in our opinion, and we look at people from those teachers with more respect. The interesting part, though, is that even those great teachers miss something sometimes and take on students who turn out to be a problem. No one is perfect. The student has choices too, and may make the ones that make their teacher and school look terrible.

In keeping with this philosophy, one person's title matters, and another's does not. Like a university that becomes a paper mill for documents and has no real training. Our system is very much alive and changing all the time. We also give a lot of autonomy to G/M's and others to define with their students what is best. For a good teacher, this is essential. For a bad one, it is problematic. Therefore, we are left with what happens. Good teachers vet their students. They make them spend the time, prove their worth, and intensify the drilling until they are sure they have a good candidate, or the person walks away, creating a good reputation. The bad teachers collect their money, take anyone, want faces on their social media or their walls for roles, and have no interest in quality because they have no quality to offer anyway. It can be a very sad state unless... You look at it a little differently.

If you come from the Indian perspective of the guru, it tends to work much better. When you enter India and seek a guru, you may find fakers, impersonators, liars, and the like, and it is accepted as part of the process. You might be stolen from and lied to multiple times. Yet, the goal is to find the right person for you. Some people crap out and give up and head home. Some persevere, while others find the wrong person and spend a great deal of time figuring that out. That is not a bad thing that the guru is doing his or her job for you by giving you that education. When it is done, you can move on to the next one. The spiritual journey is complex and is a crooked path (many puns are intended here). Everyone's journey will be different. If you look at it this way, then you are far less likely to give up or walk away. There is an expectation that frauds exist. We do the work anyway. This guy may be a bad person, or she may break my boundaries. Do I stay or leave? Am I too sensitive, or is this a problem? It allows you to develop.

Looking closer at the masks of the Stygian and the Technology of a Modern Chaos Reality specifically, it is the skull that is ever-present. Death is a constant companion, and so we make friends with fear. Then, there is no fear in the darkness, and it is like a silken dream. The things that come from it are also welcomed like guests if we, as occultists, clean and manifest the wards and have the Guardians. Then, whatever it is that has entered your world, they are disadvantaged. I have found many deities, spirits, faeries, and guardians this way. When you are at the table of the Gods and Goddesses of Death, few are interested in your presence, and so our masks of the skull are primary. Others come forth for different reasons. I use three masks for the Gods I tend to invoke and learn from, but this, too, changes over time, and there are many Gods I sit with that I do not invoke but evoke and sit with to learn from them. The masks for that are not needed.

One's mirror must also be mentioned here. A mirror reflects, but our minds both project and cut things out. Scrying cuts away at these limits. Sight becomes different. Our masks tend to evaporate. If we dig deep enough, you disappear. Study this idea; it is a radical experience.

CHAPTER EIGHTEEN

ETHICS

If you have been reading the book, then this chapter will not surprise you. The ethics of the Stygian are not those of most of the occult community. Ethics have been interwoven into the mesh of all the philosophy discussed thus far. The purpose of this chapter is to challenge the reader to consider the differences further. It is also to call bullshit on the things that do not make sense. Unfortunately, there is a vast array of these, and it needed an entire chapter to fully express them all. I am going to break them down into sections, as I have so many of the topics before.

Vampirism

No matter the system or instruction you may have discovered, when things are in print, they lose their ability to be completely honest. I challenged this in prior chapters concerning consent. Consent is the word of the day, so it must be entered into every category, or something is wrong. Somehow, openly feeding (another word they are trying to do away with) is cool, but feeding via tendrils at the bar on Friday night is an affront. These are a square peg in a round hole. If you are trying to fit within society, do not invest time and attention into occult practices. I am not a hypocrite. I cannot tell you that one is right and one is wrong. I do not own your ethics, nor do I wish to. You own them and are responsible for them. If you engage in vampirism and then set these limits, that is not vampirism. You can call it anything you want if it makes you happy, but honesty is more important than that. Be honest with yourself. If you choose to lie to others, again, that is about your ethics, but lying to yourself, for the Stygian, is a sin.

Ethics for a vampire, in reality, is simple. Taking someone's blood without their consent is theft, just like anything else. There are always enough willing participants if you look for them. Psychic vampirism is wide open. The choice and option are yours. Don't step all around yourself to make it make sense. It either does or doesn't to you. Act accordingly. I know many who cannot ethically use this method. No problem. I understand why, and so do they. Do not lie to yourself and tell yourself you are something you are not. That is where the ethics live.

Left-Hand Path

Here, we have the basis of the Stygian philosophy, in my opinion. It had to be here because it has too many components that are in direct violation of things on the right-hand path. I do not find a lot of help from this designation or any box or limitation. But I would be lying if I did not indicate that the Stygian leans in this direction. We do not draw from a classic priesthood; we do not seek salvation, and we are not servants to a deity that is the be-all and end-all. All of those aspects are present in the RHP. It is also true that many on the LHP are atheists or non-theistic. They are seeking self-deification. Many see no life after death. The Stygian does not agree with any of these positions either. So why do we fall more on the LHP? Here is a short list of the things we adhere to:

- We see the need to follow the Will, the Daemon, and to embody the Deity to enlighten or seek gnosis
- We follow a non-dogmatic method enforced by experience and experiments, and not some book or leadership from others
- We rectify that demons and angels are the sides of a coin
- We recognize and use cursing and blessings as part of our skillset
- We pull away from judgment, evangelism, and coercion to get people to join us, and lean more towards everyone doing their own thing
- We see the wanderer's time of isolation as a tool for training
- We use a combination of bodily fluids, sexuality, deep emotions, and feral practices in our rites
- We use an initiatory system and egregores in our philosophy

- We see all as teachers, we look to what disgusts us, we look to the libertine as a model, and we seek to eliminate fear
- We embrace silence and the darkness
- We see reincarnation and death as steps and not endings
- We embrace masks in our work and invoke the Gods to further our work
- We use ritual chambers instead of Pagan or Wiccan circles
- Our use of guardians, sigils, and servitors differs from anything on the RHP
- We feed on energy and empower ourselves to do our work
- We do not limit, use the phrase "you can't do that," or any derivative; we believe all is permitted
- We abide by the laws of our land, not out of agreement but because our freedom is essential to our work
- We build and consider our ethics over and over, willing to change and adapt as needed, keeping only to our own and not others
- We see sexuality as sacred, whether in ritual, lust, love, or for other reasons
- We do not seek hierarchy for the sake of it or to stoke the ego, preferring our shadow work to be mastered
- If we do take on roles of teachers or instructors/mentors, we do so to enhance our skills while testing our practices. The secondary gain is the student. This may seem selfish but it is a great way to not get caught up in trying to make a minnie me. We do not want copies. We want free thinkers.

Yes, this is a short list. I could fill a few chapters with more. As you can see, all of these items are LHP-related or adjacent. There are very few aspects of the RHP. The rest of them are more middle-of-the-road, where something like yoga or reincarnation lives. That, for the Stygian, is the balance. It is not between right and left, but more between left and center.

The big question then is often, how does the Stygian form their ethics if they are defined by the individual? It is more like a living document. Each person who is accepted into the apprenticeship is asked to write their ethics from the start, without any influence on our part or any training from us. It is what you bring to the table initially. We ask them to reflect on it and ensure this is indeed what they think and believe. Then we ask as they work through the apprenticeship to periodically review the list. It always changes, always. If it doesn't, the student doesn't make it because it shows an inflexibility in their thinking and an inability to grow. It is not wrong or right. It is about being able to learn and adjust. This skill is paramount. Again, this is in opposition to society at large and to the RHP. For them, ethics are established by family, religion, culture, society, and are a firmament. It is equivalent to faith. Accept it and forget it. Not here, here, we do not do that at all. We are constantly reconsidering to ensure we are still in the same mind frame.

We are firm believers in the idea that you cannot know what you have not experienced. The value in that is monumental. You have no limits set on you. The only exception is what you are not willing to do. For example, "people who jump out of airplanes are crazy." Have you done it? No, then you cannot have an opinion. If you have done it and hated it and feel it is not for you, then that is fine, but notice my quote begins with people... That implies all people, and that is a judgment. Now, if I have done it and said, "I do not like jumping out of airplanes and would not do it again." Here, we have a stance that is individualized and great. The problem is that we usually do the former, as society has taught us, to hold others to our standards. The Stygian Way will break you of that. Those are much more practical ethics than some dogma you do because you were told to do it.

People are still going to do it to you. They are going to judge you for using your own or others' blood or fluids. They are going to judge you for your dress, comments, and ideas. They are going to associate you with the least common denominator, and they are going to judge you. None of those things matter if you simply do not care. If you let outside influence in, then it is you who has allowed it in. You are your only gate. You can isolate, you can leave, and you can say no. If you choose to remain and allow it to marinate in your brain, then you have let it in. Take responsibility for that, and you are moving into our version of practical ethics. If you continue to take on a victimization mentality while allowing them free rent in your head, then you are the problem. Our mentors and teachers are trained to help you deprogram these societal traps to keep you in their grip. We choose to move into being the predator and not continue to be prey. We all fall short at times, but that is not the same.

The Stygian Way is not for the masses. There is no way for us to deprogram them all. Nor do we seek to. Let them have their ethics and their moral high ground that is corrupted and hypocritical. We are not missing out. That does mean that we must be able to have confidence and pride in who we are and what we are. It does mean that we need certain knowledge. This can look and feel like a form of elitism.

I look at this from a humble paradigm. I did not seek elitism. I did not seek to know more than others. I sought wisdom. Now that I have experienced some of it, I must be grateful. I do not seek to spit over my shoulder at those who have not gotten there. I have compassion for them. It is not their fault, in most cases, that they have not found real wisdom. Society is a master manipulator, and it is going to catch the majority in its web. My ethics will not allow me to then ridicule them on top of it. They remind me of myself when I was unclear and unsure, and I have a ton of compassion for them. Now, let me be clear: compassion is not sympathy and not even empathy. It is up to each person to figure it out. I will not allow their influence, limitations, negativity, or judgment to impede me in any way, regardless of their role in my life or society. People are expendable if they are not open-minded and respectful. Those are my ethics. They do not have to be yours.

I have had students and colleagues who are very dismissive, and some who are trying to save the world. I have had harsh and devastatingly rough people, and those who I see as too soft. That is what individuality is. I do not judge them. It is my opinion as to hard or soft, weak or strong, and I keep it to myself unless asked. These options are left to you. I will say that the variety is what makes the best soup. I prefer the hard person to teach those who prefer pain and need a brick hurled at them. I also need a soft teacher for those who have been utterly victimized and traumatized by society, and they need a soft touch first. It is very interesting to know that both styles hold a lot of the same ethics. Something to think about.

Societal Norms

For the Stygian Way, this is a topic for masks. We may hold these roles or norms to make money, feed our families, or excel in the world. We might use the masks to enter certain groups, organizations, or activities. We might wear them to date and find a partner or partners. We might vote and agree on certain parts of society to make our mundane world better, or for several reasons. Or we might seek a communal living space outside societal influence, live off the grid in a witch's cottage in the woods, forming our own social norms. We might gather our friends and those who think like us and do our own thing. More and more people are working and making money at home and using passive income strategies. This could allow them to prosper while working on their spiritual path. The Stygian is on board with these ideas. Our ethics play a part because many people would say we are abandoning the mundane society to their fate. They might offer up civic duty or some other form of societal morass that is insufficient.

The Stygian ethic is to be true to the self-first. It is only then that we can adjust to being around others and filter out their biases and the influence they have let control them. It is not surprising to the Stygian that the elitists could do one thing and tell the general population to do another, and the masses were compliant. We are not interested in being among that. And this is where my ethics may differ from yours. With the awareness that this is the majority, I have no choice other than to accept it. What do you do with a majority of sheep? You sheer them, that is what they want. What that means will be determined by the situation and the person. It does mean that most people want to be led.

For instance, the time-honored issue with friends and partners is: what are we having for dinner? Many years ago, I just took over. I offer two options: we can go here or there. I'm not sure, cool, we are going here. I do not like to waste my time, and if there is a lull and I get what I am after, then let's go. I also state my preference at times, and others just go along with it. Is it that I want my way? Sometimes, but usually, it is because I don't want to waste my time in the inane back and forth. When you realize who you are dealing with, then you must decide how best to handle the situation. Ethically, this is practical.

The truth is also a contentious place. In society, we are encouraged to lie. How do I look in this dress? Am I getting fat? I have learned a comeback, which is, Do you want me to answer that? People know me, and that means I will indeed tell you the truth. I prefer it, and ethically it is sound. Why? Later, I do not have to guess which lie I told. The choices and your ethics are yours. Some will find me too ethical, while others might find this to be cruel. The important factor is that each person is comfortable with their ethics.

Some ethical bounds are set by mentors for us as a training entity, and they include the rules of law. Whether we agree with them or not is another story. We adhere to them for the benefit of our members and for the ethical integrity of our work. Our integrity will not allow us to endanger the freedom or liberty of ourselves or our members. We hold our freedom highly. Our ethics are also not to tread on yours. It is important to us that our members are respected and understood. There are always limits to this due to the nature of some people who will seek to impose their will on others. That will not be tolerated.

CHAPTER NINETEEN

A DEEPER DIVE OUTSIDE OF OTHERS' REALITY & OUR REALITY

Now that masks, ethics, and the basic measures of understanding the Stygian are exposed, it should be clear why society's reality and occult reality are not the same. Societies write the narratives and inform you of their ethics and their reality. Often, it does not make sense to artists, occultists, and libertines. Their society often seems flawed, has no depth, or is cruel. It is important to dive deeper into the depths. Many people believe that they are exceptional, and that is useful for society. Others feel they are failures and can never succeed without others (also useful). The parameters for feeling these bipolar ideas are better for others and not the individual. Individuality is seen as a problem, as ego, elitism, or isolation. Society makes those people feel they cannot succeed too much or they cannot fail too much. Both lead to the need for the return to society for the person to suckle more nutrients from others.

However, there are those in our midst who are exceptional, and they are very much appreciated. They are also odd. What that also means is societal parameters are of no use to Stygians, but we must be aware of them. For occultists, the ability level is estimated by the teachers when they come to the student, and the student determines if the teacher is truly advanced. It is subjective for all the reasons I have given throughout this book. When side by side and in comparison, what may seem advanced to some may be basic to others. While some will make fun of the advanced as impossible because they cannot attain it or see a way to attain it, others will understand it quite well.

So, for me, what is advanced? Often, it is difficult to describe what comes after the intermediate because things become misty or very gray. Therefore, I am going to do the best I can. Once the wanderer goes off on his or her journey, they will go on an endless set of rabbit trails. Some will be relearning their basics, others will choose Currents they can double down on, while an entire other group will find gnosis from a different perspective altogether. None of this truly matters in the macro; these are simply growing pains to impart the next stages. It is always true that some will just walk away and never return.

What moves someone from intermediate to advanced will vary greatly, but have some or all these aspects in common:

- A lack of second-guessing will develop, and a true belief or a knowing will manifest itself (sometimes despite your agreement), this is not arrogance or grandeur, but real
- Your relationship with Deities will become "real" to you and a reflection of you
- Your breathing, lack of fear, ability to move energy, and your focus will begin to overwhelm you in a positive and respectful way
- Knowing (not knowing it all) will become predominant in your disposition right beside a childlike interest in things
- Sacred work, scriptures, and grimoire-style writings will begin to be readable and accessible or for some, you will discard all of them for experience itself as the teacher
- At times, when in the astral or other realms, you will not want to return to your body
- The balance will be attained eventually between the internal and external
- Psychic and unexplained phenomena will become accepted, common, and usual
- For some, heightened feelings will lead to deep introspection into romantic and sexual areas
- People will either come to you like a magnet, or they will be repelled by you if you take on more of a hermit manifestation

- Life will change its meaning for you, and you will see the nature of your dharma here, that dharma will mean more than any person, goal, or outlook
- You will tire of day-to-day work, and pick another profession or a way to live on passive income, and then you will dedicate your life to that dharma or there will be a discernable change from your work life to your spiritual life
- Others will not understand you, find you extreme, unexplainable, or embarrassing to them
- Due to all the changes, you will either isolate, find small like-minded groups, or seek out a personal power couple to continue the work (destroying many relationships to make new ones)
- Deities or spirits may become your Beloved, and the nature of your life will not fit society, you will develop great compassion but not a great deal of ability to talk people out of the misery that they choose
- You will cease to wish and hope and only create
- Life will change meaning to a time to manifest through Deity and spirits, time will change its meaning, and the need to care for the body as the Temple of Divine will come more into focus so you can attend to the work before your body is returned to ash
- Debating others will have lost its fire and flair, seeing it now as a waste
- Teaching those who ask is now a pleasure and a way to execute your work of the highest order
- Pacifism eventually shows up because you see the evils of mankind, but it is often too late
- The ability to have others do what you ask becomes simple, the knowledge of their best outcome overshines their want or need, and you are compelled to overshadow them, but you must retain the balance and the boundary for them to do as they will
- Pain, passion, ecstasy, bliss, joy, wonder, love, compassion, anger, and all the feelings become balanced and focused with slowing down, enjoyment, and deep consideration

- Banishment, banes, blasting, and what is considered dark are simply the same as a blessing, a consecration, and a benediction if used within the ethics of the user
- Ethics and a personal code are grounded and foundational. They can change but it is only when the practitioner is thoroughly convinced of a flaw in thinking

There are, of course, many more aspects, but these are the foundational ones I would like to discuss further in this chapter. There is never an order to any of these changes or experiences. They happen when they happen, and some are not for me or you. Humanity is typically unsure, so the change to knowing can often seem arrogant or egotistical to society, but it doesn't look like that. It is not the know-it-all. It is through experience and experimentation that one gains knowledge and a personal understanding. The person no longer seeks for it to make sense to others. It is simply their knowledge, and they earned it. You may see it very differently, and if you are open-minded, they may engage you, and the two may learn from one another. If not, the person nods, smiles, and walks away. This is part of the childlike disposition. You simply do not suffer fools. At times, your Daemon will tell you to get out of a situation or not go there or do that, and it may seem wrong to you. People ignore these things all the time. If you have accepted Deities and spirits in your life, they warn and help. Allow them to do their job. Ignoring and ignorance have a lot in common.

I listened to a YouTube person for a long time. He often mispronounced words, and it annoyed me, but something about him kept me there. Under all the language issues and the approach, there was something there. He comes from the Left Hand Path exclusively. Yet, in his case, I just saw something. He did the best reading I have ever had, except for one person, and I have had hundreds of readings. Some by the elders of traditions. The deity pulled me to him, so there I was. We differ a lot, but we do not differ in many practices and approaches. Kindness and understanding, the ability to listen, and to be open-minded are far more important. He has all those traits. He exhibits part of the childlike aspects at times, and that pulls me in further.

Deity relationships differ from person to person, but I have never met a truly advanced practitioner who is an atheist. I know many great people who are not advanced mystics, sages, or occultists. I am sure they exist, but I cannot see the work of invocation and having that experience, and saying it was then all in your head. There is also a joy or happiness factor that is not present. Don't get me wrong, I deeply love and admire several atheists, but I see a sadness, an emptiness in so many. You can also not get to the reflection if they do not exist, so in effect, you are setting a limitation, and if you break it, then you break your system if you maintain their non-existence. Any set walls or lines you draw are going to come up as limitations and thus limit you from advancing.

Many systems view breathing as a key, and it is for me too. Advanced pranayama is magnificent. Like blood moves oxygen so breath moves energy and engages the body with health and wellness. At some point, you can have a moment (I have encountered and heard this story many times), you will encounter the breath and realize that at some point it will end, and you will stop breathing. This gnosis comes to kill the fear. For some, it comes from other places, but many of my Kultus found it here. It comes at a time of high skill and a lot of practice, sometimes around the rising of the Kundalini, and for others, many years later. When it does happen, it is overwhelming; you feel like a speck of dust. It gives you perspective, and then it gives you a fire to carry on your purpose. I must sidestep and add that the Kundalini is not a milestone or even a high-end event. It is a step. That is all. Those who put heavy emphasis on it or who claim light and fun without fear have not experienced it. It always has a fear-driven part; it impacts physiology, brain chemistry, and the individual in many ways. Especially for those who have not prepared for it. The same speech is around the astral. There are many layers of the astral. Do not allow people to con you or tell you they have this experience on the astral, so they are this guru or that master. Anyone can do that. There are aspects of the high astral that are advanced and never spoken or written, and I will not write them here either.

Another aspect of the journey is reading and eating the books (a very esoteric concept). Some of the tomes many of us read are vexing and over our heads. Many of the sacred texts and even their translators struggle to fully unravel the juice of their peaches. I read one book for many years, calling it my "bible" and knowing the author is a bit of a trickster, then, when I was reading something else, I was drawn to reread his book. When I did, I was laughing my ass off. He was quite a character, and the information I was seeking was right there in black and white. Because of my newfound access to those gems, I could open other keys and continue to open aspects of Taoism and many other Asian traditions I love in this way. Sometimes, they do it to us on purpose, like a test or a riddle. Other times, it is to make sure the right people pick up the trail. When things begin to open, it becomes much easier to gain and eat the knowledge from books, people, and sources. This one does not seem gradual, but more like a switch is thrown or a never-ending combination of switches. My experience with the writings of Crowley was exactly like this. With the help of Lon Milo Duquette, who allowed me to navigate through Crowley's books, I learned how to read Crowley effectively.

This is not just an esoteric concept. It fits all kinds of literature as well. The works of Shakespeare and other prose can be just as difficult. Words mean different things now than they did then. I would also say that it is the same with influence from all sources. You have to know how to read it, and you should read it and not watch it. I believe we are much better readers than we are consumers of vast amounts of media. I did some experiments of my own during the pandemic and concluded that people are much more discerning with the written word than the spoken one. That depresses me on some level, but it does explain why people can listen to their preachers and cross the street and buy porn. The mundane and spiritual can be very intertwined or not. The choice, your filter, is YOURS.

We spend so much time in our bodies that when we finally get out via some method like meditation or astral work, going back may seem difficult. Especially if we have health or physical limitations that cause us pain or discomfort in the body. I remember learning lucid dreaming before I knew what it was. Children, if they work at it, can become rather good. They do not have all the rational garbage of the modern world, work, and other stressors to prevent them from magick. Not to mention all the garbage that grounds and grinds them into the earth. For many who start later in life, they often freak out when they look down and see their own body just lying there. It can be addictive or intoxicating to be in the astral. It is like getting to see what lies beyond and then going back to Kansas (if you get the *Wizard of Oz* reference), where things are, well, not the same. Once you are aware of the possibilities, it is difficult to return to the mundane with much gusto.

That is why the Bodhisattvas are so important. It takes a hell of a soul to return when you know where you are going. The selfless nature of the act is beautiful and so needed for the rest of us. It is at some point on this journey that a couple of these bullets take place. Because you are going between worlds and your travels are thinning the veil, you begin to balance the internal world and the external one of the mundane. This helps with your ability to measure your time and set your goals on either side. With the thinning of the veil also comes the ability to experience the spirits on each side. Some claim the spirits come with them. Others state they just begin to see or feel more spiritually. While others gain psychic or prophetic visions or experiences. For me, it led to large expanses of work in scrying because the spirits were so close, and the trail was well-worn.

There is another side to the last paragraph, and it is not a pretty one. Some cannot walk between worlds mentally or emotionally and begin to break down. They do not balance. They fall apart. They become plagued with the very emotions and negativity they carry, and their minds cannot handle the strain. Their visions may be horrific or demonic, and they may see themselves as being persecuted, which leads to paranoia and psychosis. Once this slope begins, they need real help, and some will not return. This is the major reason that many good teachers in the occult community who are honest require the basics to be mastered. It is through the basics and the vetting that teachers learn who is going to be fine and who is going to be broken. Many do not listen to the good teachers and seek their peril or find a poor teacher to guide them. It is simply a possibility for any esoteric or occult path where mysteries are involved and uncovered. Awakening means you can now see. You cannot go back to being asleep. I find many modern teachers state that there is no evil or psychological peril in the work of the occultist. They downplay any real concerns and offer up a very limited palate, making them correct, because they are not doing anything beyond the basics. Be wary of this. Be wary of teachers who have no experience with spirits or deities. If that is what they are teaching and then spouting on and on about demons and their astral journeys, you have to begin to ask how all that works in their heads. Any kind of severe rebuke is always a sign of limitation and the inability to deal with the truth.

There is another avenue of interest that the Kultus and Stygians have an interest in. The art and practice of sexual magick is a method to open the mind, walk between worlds in ecstasy, and embark on a dual journey through the use of group, partnered, or individual sex to maximize the connection with the Beloved. This is done by invoking spirits and exercising sex magick to create the magical child. I feel the need to express here that I am not referring to an actual child or procreation in a mundane sense. This is often confused by people who are not occultists or sex magicians. The magical child can be many things: a spell, a servitor, or many other outcomes. The entire corpus of work in this area is not simple and has yogic, Taoist, and other sexual, mental, and physiological aspects that must be mastered to effectively reach long-term goals. It is not concerned with the mundane use of sex, but it is the physical mode to get there. The concept of the Scarlet Woman was made more famous through Crowley, but the idea was around well before him. It is always true in the more advanced practices of sex magick that the merger of fluids is the elixir sought. It is also true that this is not the only way. This never precluded same-sex work. Those who know Crowley's history are very aware of this.

Reaching or restraining an orgasm can be part of the work. Some reject this, but some see it as essential. The use of ordeals, kink, and pain and pleasure are also meant to access these aspects. The practice of holding orgasms for long periods can be a very powerful magical aspect of increasing power and securing higher levels of gnosis. It is also very common in the sex magick corpus. At the same time, the orgasm, known as the little death, can also be moved into a multi-orgasmic place and also raise the level of ecstatic joy and trance. This can be a very powerful practice and has been taught by the Stygian since the beginning. The Kultus expands this view to many other practices beyond the scope of this book.

Yet, still, for others, there can be very deep muse relationship, aspects of finding the Beloved, and an affair of the heart can be found in the spirit world. It can include a deep understanding of true romance, of sexual or non-sexual love. It can become like a marriage, a love affair, or a devotional relationship. The muse is very interesting as the inspiration of an entity leading to many overwhelming and highly erotic experiences. It is also close to the heart of the artist and so a reflection of the Kultus. For a person with artistic or creative leanings, it can be rather amazing. One must always remember to treat the muse well, or the same loving relationship can have a rather ugly turn. You may want to believe that these are just folktales or stories. Don't test this, trust those tales. The Technology of a Modern Chaos Reality is particularly interested in this area because of the artistic aspect. We are deeply connected to the arts, all of them, and we keep to an artistic flair. For us, this can be highly magical.

Due to all the changes at the advanced levels, the meaning of life and the purpose of your time may radically shift. Some tire of the day-to-day, and some seek a muse to alleviate the financial curse of the modern world, while others balance well. You may also completely change course, professions, partners, countries, states, and many of your other patterns. This will cause others to react, judge, and possibly seek to shame you because they do not understand. Your magnetism may reverse, those who were pulled to you might repel, and those who did not even notice you might be pulled hard. You may also wish to retreat and move further away from society to do the work. Your dharma becomes clearer and clearer. It is no longer a thought. It is a mission that is very clear to you. It is like trying to explain parenting to someone who doesn't have children or sex to someone who has never had sex. It is not possible. It is the experience itself that is the initiation, and it changes you. You will have less time and attention to the mundane issues of the day and those who put great stock into them. Debating people over any of these issues will not even be a consideration. You choose to spend time with those who can hear and understand. At some point, some do transition back to the mundane. Often, it is because they see themselves fully or see something in the dark that makes them fear again. They flee and return to "safety." After they work through the advanced, some become teachers, and their compassion returns, so they can take pleasure in teaching.

There is a very deep thread to the idea that wishes and hopes end, and the advanced teacher takes the role of a creator and destroyer. It is no longer necessary to hope and plead. The teacher manifests and removes as needed. This sounds much different than a dramatic representation and is subtle, but the way it happens is monumental. The power and freedom this offers cannot be explained. The teacher becomes the temple more than the working altar, things come more into focus, and then eventually the body tells the teacher it is time, and that lifetime ends. Some deep esoteric tales and traditions state they can move the mind, awaken the mind, or recall in the next life to further the individual along their path quicker. It is interesting to me that so many traditions talk about this in their writing or claim it outright in some aspects of Buddhism and certain yogic teachers, for example. It also shows up in the Greek myths of the Underworld, where some can maintain their knowledge depending on where they drink.

Warriors and monks are a theme within many currents, and that happens for a reason. Once you see all as part of the One, no one seeks to kill themselves in anger and rage. You also have compassion for the stages, remember your journey, and see that they need the time and resources to do what you have worked so hard to do. There will be a divide and decisions to be made. At some point, you will want certain parts of the One, cut off from you, removed. You will see the cancers and the parasites, and like anything set to kill you, you want it out. The body is the temple, and the temple is the metaphor for the One. While feeling compassion increases, realism also increases, and with it, the ability to discern. You must cut away certain parts even though they are "part of you." I sincerely believe this is an inner mystery around capital punishment. Some feel it is needed to literally kill away what is a killer or fiend, while others feel the deep connection and know that person is part of them, so they can never kill a living soul. What is right and what is wrong is an ethical dilemma left to the individual. It is also true that humanity likes to remain the same without change, so some warriors will always see war as the answer. Growth and empathy seem to come at the same time or not at all.

Working with others becomes much simpler. This presents problems for some who are still holding onto egoic means that often lead to a megalomaniac. If you take a moment and look at cult leaders, this is often where they begin to buy their own press, add drugs to the mix, or begin sleeping with everyone. They may be true mystics, true avatars, and amazing, but they allow the god-like position to go to their heads. Instead of the betterment of the group, community, or all, they revert to me, just me. The True teacher laughs at themselves, finds humor in being put up on a pedestal, and will never take it seriously. This is the problem with most religions that think they are better than you, but it is worse because they are not enlightened beings; they can become used car salespeople. They are selling you the same lemon they bought.

What is required, and the mark of a true teacher, is that he or she allows the person they encounter to take their own time and method to arrive when they are ready. There is no need to press, scare, cajole, or manufacture consent. Allow the person to decide their will, help them to find out the way to learn their own will, but then let go. If they don't like your way, that's fine; offer them a referral to something else. It is not personal for the teacher because your goal as a teacher is that they get where THEY are going, not where you want them to go. It is highly arrogant to believe you know better than their Higher Being. They are a vessel embedded in their Current and nothing more. Ego tells us we must collect others or get them to see things our way. This is false teaching. I am forming adults, not children or robots. I do not want those who have come to the wrong place. I must send them where they are supposed to go, not impede them further. It is never my job or intent to change your mind or manipulate you. When in doubt, release.

Then there are the feelings, and there are a lot of them. They are neither negative nor positive. They are as they are, balanced and equalized. It is what you put into them that infects them, and then you judge those feelings as positive or negative. I must digress to say that I am never talking about mentally and emotionally charged individuals who will be unable to make it to this stage or who, after being led astray by nefarious actors, may have driven themselves to madness. These people are broken under bad training, poor leadership, and acts of egregious cruelty by the abusers who have unceasingly sought to control them. If you have a teacher who wants to control you, get out! Leave! You cannot gain this path through this methodology. I am talking to those who mastered the basics, worked through the intermediate, and now stand to witness the Gods and Spirits in their glory. Those who no longer live in fear of what lies between. Those who are fully accepted as priests/priestesses/magisters/dames/devils on their path. Those who know their Daemon intimately and who have merged the three souls, powers, and with them the chakras, and who ratify this work weekly or daily, and for some, monthly in the moon. I am also not stating that people who have mental health issues are not allowed in. On the contrary, it is often through the work of the

Dark Night of the Soul, the dismal depression, and the horrible anxiety that we can then come out the other side and be more robust and able to manage anything. However, we cannot move on to an advanced state without conquering these dragons, or they will constantly impede us, disrupt our visions, and sabotage our overall journey.

For those I am talking to, the feelings you experience are balanced and wondrous. Pain and anger in the list may have stuck out to those who seek the light side alone. You may see this as beyond you or wrong or have some other negative connotation, but these come too. Pain can be very comforting to some, from the hooks of tribal traditions in the flesh to the flail to the accountability that is essential for seeing clearly; pain is a teacher. Anger, too, comes to show you your boundaries, dealbreakers, and what you cannot accept. Anger can be very healthy. I recall the sentiment from a martial arts teacher when I was a child: *I am peaceful in all things, but if someone were to breach my space and offer violence, I would return the violence to that person. If they persist and I deem it life and death, I must destroy where I had no intent to do so.* Anger can keep us awake, active, and focused. Fear is the sibling of anger, but one we cannot abide by as it breaks us down and destroys focus, accuracy, and intent, and opens cowardice and non-action, our enemies. The cliché that fear is natural and people with courage act when fear is present, are not magicians. And in my experience, it is not true. Fear is a poison that saps you of control, and it is a detriment; much like worry, it is useless. This is why, in my opinion, the Vikings were fearless (at least in legend) because they believed their fate was already set. It had little to do with them. This eliminates worry and fear as a whole if you truly believe it. Occultists, mystics, and magicians see fear as a poison they must eliminate in total.

The last two points often divide people. The first is the idea that the bane and blessing are simply two sides of the same thing, which may not be palatable for some. If it does not fit, you can choose to reject it. However, my challenge is simple. What do you do when your daughter is raped and killed in the street? What do you do when your partner is imprisoned for something they did not do? What do you do when a drug-addled brain beats up your children as you look on, horrified? What do you do with your anger? I attest that a banish and binding for certain people is a blessing. I attest that fate does not always show her face to those who act out of sickness, dysfunction, and evil. Justice does not always tip her scales to make things right. Yet, the Deities I work with will take on justice, the bane, or the blessing that is needed. They do sometimes see things differently, but they will know our hearts. At times, my hand is stayed, and I hear them. At other times, I feel the power overwhelm me to do the work, knowing it is right.

The last point concerns ethics. If you read the chapter on ethics, where I defined some of this already, then you will understand. The Kultus and all the traditions I am associated with see ethics as personal. The tradition does not list or state a dogma or set list. That is for good reason. If we accept the fact that we grow, then just by that fact alone, our ethics will change. A young girl might think boys are yucky at four but seek a boyfriend at six, see sex as gross at ten, but be making out at fourteen. These are childhood developments, but we do the same as adults if we are awake and paying attention. The opposite is easy to spot. The Western mind believes we master things, and then we no longer need to grow. What they do not know is that this is not mastery, it is entropy. This is the reason for returning to the mind of a child. We must continue to have fun and have a sense of humor while holding on to the keys and maturity. We keep our laws and our ways until we grow out of them. War seems like a good idea to many groups when they are younger. Fighting and being dramatic seem okay. Stealing or taking things from others might be normalized. Buying into certain authorities, medical, legal, educational, or paradigms, might seem appropriate until you see the humanity of all people and their flaws and faults. That is when we grow. I always believed Asian and tribal communities understood the elders better than anyone else. They see them as tomes of knowledge and needed. They also saw them as human and flawed. They need to be cared for and loved, while so many other cultures put them away or allow them to die.

At some point, if you are awake, you become aware that your beliefs about other people are pie in the sky. We were all naïve once. You thought that doctors had all the answers and were somehow smarter and more resourced than they are. You believed that all the imprisoned people were guilty, that the legal system always got it right, and that the police and the authorities were there to help you (for some). Then, one by one, these things are kicked over. You see the nature of people, the idea of "following the money" is accurate, that the authorities are just like you and often worse because some seek control over others, and your visions are dashed. Also, we are trained by society and its nature to idealize certain professions and people, to see them as deific and untouchable. This is enforced by many parents and society in general. Even the very idea of "trust the science" is embedded in this belief, when any scientist will tell you science doesn't work that way. Much like magick and personal ethics, it is a moving target. What is the science, meaning the truth today is often disproved tomorrow? When anything becomes a political or societal hammer, it is negative.

The surer you are, you can be sure the more wrong you will be unless you do the homework. If your source is social media, media, or a biased person, the likelihood is that it is wrong, or there is a problem with it somewhere. The truth lies in the in-between and never at the margins. It is also true that the margins are not in a line but in a circle. Eventually, both tyrants meet and agree to the same rampage. This breaks the system: civil wars, deaths, cruelty, destruction, and eventually rebuilding. Due to all of this, ethics must be in constant flux and must be challenged and understood by all practitioners. Being wrong is never bad; it is a gift. It tells you that you are still awake enough to hear, to listen, and to understand. Without the impact of being wrong, you can be sure you are going into entropy and that you are delusional on some level. Do you listen or run away? Do you hear or convince yourself you are right with no evidence for it? If you do this, then your ethics are broken. Reconsider your positions often. I do this every new moon. What is not in movement dies.

Ethics are always a difficult topic because by their nature they are limits. My tradition as a whole is the breaker of limits. However, you cannot have one without the other. I will not pontificate on what your ethics should be, but instead, I will offer you a version of my current ethical standards.

- I will not teach or seek to educate someone directly without their consent; indirect education is through example and cannot be avoided
- I will not force my opinions or ideas on another with the intent of making them like me. I will speak my mind and present my positions when appropriate to do so

- I will give all people the benefit of the doubt, seeking to make friends and meet people where they are in all I do
- I will only banish or send away entities or people who seek to harm; all others are welcome
- I do not recognize the societal norms, laws, or the elites of society as having power over me or as my lords; I accept them in their roles and adjust to them according to the limits I must and no more, Caesar unto Caesar
- I offer love and guidance to those who seek it without expectation or control; their Will is their own and I respect their Will and the limits they set upon themselves
- If I am under attack I will not hesitate to blast, conjure, or bind as needed. I will not follow an even policy but offer destruction to those who seek to destroy me, knowing I am destroying part of myself in the process
- Integrity is a primary responsibility of my path, not sincerity, consistency, or truth as all of these can and will change based on growth and situations
- As a priest of my temple, I have oaths, rites, rituals, and work to attend to, and this is and will remain my primary purpose in this body
- Sexuality is sacred and part of my work, my life, and the blessing of the body. It is not perverse or deviant; it is not sin; it is a sacrament.
- My practices ensure the work on this plane is complete, so it overshadows all other things, so that I may end the wheel of karma
- Refining, reconsidering, and taking in new ideas is ethical; the work cannot grow in an echo chamber
- Allowing people to suffer, fail, and struggle is human nature; if I remove these factors, I remove their ability to overcome, grow, and learn. My ethics prevent interference without request and sometimes even if requested, I must allow others to learn the hard way
- Judgment and castigation are not part of my path, do as you will
- I recognize other paths, we can all be going to the same place and using different roads, the difference is good!
- Question everything, do not accept things as stated, do not honor someone with authority unless they earned it, and even then, check first

- Remember the divinity within is who you are, do not allow the masks, personality, defects of character, and ego to manifest, allow the divinity to manifest via your Daemon
- Remember, you are radical and in good company. You are not radical to be radical, but to cause sense and balance, since it is the world and society that are extreme, and the radical is more awakened
- Keep your personal responsibility always; if you offend, take responsibility for it, and if it is deemed right, apologize. If you see nothing wrong, do not. Others' reality cannot and are not allowed to dictate your world
- Eat well, breathe deep, love well, have joy, seek happiness, and find wisdom
- Take in nature, ground yourself, test yourself, and experience peace and serenity daily
- Do not avoid conflict unless you are dealing with the convinced; allow them to suffer, and walk away, but those who are open and can grow, argue with them for the goal of two people learning
- Refrain from seeking mundane wants, focus on the needs and the progression, the Gods know my needs and will readily offer their gifts
- Wealth is not evil nor is poverty; neither reflects happiness or sadness, the more one has the more that can be taken away
- Reduce the mundane to necessity, and joy, and then return to the real purpose of life
- Meditate daily, ritual daily, connect daily, and practice daily to stay in the Stygian Way
- Always be the artist, see as the artist, and see the deep beauty, do not miss it
- Take pleasure in the darkness, in the death current, and the macabre

These are a shadow of my ethics. What would your list look like?

CHAPTER TWENTY

THE BLUE FLAME AND HER NATURE

In this chapter and many that follow, I will be moving more to the practical side and away from the philosophical. I will discuss more personal practices and allow the reader a more inside look at our tradition. In offering an honest assessment, it is clear we are all influenced by teachers and past experiences. I am not immune. Therefore, I will disclose the influences I know have permeated into the Kultus especially. Part of that is the disclosure of the sacred flame we utilize as our closest point to the Dark Mother.

I will offer categories of my foundational knowledge for those who would like to look at source materials. I will also offer a further reading list in the appendix. Like all influences, some have moved on, and some remain in my daily practices. Sometimes, I have moved over an entire method, and other times or I have refined it to work for me. The immensity of "my religion" has taken a lifetime to unfold, so it is going to seem like a lot of pieces to most people who have not done that. I hope by the end of this chapter, you will have a firm foundation on how it all fits together, or you will have a lot of research to do if that is an interest for you. My goal in sharing this is not that you form your method and system based on anything I write. My goal is to either give you ideas or get you excited about your process.

All versions of the occult are based on the master and the student mindset. One is beholden to a lineage or teacher. It is their order, their tradition, or their way, and that is sacred. If you leave, you are a traitor. This method works for the green or wet behind-the-ear new person who has no idea what to do. That is the purpose of the 42 and foundational learning. Once these basics are in place, the work of the Stygian changes direction. We no longer adopt the loyalty or indentured slave mindset that we must keep to our box and stay in our lane. We are told that mastery of the system and not the self is the point, and frankly, that is a lie. Mastery of the basics is needed, but then it is the questioning and self-discovery where intermediate skills are formed. Then, the advanced notions come through the knowing of the Daemon and allowing that alone to become your guru and master, meaning you become the master of yourself. This is the only way. I do not say that lightly. There are innumerable ways to get to this point, but once there, you must do it yourself. It can only be that because no one can see what you do. No one has your experiences, and no one is the Universe you are. Telling yourself you must lean on another is a weakness and folly. It keeps you dependent. There must be a transition from student to colleague with others, or you will never grow fully.

Let me say this a different way. If you are quietly relying on another, you are watching them attain mastery while you look on. The reason it must be this way is because no one is you, and you are no one else. This comment is tricky as we discussed the All or the One and that you are indeed everything or the Universe. But this is a learned concept. We all begin with our lens in the world, the individuality. We start there, and remember you cannot just jump ahead. You are forced to look at others to assess, experiment, practice, and experience, without these experiences, there is only theory without action. This is known as the mirror method. It is through seeing "others" and remembering others are aspects of you and them that the growth begins. This helps with memory, direction, and all decisions and ideas because they are all illusions anyway. Because of this esoteric truth, without this discernment, you see others as others and cannot understand or move on to more advanced work.

I offer another martial arts example here. A long time ago in an old factory building in the New England area, I was the guest of an aikido teacher. We were sharing information when one of the students in his class challenged him. In those days, it happened a lot and most teachers simply ignored it, threw them out, or allowed a high student to practice with the person. This teacher did not, he smiled at the man who looked sincere, and they got on the mat. I watched the younger man get into stances and knew he was a karate guy. His stances were low and deep. The Aikido teacher did not take any stance and stood there. He asked the man if he was ready. He said yes and before the student could move the teacher was upon him and kicked him to the side of the chest sending him flying off his feet and landing on his backside. The young man was shocked, got up, and ran at him. When he did the teacher waited until he was on top of him and spun on his back leg catching the arm of the man who was again sailing in the air. Moments later, it was over.

I noticed both moves and neither was from Aikido, at least none I had seen. I asked the teacher why he chose those. He smiled saying, "The art of surprise is much more important than styles. I was challenged as a man, not as a teacher in this dojo (school). It was personal and now the student will learn from this. That is why I accepted the challenge. The kick was from karate I learned many years ago, and the throw was from jujutsu." We laughed but the point was there, right in front of us. The teacher must not be restricted by style or rules. They must explore to the highest degree and make their style the best they can. Magick is no different, and neither is the spiritual path.

I will break down the systems that I studied into Eastern and Western traditions for clarity. The MT listed refers to "my tradition," meaning my prior religious order or prior initiatory work:

Eastern

Buddhism, Taoist, Yogic, and (MT) meditations

Tai Chi, Chi Gong, Bodywork, Reiki, and several martial arts systems

Taoism philosophy, health/wellness, magical system, and energy work

Tantra Yoga philosophies, Interfaith Seminary

Western

Traditional Crafts, including folk traditions and others

Hermetic philosophy, Theosophy, and similar traditions, including MT

Chaos Magick, shamanistic style training, shadow work, hypnosis, NLP, psychologies

I have been an academic and writer for some time. My training includes many different philosophies, including metaphysical, theology, systemic ideas, and psychology. I have been trained in hypnosis and NLP by three different systems.

All of these are foundational to how I see the world, my meditative and astral work, and my practices. I am not a traditional therapist and do not see the world as most of my colleagues do. I have been influenced by India and all her beautiful sounds and pictures for decades now and she is always my Beloved. Her Tantra and the Chinese Tao are the deepest of my understanding of philosophy and wisdom with the grace of the systems of yoga to move her. Yoga is the most widely used method and for good reason. In the early 2000's I came upon something I would later know as Trad Craft and then I fell upon a second version and both are crucial to my path. Both appealed to me, and both began to take up some of my time. Their influence is very much a part of me from the feral ideas to the sprites and spirits. Those spirits were the ones who spoke to me and not the demons of the Goetia. This is what dropped me on the River Styx and what led me down the road to the Stygian Way.

I have no idea why it opened up a Gothic mystique or a very dark journey to the Underworld and the understanding of death. All these things are locked together within the philosophy and manifested in the Kultus. I could not have any one of them work without the other parts. The artwork called to me from local artists to Gothic photography, to the world of Kink, for me, it is an expansive and beautiful darkness. In the same way, I could not fully understand martial arts until I understood the need to truly have your own style. Or the understanding of what the Beloved is, without fully falling in love so deeply, I would happily die for another and endure unfathomable pain.

So, what does this all have to do with the name of the chapter, the Blue Flame? In the Kultus, we refer to the Blue Flame. It has a lot of different meanings. A flame must be given oxygen or breathe to exist. If you remove this or snuff it out, it goes out. In the same way, all of us have a flame, and it is fed by our training and experiences. I have shared with you what created my flame and how I keep it burning, but that is only one aspect of the symbology of the flame and what it means.

It is blue because that is the hottest part of the flame and is always inside. It is light blue with a gaslight (another key), and it is an element that is primary for my work. Closest to the wick and used as a metaphor for the Daemon or soul, it is the flame of wisdom, gnosis, the one we stoke in all our work. It is also the hearth, the home, and the destination sought. It is also the Beloved, and

I identify her as a she. Some refer to her as androgynous, and others as male. For the Stygian, she is honored with a large black pillar candle, and she is referred to as the Dark Mother. What is much more important is your relationship with her. She is also a manifestation of the Goddess, Deity, and is specific to the Stygian and the Conclave. Her nature is primary to all the work. Her nature is the creator and destroyer, life and death, art and science, breath and steel, mantra and silence, acceptance, and cultivation, and many other symbols and ideas. She is both the hearth maiden, the elder witch, the cosmic powerhouse, and the aged grandmother who comes when you are most in need. She is seen in the blades of Sehkmet, in the beauty of Aphrodite, and in the horrors of Kali. This is all very subjective. The objective aspects come early and show the connection to the Deity from the Stygian Way. Once this is secured, the bird leaves the nest and must explore and grow. In doing so, visions change and refine.

In the scales of Maat, Anubis, or the Lady Justice herself, one must balance. If you blindly follow, there is no balance. If you do it all yourself and never adjust or listen to others (and remember others are you, it is your mirror, and you need it), having no foundational basic knowledge, there is no balance. If you have it all figured out, you are truly lost. But if you work through each part with effort, attention, and practice. If you manifest the beauty and other aspects of a Craft or the Arte Magica, and you modulate, refine, and adjust, then you can slowly move to a deeper abode. In that space, there is no need to force others to understand you. There is no need to edify yourself to those you speak to and teach because if you teach them well, they have the foundation to rest the higher knowledge upon. Even if they disagree, they can gain from it, and here beauty intensifies. Some thrive in the dark, others in light, and still more in the never-ending kaleidoscope of grays.

My greatest place within is the astral or mage tower. It is fortified, and the stones are so black that people can walk into them in the night. It sits in a wood where I grew up in my fantasies and my playtime. A brook runs to one side, and animals abound. A large outdoor altar is dedicated to Mother, but many in the Conclave come to it. No statue litters its top, and a brazier is always lit. On the other shore are the black rocks and the death of the River Styx. Nothing lives there, and it is always gray and colorless. Inside the vast and massive cedar and steel door lies my inner circle. The first floor is dedicated to the library, a writing desk, journals, papers, divinatory tools, and puffy, comfortable leather chairs and ottomans. Teas and coffee are always available, and the windows are always open to the ever-present autumn, where the lilac smell is strongest. I am there at dusk mostly, so it is always the end of the sun and opening to the moon. Candles litter the walls and the desks, needing light to cascade them in a way to read, write, and work. The second floor holds two distinct rooms, a bed chamber, and a devotions room. In the high tower lives the temple. All my astral tools, the altar of dreams, massive chairs, tables, and useful items from the Conclave and other traditions. The symbols of the work are cast and hidden. They do not remain. The defining sound of silence is ever present, yet when I call, the minstrels set to their work to surround the room with their warm strings, chords, and sounds. My guardians are present in true form, my servitors are present for the work, and my familiar has free reign.

I do not share the most important elements, but this place is not for you. I share it with you, so you have a way to form your own. Do not allow the mundane world to limit you. Think as the Gods, without limit. It is difficult to do. If you can think it, envision it, and do your work, you can manifest it. Do not slink away or draw fear to you. Break through the limits, if you dare.

Pan and many of the tricksters have been with me for many years. He comes to me differently. I do sometimes see him with the nymphs and by a pool, but most of the time, he shows up as the romantic. He is jovial and sometimes stern. His eyes are pools of green or blue, but not of colors of earth; they are filled with magick and power. He carries the universe in his eyes but plays it lightly as a flute. His words are ever pleasant, and his voice is warm and comforting or utterly vulgar. He is sex, lust, and with deep intakes of wine, flirts and plays at the boundaries of gender and identities. He divorces people from their cultures to see the deeper identity of fate and the long game. He heartily cries and laughs without embarrassment or limitation with and for those he loves. As passionate with his games and trickery as his love, he is also engaging. He is with me due to my romantic nature and how I love. When I move from that style of love or resentment where it takes me, he scolds me. He was so much easier to embody in my youth because I was unfettered. Age and struggle create limits that he finds offensive and brutally stupid. His vision is not fettered by time or circumstance. I intensely need his view and distinction, and I am grateful to him. When he sheds the clothing, his phallus always erect, pulsates in the winds. He is as comfortable naked as clothed. He seems one with the Dark God.

The Dark Mother, whom I will not name from the Conclave, holds the face of many of the Goddesses of old and many of their characteristics. A moon Goddess like Hecate or Diana, a love Goddess like Aphrodite, and a necromantic and underworld Goddess like Hel, she is many-faced. The idea of the three is not three; the ancient idea was that there was one, the two lead to the duality, and the three meant it was poly, or three or more. The Mother is a kaleidoscope and is not limited. Limiting her strips her of her deity status. The grandmother/elder, the warrior, the maiden, the sexy or the austere, the vibrant brilliance or the utter darkness, the great witch at the cauldron, the embodied statues of the great temples, and on and on I could go. The reason for esoteric and scroll-style writing is not to shade the truth from people. It is to illuminate what words cannot wholly touch. She is the Dark Mother for me because that is her usual appearance. She is more a vision and my Beloved than a consort to any God. I have not seen her engage others as she has me, but I have seen her tolerate many others, be close to them, help them, and heighten them, and when I wonder why, I feel that she is with me. It differs greatly from Shakti and Shiva, who fit like a Yin & Yang together, and energies interlock as a great majestic puzzle. This Mother is "One" alone. She can work with others, but she is indeed whole. She is my Matron, Beloved, and the foundation of my universe. Other aspects of her impact me and my work, but this aspect is always primary.

The use of the concept of Shiva and Shakti comes as Baphomet might be used by the Templars or modern occultists to articulate their work. It is not the entity of Baphomet who does the thing, but his sigil or being that is an embodiment of the work. Of course, this is an outer shell only; the more you dig, the more that Kali reflects into the Dark Mother as well, for some, she is the principle. Shiva can easily turn into a reflection of the Dark God. It is another manifestation. It is not a coincidence that, in many aspects, these deities are also blue. It is also not a coincidence that the Black Kali also speaks very loudly to me personally. The snakes, destruction, creation, implements, and intention of their statues, holy scriptures, and intimate correlation to many aspects of sacred traditions, including yoga and Tantra, are ever-present. I could easily write down my manifestations, but this creates a lock or block for the reader. You must endure and engage yourself. My experience is quite unhelpful for others because the nature of people, even occultists, is to mimic. I am also very much aware that most Westerners struggle with Hindu or Tantric deities due to the truth offered by many psychologists, including Jung. We tend to do better with our own religions since it is such a stretch to understand and see another culture with such clarity as to understand its religion. In my case, this was just not accurate. I also do not like to project my image onto your work because that is not helpful; you need your own.

One of the teachers I had in the 90s told me to stop looking at pictures in history and religious books. When I asked him why, he told me that I was just copying and pasting in my meditations, and he wanted the pictures to come from my own creativity and inner world. I had never heard that before. We had a deep discussion about why magick was so much more powerful and active before writing or pictures. People had to tell stories and draw their own pictures in their heads or on their caves, walls, or the dirt.

Years later, I took a psychic course, and the goal was to develop a relationship with my spirit allies. I recall thinking, *Oh great, I am going to just see my pantheon show up, and I won't be able to share anything.* I was wrong. I got several scenes I had never seen before, and I was confused by the presentation. I explained it to the group, and no one had a clue. I went home and did some research based on the symbols and the display. I found him, and I was shocked that although the images fit his symbols, he looked very different. In recent years, I have met teachers who claim that we just project the visuals we know in our minds. They are right. My old teacher knew this in the 90s, and his wisdom taught me not to do that. Most people interested in the occult do not engage in this way and read all the books and ideas, filling them with limitations instead of challenging their personal experience. They are moored in the symbols and icons. They are very unaware that they are limiting themselves. It changes the mind. We then believe it must look like this, and then copy and paste it from the book because it says so. Even worse, we become know-it-alls and seek to limit others by telling them it must be this way.

Many years ago, a yogi told me the same thing. We were talking about spiritual ideas, and I asked him a question about a sutra and the Gita, and he laughed. He told me he never read them. My first (very Western) thought was, uh, oh, he is a fraud. He explained the same thing my teacher did in the '90s; he told me he allowed the Gods to write the sutras on his soul. He lives them; he does not read them. He also reminded me that most of the world is still illiterate, and it was arrogant to think only those who read have access to enlightenment. He further chastised me and told me that it was those who used words as weapons that limited their access to the greater mysteries and beauties. That is why I never sought ceremonial magick and stuck to the folklore-style Craft traditions and others that allowed for a direct connection. I have seen many in these areas brag and have vast stores of knowledge, and I am very happy for them, but that is not what I am after. I also see a lot of burnouts and a lot of assumptions on their part about how things work. I look for results, growth, and difference. I also did not downsize my library. Those aspects worked for him, but for me, studying and processing are still important and feed me.

The Blue Flame is the essence of all these concepts. For me, it is the advanced nature of a more wild and visionary system and not an organized and set way. After all, it is in the Chaos Current. It could not be otherwise. The metaphor for trying to capture water comes up again. The more you close your hands and seek to control it, the more it just runs through your fingers. It is not captured, but it is present. Bottling it or stopping the flow is not natural. Even within us, being mostly water, it must pass through. The term "living water" is very important to the work.

CHAPTER TWENTY-ONE

SATANISM/LUCIFERIANS: NOT COLORED IN THE LINES

This chapter may be a difficult one, but it is needed and part of the philosophical foundation of the Stygian for multiple reasons. They include:

- The bipolar notion of the left and right-hand path augments a determinism of what is orthodoxy and what is not, forcing the Stygian to the left
- The modern ideal of black and white, good and bad, again, a bipolar determinism pushes the Stygian to the black
- Christian, Jewish, and Muslim religions espouse through their mythos that mankind was made and the angels were forced to bow before the creation as lesser than, and many angels did not. This dividing line created demons, which were angels who rebelled.
- Just as in the heavens, we are faced with the same choices and doxology on Earth. We are either with the status quo or we are in opposition. Satan means adversary. Therefore, groupthink is defined as good and opposition as evil. Lemmings falling off the edge of a mountainside is positive, and standing up to authority is evil. Really? The Stygian must then choose to be with the opposition.
- Scapegoating and relying on scriptures and dead religions are used to firmly associate people with evils if they do not do as the elitists instruct. The verbiage makes little difference: *follow the science, no more taxes, I need 50*

million, or I will die, and Jesus says I will get it, the Hurricane was sent by God for the sins of New Orleans, or whatever incendiary claptrap winds you up. It is all a foundation of us versus them.

Luciferians or Satanists have long been confusing to the world at large because they are seen as wackos and insane. Anton LaVey cultivated some of that in his carnival barker style, but at his core, in writing and intellect, he was not that. As the founder of the Church of Satan, he was just a man of his time with a deep insight into common sense, an understanding of what magick is, and a realization that the dead religions had brought so many problems to society that he sought to rectify them by literally offering the alternative side. Sure, he poked the Catholic Church, the big religion, in the eye. He made fun of them, but it was not just fun. It was deeper than that. Satanism did not begin in the 1960s. There is a deep history in France, and LaVey knew that.

Many other Satanic systems modern-day occultists are familiar with came behind him, including Michael Aquino's The Temple of Set, Michael W. Ford, and The Temple of the Ascending Flame. I could take this chapter to list out the rest of them, and I would have to include organizations that even I am confused by, so I will leave it to my audience to seek out further options if they so wish. For me, these are the major players. Many authors and other people have gone their own way and developed their methods, like Ford. However, there is a lot of overlap, and often it feels convoluted to me. Other times, the work itself feels washed over with a Satanic paintbrush.

I have added a chapter on this topic because of the misinterpretations and bipolar nature of how the world sees things. These together force the Kultus into a position of the adversary. We are averse to groupthink, following the crowd, believing lies that are convenient, or seeing any authority as the be-all and end-all when they all put their pants on, just like any of us. For the Tantrikas of old, this makes us left-hand path practitioners. It makes us Satanists to some. Philosophically, I cannot deny these labels when used in this way. Are we following some church, wearing horned caps, and screaming "Hail Satan," no! But are we adversarial by nature, think for ourselves, and actively engage in self-discovery, absolutely! Labels are a way of caging people. I have written about this concept all along. Do you see how easy it is to set this trap?

OMG, you said you are a Satanist! That is often the response because nuance is too difficult. It means you cannot cast the whole thing in a box and call it A, B, or C. You have to think and consider. That is required in the Kultus. We work and live in nuance, not absolutes.

Satanism of the 1960s was a reaction, and it served its purpose. It morphed for many, and it went in a different direction today. It spun out into atheism. They moved away from actual Satanism and moved to an atheistic cabal. The changes were not the direction Aquino wanted, and he writes about this, so he left and did his own thing. The Temple of Set is very appealing, especially as a magical school for some. I deeply enjoyed reading his books and many other tomes from the adepts from the Temple and the CoS, including Stephen Flowers, Don Webb, and others. The issue around labeling yourself a Setian, Luciferian, or Satanist is that no one listens to the definition of what that is; people react to what they think it is. For some in this group, they have no problem with that, and like the provocation, it causes and stirs. For others, they use other names, pen names, or the like to continue to write, but not cause themselves the reaction of a world that sees these people as bad or evil.

I will share with you a secret. The big bad Satanists might hate this, but it is very true. I have been around many religions, working with interfaith and many kinds of people for a generation. I can honestly say that I would much rather be in a room with high-level LHP practitioners than any other group on the planet. The reason for this is simple. From high clergy to Pagans, from mystics to Gnostics, and all forms of witches, I can count on these LHP folks to show up. I can count on them to be kind. I am overwhelmed by their generosity, their common sense, and their ability to smell shit a mile away. They are honest in their affairs with others within their circles, and if they say they are coming, they are coming, or they are dead. Why is that? I have my theories. The most important ones are:

- They are trained to think for themselves
- They have been beaten down and harassed so much that they see their LHP folks as family and treat them as such
- They do their shadow work
- They know who they are

- They have been to the mill and have gone through the gambit, they have the tee shirt, as we used to say
- The kindness and care are reciprocal or people are cleaved off like firewood
- Holding others accountable is acceptable and even required
- There is no set belief system therefore, we are always learning and open
- We have no problem with the hex, banish, and curse mentality so people don't tend to show up unless they are stupid (and we usually have pity on them) or ready to do the work
- People are afraid of them, the dark, and all that they have heard so they only enter if they are willing to face those fears

The reason this creates a wonderful foundation of nice and approachable people is that no one is trying to box anyone else. It is the opposite of most witch or Norse platforms, where so many people are telling everyone else that they are doing it wrong. The philosophy is the opposite. Is it working for you? Great. Are you saying it's working for you to get attention? That's not going to work because, as an LHP person, I am not here to blow sunshine; my response is usually, "Great, keep working on it." This is not a social media platform. People who work alone or in pairs, think for themselves, constantly challenge ideas, and do their shadow work are not going to just follow others. In the eyes of the Kultus, they shouldn't.

Why even mention Luciferians and Satanists at all? It has come to my attention that the Death Current of the Stygian is happening at the same time as some Satanic currents have been bubbling to the surface. In some instances, we have a lot in common. I have reached out to some of them, and it does appear that the Satanism of the past and what is coming is maturing. There is nothing wrong with the good fun of the Church of Satan or many of its contemporaries, but now there is a theistic Satanism that has much more teeth. It is no longer about just being the adversary. It is a drive to a deeper understanding of why humanity might have been duped by the wrong team. Why did those who formed and wrote these religions down have a different agenda than the founders, or in some cases, has the message been subverted? Gnosticism and the LHP confused me at first, but it makes a lot of sense. These philosophies are both saying a lot of the same things: God is a fraud, Lucifer and Jesus were both called the Morning Star or Light Bringer, Christianity that grew in power got so much wrong, and many other convenient facts of history.

However, the Kultus draws the line there. We, as the Technology of a Modern Chaos Reality, are not within the Satanic Current as such and, more than that, steal away from all things from the primary religions of the world in general, including angels, the Kabbalah, and their mythos. It is not that practitioners cannot engage the material, but it is not primary and would have to be explored outside the realm of the Stygian Way. You might say in the same bipolar way we have tossed the baby out with the bathwater. Instead of working from the middle and taking parts, we jettison the whole mess.

I never understood why a modern occultist would forge a bridge to the Jewish Kabbalah, to angels and demons, and the paradigm of a system they state they are opposed to. I hear occultists speak terribly about Christians and then make the sign of the cross, wear crosses, and use many of the rubrics from the Christian church. It's like saying you hate your family for all the terrible things they did to you and then revisiting all of it on your kids. Have you learned nothing? And before I get letters telling me the cross is far older than Christianity, I am very much aware of that. However, they usurp it, and now it is theirs, just like mysticism and monasticism for the most part. If you do not like it or hate it, why do the opposite? For me, that is a compliment. If you are in opposition, walk away. Do not give it a moment of your time. While you may believe doing the opposite is blasphemy because they told you it was, look at what space it still has in your head. I do not offer space in my head for such things. The Gnostic Church of Crowley feels like the same thing to me. Although he was much more creative than most. Both the Gnostic Mass and the Black Mass are published in various books. Look at them.

The Stygian Way prefers a clean slate. Our rites and rituals are made for our people alone. They will never be published. The only reason to publish them is to give people the incentive to do what you do, and we are opposed to that. So, in like manner, we differ.

Yet, just like Pagans, witches, or even Satanists, we find them as brothers and sisters along the path. We might not use their methods or philosophy, but we respect the differences of others and work to see what we have in common more than our differences. I felt a need for this chapter in the book to highlight this area of the occult in particular, because so many read Satanic ideas in the work. Now I hope you understand why and where the differences lie.

CHAPTER TWENTY-TWO

HYPNOSIS: DIVING INTO THE SACRED SPACE

I will direct you to Dr. Christopher Hyatt from the beginning, as well as *Monsters and Magical Sticks: There's No Such Thing as Hypnosis? (1987)* by Steven Heller and Terry Steele. Hyatt is far more esoteric and expressive in his writing than most hypnotists/occultists and covers far more depth than I can touch in a single book, never mind a single chapter. I find him to be an excellent mentor and educator for those inclined to do their work. He played with hypnosis and Reichian Psychology/therapy, as did his mentor, Dr. Israel Regardie. He plays at the dividing line a lot, at the point of madness and insight. I found Austin O. Spare to be similar and loved them both. I never reinvented the wheel, and I don't have any need to do so. You could never do it with Hyatt or Spare, even if you wanted to. There are mountains of work in hypnosis, and before it was pushed to the side, all the leading psychologists/psychiatrists used it, including founders like Erickson, Freud, and Jung. It was removed as a common modality a long time ago, as were the more esoteric or systemic models for medical ones. That was an error. We have massive evidence to prove it to us today in the psychological profession, which is not just lacking but, in many cases, moving further and further away from the philosophical standouts to embrace newer empirical systems. Those systems are biased and more closely related to the medical model. The easy target is the one most embraced today, CBT or Cognitive Behavioral Therapy. If you are interested in this topic, consider the title by Farhad Dalal, called *CBT: The Cognitive Behavioral Tsunami: Managerialism, Politics, and the Corruptions of Science (2018).*

Like all things, psychology, as an institution, backed the wrong horse. They followed the logic of the money and the medical profession, and not the facts, the client, or movements like systemic therapy that produced many icons. They followed the big pharmacy corporations and the medical associations. They moved further and further from personalized care for the clientele, who, for the most part, do not understand that they are no longer being given the essential models. They are given a watered-down variant with a massive number of drugs over behavioral and developmental change. The same is true for herbalists.

So, the hypnotists stay in their lane now. They do not want to be put into the same category as Hyatt, Reich, and those who saw some light for people in general, and wanted to go in a very different way than those corporations wanted them to. Even those psychotherapists who do both therapy and hypnosis often separate offices for legal and licensing issues. For those hypnotists who are very good and track their numbers, if they are honest, they will tell you two things. First, hypnosis is far quicker than traditional therapy, and second, the outcomes for those who are motivated for success are far higher in all cases. Hypnosis clients have a far cleaner second-order change. Not somewhat higher outcomes, but in some cases double. Why? Because the work goes straight to the psyche, straight to the unconscious, and to second-order or belief change. So, why do hypnotists who are also therapists still do therapy? I have asked that question many times, and the answer is probably obvious by now.

The first half of the people who would attend therapy would never see a hypnotist because they see it as “woo woo” and, therefore, not real or productive. If they just did hypnosis, they would only get those folks who understand the background I am currently speaking to, which is a very small portion. The second part of the people understand and have some connection to meditation, astral work, mindfulness, transcendental work, or even bodywork. These people would come to hypnotists, but often do not have the funds to spend what hypnotists must charge because insurance will not recognize them. This catch-22 is common for those outside the maws of the medical model.

Why is this chapter here? Well, because it is just another nail in the coffin of the general public, who are outside the loop of such things that can assist them with zero side effects. There is no way to make billions here because we get shorter-term solutions. It is also completely opposed to modern society. Hypnosis requires attention and focus to enable the person to take control back. This is opposed to social media, to screens everywhere, to distractions, and wasting time. In its place are focused practices, cognition in real-time, and direct engagement. It is also a method that a lot of those who are depressed or anxious have a shot at teaching themselves. It has been known to help in areas of addiction, behavioral modification, and even obsessive or compulsive areas, akin to mindfulness. On the topic of mindfulness, I would assert that these two are siblings. Both have excellent properties. Mindfulness snuck in under the umbrella of being trained and studied in universities. It pulls slightly away from its Buddhist base to keep it open to a wider Christian audience. This chapter is also here to illustrate how important it is to advanced work. It is not part of the basics, although it could be, but it is essential for higher encounters.

Here I list some studies I would love to see happen, but never will. If I missed them and they are out there, please notify me. I would love to read them and use them. Here are a few, if any of the readers are so inclined, or who are within the new occultists and witches within academia.

1. A study on the difference in health and wellness of the self-identified Pagan/Witch/Occultist versus those who are self-identified as one of the major monotheistic religions, who are all hypnosis clients
2. A study of hypnosis clients who are deemed to be motivated and clients in psychotherapy who are motivated, for a long-term 10-year study
3. A neurological study of the brains of people pre- and post-hypnosis, and the results of the work with a broad audience, looking at outcomes and the satisfaction of the participants

The hypnosis I am referring to is not the stage version. I am referring to a very engaged pattern that is used to work yourself or someone else into a trance. Trance is common in many tribal, shamanistic, folkloric, and other religions and traditions. Trance is essential for flying over the moon, for the work on the astral, and for the invocation and riding of spirits and deities. They cannot be separated from one another because the ways of the shamanic practitioner are self-hypnosis. It is a universal method. Learning the skills of self-hypnosis or, for a group or coven, group hypnosis by led scripts or stories is essential to getting things to align. Recording your voice or using another can be very helpful in lulling the person away from their body and into the in-between. The more you practice this work, like anything else, the easier it becomes. But it is not just about ease, it is about detail, and it is about depth. The more you do it, the more you can pay attention to the needed aspects and learn and grow from them.

This is very important when you are engaged in scrying, meditation, working in the astral, or engaging in invocation or evocation. Being spooked or frightened can happen, and one must be grounded. Hypnosis teaches you how to do that. The more you are well seated in your stance and have experienced and seen some things, the more you can endure. If you do work with demons, tricksters, or other unmanageable spirits, the more aware you are that you must have your wits about you. It comes full circle, though. As much as it is for the astral and inner workings, it does translate into the mundane. I have seen the meek and the passive after months or years of good trancework utterly change personality. If they can face a demon, screw that guy at the grocery store!

Dreamwork is close to this, and the same framework of training and learning is true, but is more like lucid dreaming. On a scale, lucid dreaming is child's play when comparing it with a deep meditative trance. This is why most occult traditions teach dream journaling as a constant. The more your mind becomes used to writing down and capturing ideas, the more it allows for it. The more accessible information becomes, the better able we are to recall it and use it. That is why journal work and dream work are a good jumpstart for the retention of recall on the higher planes.

Trance can be found in gazing, off-focus presence, raising energy, dance, drums, music, mantra, ritual, and many other forms. All advanced work for me is via trance, within the planes, or the liminal outside of the flesh. The work in the body can also be advanced, but it is done not just here but in both realms at once. Eventually, an altered state begins to become more normal and then more common. It can be almost like a switch you throw. Grounding and connection are ever-present, yet it is not the grounding that enhances us. It grounds us to the earth as an axis. Just like the umbilical cord holds us before birth to our mother, so does the grounding cord hold us to earth. Bonds and the same kind of "cords" must often be severed so we are not encased in a web of what we must release that entangles us and keeps us from our truest path (placenta). All things must be in balance. All things are a cycle.

Without the fortitude to fully function, all of this is a moot point. Freedom and liberty are not simply words in a song. They are fundamental to the occultist. It is not only from the oppression of a state and religion but also from the very webs you have woven yourself and stuck yourself with. We are truly our worst enemies. Cutting away limitations is a ritual I highly encourage, and that has always been part of my private practice annually and as needed. Then, when you work with trance, you are not pulled in all these directions because you have already burned away or cut away and sealed those exposures. Traumas abound and always have. What we do with them and how we treat them will vary, and they should, but they must be dealt with in shadow work, or they will surface when you least want them to.

I recall many films, usually horror-related, where the demons or the devils show up and know everything. Ironically, their usual method is to tell the truth. They simply pull on the strings I am referring to as a web in the last paragraph. What if the person had severed them? What if they had forgiven themselves and accepted their responsibility? Would the demon be able to pull it off anyway? I don't think so. The latent thoughts, the reflections, and the carrying around of the baggage are visual for those who are aware. For those who are psychic and for parasitic spirits, it is like a beacon calling them to you. But if we dealt with our traumas and resolved our shadow work, they would no longer confuse us, confine us, or retain us. This, in a nutshell, is what hypnosis can do. Don't get me wrong, Hollywood fans different flames and dramatizes, yet just like a good joke always holds truth, so does a good film. It is on that foundation that they build the laugh or the drama.

When you look at methods of hypnosis, it is a bit like looking up a diet. There are so many varieties that one can be mesmerized (pun included). If you are looking for a recommendation, I would begin with the National Guild of Hypnotists (if you are in the USA) and the work and organization around the late Milton Erickson. I would not use any of the methods that have no direct association because of the diet idea; many have sought to monetize and water down the work, and their methods are less than. The three teachers I have used have all been associated with one or the other or both and have very good reputations. Certification in this area is usually worth as much as the paper it is printed on. It is far more important to know the craft and be able to have results with people and yourself. It is important that you can do both. I am coming at this topic from many areas, but it is important to the Stygian because of the occult aspects.

It is a very deep topic because of the inverse hypnosis we all get. Some would throw me into the crazy theorist of conspiracies here if there were not heaps of evidence that it has and still is being used. It is taught in marketing and advertising. It was expressed in documentaries and films, and ironically, people still do not believe it or pay attention to it. Hyatt was a very large speaker on this topic, calling the general populace monkeys. Other traditions would refer to people as sheep. The reason for these monikers is that people are not awake and do not pay attention. Because of this, it is very easy to do horrible things to them, as modern times attest and history further attests. Those who are in control then create a divide and cascade hate and seek to divert people so no one is watching the real problems going on that are far more sinister. That is a form of hypnosis. That is the form most people fear when they come to a hypnotist. They are worried they will be manipulated by them and forced to do something against their will. The irony is that society itself is doing that. The hypnotist is teaching you to break the patterns and to be empowered so you can get what you are seeking, enforce your own will, and generate a link between that will and your intention. Therapy was also doing this. Why was? Well, some therapists have taken up the messaging and the direction as good "monkeys." They are now selling the same problematic dispositions as a society, compounding your problems and furthering the clients' addictions to them or their drugs. There are still good ones, but they are typically under fire and left out of the mix for jobs or not awake themselves.

I do not expect my audience or anyone to believe me or take my word as gospel. That would make me no better than the powers that be. What I would ask is that you investigate it. Look deeper. If you are not aware of any of this, or it is very outside your profession, interest, or point of reference, I would ask you to look at the books in the appendix and consider your options. If you reject my words out of hand or you are pushing back, you might ask yourself why. What would it mean if states' propaganda and hypnosis were infecting you, and you did not know it as an occultist? That would indeed be a rather large problem. Are you fearful? Have they implanted that? Do you see the game, or are you in their game? Honestly, I do speed through social media at times, and it shocks me how many highly intelligent people are sucking at the breast of the narrative of government and media. These are the same people who will shift with the tide, holding the other side responsible and calling the government evil when their person is not in charge. Really? Perhaps you missed the point. The very idea of being an awakened being is to be above such team-driven tribal bullshit. Apparently, the memo was lost in the mail.

A long time ago, through the advice of a friend, I watched the series *Babylon 5*. It is very good. A certain episode stood out to me that is important here. There is a race on their space station that, once a year, gets their silk scarves out. It is random, and both stick to that team and are set to kill the opposition. When asked why, they do not know. It is a cultural thing and a tradition. The earthlings make fun of them and find them frustrating, so one of them becomes the leader of one of the opposing teams and finds a way to end the conflict. It made me laugh that these earthlings found this to be so strange. We do the same thing with governments, races, politics (basically everything) all the time. You're in one day, and the next, you're out. Look at the history of France, England, and Spain. They did the switch over and over and, through their ministrations, killed many over a flag or religious denominations and the whims of the sovereign. Are we so different? China is bad, China is fine, this country is good, oops, we have to invade them now. We do this with sports teams. Is it any surprise that there are fires and violence even when their team wins? We are still doing the same stupid shit.

Doing this, acting like this, responding like this, tell those who would offer you suggestions that it is still working quite well, and they can control you by your emotions, anxiety, fear, panic, and opposition. It is a lot of work to push back against such massive machinery. Self-hypnosis, focus, intention, discovery, and an internal locus of control far outweigh the impact of entertainment and media if and only if you choose to do the work to de-program. Why does what we might view as "evil" speak the truth? Think about that. It is a way to tell us or suggest to us that the truth itself is evil. In the religions of the scapegoat, the evils are dumped on other things to rid ourselves of them. The idea of the Sin Eater, the methods of the black goat or ram, and the long history of sacrifice are so common in our cultures. Why? Because we fear the truth, our frailties, and our mistakes. We look at them based on society's words, and they become awful. This needs a rewrite badly. I will offer one here. What if sins, mistakes, and screw-ups were opportunities? What if they were our nature as human beings and simply ways to improve ourselves? Some have taken this idea and stupefied it. They now do things wrong and defend them, and do not take responsibility for anything. That is NOT what I mean. What I mean is that I tried this thing, and I failed. Why did I fail? Did it hurt someone? Apologies for that, I will not do that again and mean it. Learn from your mistakes and grow. If we do that, then sin is sought. We want to get it wrong. We need to so we can grow. From my mindset, this is the most basic humanity: to make mistakes. The idea that we never grow from our mistakes is toxic.

I think this is an important point. People hypnotize themselves in interesting ways. Some tell themselves things that toxify and limit them; here are a few...

- I do that because of X relative, it is just who I am
- I am too old to change that; that is who I am
- I was raised this way
- I can't, shouldn't, wouldn't, couldn't, etc.
- I am just a cranky, mean, or hateful person
- I do not accept how you see yourself (gender, sexuality, identity)
- You don't act, behave, or do what I want you to, so you are bad/evil
- My religion tells me to judge you, so I love you as a (religion), but not your sin
- I cannot accept this part of you, but I do love you
- I am not well-educated so you cannot expect much from me

These ideas fully toxify the individual and their surroundings, creating personal limitations of all kinds. You are negatively hypnotizing yourself, or you might say you are your saboteur. These cliches become your negative mantras. At some point, you are beyond how you were raised unless you choose (yes, it is a choice) to hold on to it. If you do not differentiate, that is on you, not your parents or where you come from. You are not cranky or rude as some cute thing. You are that because you saw it and wanted it, and now you have it. A gentler answer would be to say that is all you know, but that infantilizes you, and I don't do that. If you look to others and judge them by some form of standards, as if you have some authority, you do not have. Always consider the founder of your religion or your highest philosophy. In some cases, this outcome is worse. For others, you will have difficulty with dogma and hate. In all cases, it is those who are asleep, those who are shut down or "stuck in their ways" on purpose, who are not willing to expand or grow. They make their hypnotic suggestion correct. Be aware of this. Family curses work because the children are programmed, and they pass it on, not because it is some occult intervention. There are many reasons for this, and I will not explain here. The point is that we carry on most of the hypnosis ourselves, with society reinforcing it.

Even in the Japanese culture that I love, the code of the samurai (Bushido) was to kill yourself if you offend or lose, or do not do your duty. Shame is inherent in people. We allow it to kill our passions and our souls, and for some of us, end our lives. Society always breeds this, yet there is also an ironic truth. Those who are elitists and leaders tend to be the most depraved and have no qualms about it. It is a very interesting discovery to learn that the elitist and libertine share this. However, not for the same reasons. The elitist does it to enslave and control, and the libertine does it because they see the rules are random and created to control. The libertine rebels against these random rules with purpose and flair. Yet they still see the need to be open so they may do some of the same things. This generation has caught up with some of the elitists, but they still exist. Occultists must render themselves to the same level, not to dominate others as elitists, but to hold themselves apart from the society formed to enslave their minds and destroy their passions. Society wants the population to be like crabs in a barrel. They turn on one another, they do not use the village to raise the child, they do not empower and support one another, and they are at each other's throats. No matter the phrase, keeping up with the Joneses is a well-used concept to have you looking beside yourself to determine your shame or position in society.

Take a look at how Communism works. It is a very simple idea. The work of Michael Malice is very helpful here in both his books. One about anarchy, one about North Korea, and the other about Russia. Watch the patterns. It is clearly described. People are paranoid because they are worried about being turned in by others. It is set up that way. Rumor kills. In contrast you go out of your way to stay away from what the government deems to be bad.

I can take this to an idiotic level. Military formations used to line up and attack one another. There are some good reasons for this, and it certainly worked for the Roman Scorpion, but in modern times no military has done this in generations. The loss of lives was an obvious folly. They moved to Guerilla Warfare and never turned back. Yet I am sure when the Indian tribes met the Western soldiers, they found the Indians to be poor soldiers. The truth is, they already knew more. So why is it that if tribal nations and magical communities have such great power, why are they not in charge? The efforts of divide and conquer, showing their religions and ideas as demonic and evil, separating them from each other, killing them off, murdering their families, and making it about race, culture, and gender, all nullify the connection of people and make us stop and pay attention to our problems with one another as the overlords continue to feast on our bones. When all you have is a long history of tribal differences, it is difficult to reform, join forces, and destroy the invader. Take a moment now, and think about the major topics in the West today; gender, race, culture... hmmm, very interesting. The same methods of division and conquering in a new wine skin.

Tribes didn't fail because of the tribes; they failed because of the tactics of the invaders. It is interesting that in modern times, we feel bad for the natives of our lands but do not seek to see their wisdom. It is all smoke and mirrors. If we do have reverence for them, why not change the horrible methods we employ and look to excellent tribal societies that are far healthier than we are? The answers, of course, are simple, and all begin with power and money. The goal is not freedom, health, wellness, and happiness. It is greed and power, and so we are left with the results we inherit. The Kultus is not interested in that and cannot waste its time on the tiers of power. Instead, we seek small villages and homes to invest in themselves and others. We use hypnotism to de-condition and to actualize people.

People often believe the ideas put forth authoritatively because the world overall buys them. Concepts like time, taxes, prisons, capital punishment, the law, limits to speech, limits to what is proper or accepted, and homes that can never truly be paid off due to property tax that never ends, meaning your government owns your home. I could of course go on and on. These are all suggestions we have accepted over the years. Yet who says we cannot live as they do on Risa, a world from *Star Trek?* Or in another world from myth, legend, or Sci-Fi? Society does not make our world look like this. It prefers what we have. It prefers wars, to destroy the planet on a global scale, it prefers poverty and wealth, and it prefers slavery in some form or another. With these preferences, the elect will always retain their power and the masses will be scattered. So, what are our options?

We can turn inward like so many religions and focus on our work. We can be those who change the terrain of the world and reshape and redo. We can make the mad decision to get the spaceships going and move out. We can come together as like-minds and force the changes so we move closer to real change and freedom. And there are many other options. We can also do nothing and allow it to remain the same due to our laziness and inability to correct. The problem is that it seems we lean towards the latter as a society. It is also a sad truth that the lowest common denominator tends to inherit politics, religions, or negative ideas. We do not seek better or retrain our brains, which would be the best way to implement positive change.

If you recall, throughout this book, I pose options and solutions over and over, not just the problems. Here, again, the Kultus has its vision and direction. If we believe in our work as creators and destroyers, if we believe that "I" as the All is the Universe, then we have the real power. The mistaken mundane illusion of power is of no consequence then. It is a simple veil thrown over our eyes we can react to but should respond to instead. I remember watching the films on martyrs and about Jesus in elementary school, and there was something about the integrity of those people in the face of death. I recalled some of the same faces in the concentration camps around Germany and many other faces over the years: Native Americans, the Rom, the Yezidi, Black slaves, and other persecuted races, tribes, and people. That look is both disturbing and understandable. When you take everything from people, and it doesn't matter to them, when even life does not matter, what can you truly do to control them? It takes something beyond faith. It takes gnosis, and they have to know in every aspect of their being that their cause and reason are just. That creates courage. And only that level of conviction. To know that "I" am the universe releases you from all the chatter. It is freedom beyond measure, beyond death, and so it is a powerful understanding. When you truly accept it, then you do not look to the mundane. It is a pointless blur. Its only purpose is the work, just the work. If you have your body, you can do it anywhere. When you give up the mask, the flesh, you can continue to do the work by taking a new one or moving on to the next stage of development. Those who believe in reincarnation also get this. I have seen it in the eyes of yogis and Buddhists.

Breaking patterns and moving to a more health-driven direction would be best. Then again, I would choose yurts in small villages to revitalize the planet and change much of the direction of greed and technology. Never let a person with the vision of peace and caring for one another while maintaining personal responsibility rule the world. It might end up being a happy anarchy of sorts, and we can't have that, there is no money in it, and it's all an illusion anyway. Maybe it is an illusion but it is a current reality for many. It is also a trance state for many others. How we hypnotize ourselves matters. Just like what we sell or say to others to influence them matter. Words matter.

CHAPTER TWENTY-THREE

PRESENCE, LIVING IN THE BODY OF THE OCCULTIST

The alarm goes off. I turn to shut off the phone. It is 4:30 AM (I am lying here. I am a night owl. It is 9:30 AM. This is an inside joke for those who know me), and I rest back into position on my back. I am attuned to the breath and scan my body. With age comes pain, and I seek to release it. My bladder has other plans. In the end, it wins, and I get up. When I return to the ritual chamber where I sleep, I walk to the altar and set the positive missive for the day. I may write dreams down or do small amounts of stretching and movement so the blood flows. A short meditation and I am off.

Cleansing comes next. A shower or a clean-up for the day at the sink. Focus on my eyes in the mirror. Grounding to self. Intake of water and the brewing of coffee come next. Then it is off to my desk. Soon, I am sitting in front of a screen, preparing to do work. I often light a candle and offer incense; other times, I organize. Again, I center myself, ground, and I am fully there. At set times, a chime sounds, and I am one with my being in the moment and meditate for 30 seconds. Hours pass, and I find myself with time to get away. When that happens, I either nap, read, write, or meditate. Two servitors sit in front of my screen as guards and health beacons. Behind the screen is a giant picture of Kali. Pan is to my right in a statue form, looking as if he were to come through the wall. Behind me is the altar dedicated to my ancestors, teachers, and guides who were once alive. On the bookshelves are other altars dedicated to various things. When I leave my office, I return to the side bedroom where I woke hours before. It always smells of incense, candles, and the ritual nature of the night before.

My schedule will have teachers to meet and students to meet. It will have people I mentor and people who mentor me. It will have rituals scheduled, moon cycles, and other daily works. In the office, there is a whiteboard directed to each month's work. In the closet of that room are ritual attire, items, storage, and other items not displayed openly. The ritual chamber has blackout curtains and is always dark and cool. These surroundings are excellent for my work and have only come after many decades. I used to use television cabinets and other things that were closed off and hidden. I am no longer hidden in my own home.

I must meditate three or more times a day. These moments are solemn and sacred to me. The ability to focus is essential. It means that I lose my phone a lot. It means I often leave it on purpose. I am often in silence and quiet. One might think it is a monastery, and that is not an accident. If it is not silent, there is usually music from jazz to new age, fiddles to flutes, folk, or the voices that cheer me in chants. At other times, the music is haunting or metal if I need a little high-end motivation or I want to sing. If that is not the case, I am listening to podcasts, presentations, audiobooks, or YouTube. I also listen to teachers, and for some, I take a lot of notes. My rooms are littered with notebooks and pens. I am constantly making notes and writing. It is not enough to take in new and exciting information; I need to understand it. This might include research in certain areas and has led to quite a library. Monthly or more, I organize the notes into items I can use, and they enter my Grimoire or the principal book, or are organized into other notebooks based on their purpose and subject.

I further take a week off each year to reconcile all those notes, notebooks, and ideas and synthesize them further. It is usually then that I dump a ton of files and folders. I dump a ton of things to keep to the path. As I have gotten older, I have a lot more stuff and a lot less time. I see the need for a student or students. I would have given anything to be a student of someone as open as I want to be. Thankfully, I was blessed with two teachers like that. It is not because I am some great guru or teacher; it is simply because it is so hard to find someone who wants to share it all. All those I encounter are not interested in the work, just the results of the work. At this point, I would prefer someone who lives with me for a season. There is nothing like hands-on experience. That is how it is done best. I have been very close to a few people where this was possible, but for me, it only happened with my teachers and not with my students. The times are different.

Living within this body has been interesting. It is best explained through behaviors and attitudes, actions and experiences, and through stories. My body began its betrayal around age thirty and has progressively increased its insult every year. It began with posture, then neck and back issues, which led to knees in my forties. It was once a work of art for me to play with. It offered amazing sex, movement, power, and poise, but the Gods have their jokes, and gravity and wear and tear eventually break it down to a remnant of what it once was. Oh, you can soften it and silo it for years, but that means you must see to the body over the mind and the spirit, and that is not going to happen for the mystic. I chose to allow it to go where it would if it were reconciled to allow me the years needed to pursue the work. I recall seeing Crowley in yoga poses and, as a youth, immediately thought about how fat and out of shape he was. Now, I fully grasp the concept because he, too, chose the mind and spirit over the body. He still did the work, as I do, but not to refine and turn into some form of Adonis or Apollo, but to simply get by. My attitude and behavior are consistent with the occultist. That covers the outer covering of the work; let's move on to the internal side.

The real work is on different planes of existence where nothing else is required. You cannot take any items with you in the mundane aspect, yet you have them all and more. There are thousands of different ways to do this. My favorite comes from Taoism and is from a Cave. I use it to create the temple and spire that I shared with you earlier in the text. It is here that the deepest work is done. There is no replacement for it and no other options for advanced work within the Kultus. The connection and consciousness to do this kind of work can be intense at first, but like anything else, you get used to it.

The occultist, in my opinion, is a builder. The idea of the mason is not lost on me. The steps of the building are very important, and like martial arts, you must always practice the basics (the first few steps) over and over. These seminal steps are the foundation, and without a firm foundation, the house will fall. The result of the house falling varies. It could be your magick never works, you could never reach a spirit or a deity, or you might get frustrated and walk away. There is no set formula, per se, but there are foundational aspects that cannot be ignored. Once the first steps are in place, the adepts are free to articulate their preferences as they grow with their Higher Self or Will. As these unite, again, yoga or union is not lost on me either; one begins to seek deeper and may either survey the landscape or go deeper into chosen areas.

I surveyed for some time (read this as working through paradigms). It was important for me to observe and use Chaos Magick as the means to explore, try on, understand, and either retain or move on. This was difficult for my colleagues and those I worked with because I would change a lot, and they could not keep up. Some found it to be wrong, blurring, or difficult for them, and they left me or did not want my input or counsel. Others found it fascinating and took on some of it themselves. For those in the middle, we usually enjoyed the basics together (meditation, self-care, etc.). Then, over time, things would develop, and my keys began to build a small chain for me. These were my deities, my spirits, my go-to, my teachers, and those philosophies and techniques I could rely on. This is where the creation of my system began. Once the parts were in place then I began to dig deeper. I no longer needed to divest into different systems with Chaos Magick. I could now focus on the ones that proved to be my Higher Will and the deities who spoke to me. Candidly, this is the development of working through multiple paradigms and designing my own Stygian Way. That is the goal of each Stygian.

The deep dive is the essence of higher-level magick and the occult, in my opinion. This is where I live now and will remain in these towers until I return to dust. The lower steps are filled with the remnants of my work and formulae of things I tried. Some were marvelous failures that taught me a lot, some were simply boring or fruitless, while others stimulated me and held me, and those are the ones I would retain. I can honestly say I have spent years attempting things that did not work, and I do not regret them. They taught me patience and fortitude. Sometimes they taught me what not to do. I have also had many great exchanges with wonderful occultists, Pagans, and witches who have taught me a great deal about what my options are and how to rectify issues that might arise. I am indebted to them beyond words.

My teachers are my heart, and they remain, even in the ether. Their whispers are my support and guide me when nothing seems to work, and all the other lights are out. The occult is a morbidly lonely path at times. For those introverts like me, that is like a warm bath I want to get into. At other times, I simply miss laughter, debate, and fun and games with others. It is also immensely difficult to see things, to know things, and to be unable to share them with others because it will upset them, trigger them, or cause them pain. This was hard enough when I was cutting my teeth, but now it is nearly impossible. When the veils come down, you cannot put them back up. You see the illusions for what they are. You see the game that is afoot. You register the evils and the victims, and you see the hand in so many things, as I have expressed throughout the first part of this book.

It is also very true that this book and my experiences are not considered the norm within the occult community for many reasons. Many occultists are atheists or agnostics. They have no interest in deities or any form of enlightenment, so most of my commentary would appear to be in my head to them. Many occultists view mysticism as inferior or in opposition to them. Pagans also, many of them, are not interested in forms of the Higher Self in the same manner, and instead are on a different path and may not understand or respect any of what I am talking about. Witches differ wildly and may fit very well into my patterns, or feel they are on a very different path and direction. I make no bones about it. I do not intend to be like others. I am not trying to be this or that. I am not trying to entertain others or seek a path where I can pull others behind me. I am expecting loneliness. I ask the Gods for a partner and a playmate on occasion, and to their credit, they have offered me excellent options and people I will care for and love forever.

Please do not misunderstand me, I do not lament the difference or the lonely aspects. I knew the road before I took it. I was well-warned and prepared. I was gifted with honest and upright teachers as well as the sullen, cruel, and disaffected ones who bled me and toughened me up for what was to come. I am blessed by all of them. And they all remain in the shadows.

As I turn to the last chapters of this book, I will open a new pattern. I will offer up the practical nature of the Stygian Way. I am doing it to point out that new systems can and should be created in the occult, and the Currents cannot only handle them but need them desperately. We need new blood, new ideas, and new aspects of the old systems. Looking back too much allows one to trip on what is right in front of us. Gods and Goddesses should not be limited to what was. I tip my hat to the wonders of people like Josephine McCarthy and her Quareia. Some are doing it, and their impact is felt and appreciated.

CHAPTER TWENTY-FOUR

THE PRACTICAL APPLICATION OF THE STYGIAN WAY

The Stygian Way is different. It finds its foundation on the river Styx, the place between the darkest of dark, gloomy, mist-filled, Gothic paradises. It has a representation of water, the moon, and the chalice, as well as a short trip from the Underworld, Hades, and the Death Current. It is a Goddess-based way that is engaged with fire and the Dark God. The Stygian mythos is from the Greeks, and this has reasoning and symbolism from it and other areas. The river was used to take oaths and was itself a Goddess, a common mythos in many different cultures, East and West. The following are some of its aspects:

Standard Tenants

- The cosmos is the One Universal essence and consciousness, manifested in a rainbow through black, and by it are the symbols of all things
- Within that one Universe is the Self, and this One is All
- Our primary symbols are the Dragonfly and the Seven-Pointed Star
- All is One, individually still exists in the One, and the Self is a mirror
- Reality is a play, an illusion, and a staging ground of the God-nature within you that you must raise from its slumber. The planes are its training ground.
- Life is a way to wisdom through enlightenment by embracing the darkness of the inner road, the Obsidian Path, which leads to the River Styx. It is by

the destruction of duality, lies, and the knowledge that we are already the Universe. It is only by awakening that we can link to the Stygian Current.

- Enlightenment is for those who seek it through their actions
- The body is an instrument for rites, rituals, joy, ecstasy, and connection of purpose through your sacred unfolding; it is a mere vessel and mask
- Identity is a trap of society and a limiting mask; discard all for purpose and intent
- Liberty, sanctity, and choice are primary concerns, but only useful if one is aware of how not to be enslaved
- Our Deities are guides, lovers, teachers, and friends; they are not untouchable things to worship
- Divinity is present in life as the spark of that life and it is vibration
- The mundane world is a manifestation of the Divine, its training ground, its dream, and as we grow to understand, we are the dream, the Universe, "I," and by that, the Dreamer, then it moves, there is no I, no Self, no me, but ALL, One.

Praxis:

- Practice creates belief, experiences, conceptions, and the open-mindedness of each individual is a key factor in developing into manifestation
- Rituals are stimulating, ecstatic, trance states of movement and action
- Meditative trances illuminate gnosis deep within us by exposure
- The use of many forms of substances, from oils, scents, blood, fluids, salts, and water, is used with the infusion of powers to be the vessel of the Deity
- Initiation rites are variants of rising from the dead, crossing the river of dreams, manifesting aspects of power, and becoming
- Meditation is practiced daily, including breathing, swaying, and stone methods, it comes from the Blood Throne, the seat of the meditator
- Magick is practiced in many forms, specific to each person. The thread that identifies it as the Stygian Way is a deeply guarded aspect of our power and shared via initiation only

- Study, art, praxis, and meditation are the square we stand on. We study to gain deep insight into our nature and process. We are artists in our way to understand the Current fully. We practice in many areas. All acts are dead without action.
- The breaking of taboos or norms is essential; the standards of society are created to enslave. Breaking these allows for freedom of thought and the gaining of insight. It is with this insight that we are awake in the world and can balance the body and the spirit. This is done via praxis and experimentation.

Philosophy:

- Embrace the freak, we do not run from the differences; we seek them out
- We do as we will, our law is self-imposed by personal ethics through compassion and experience, and not handed down or assumed from others
- We indulge desires for purpose, not to lose our will to addiction, we also indulge in what disgusts us to keep our balance in all things
- Death is but a step on the road; we know he is coming, and offer him tea when he arrives, so we can begin again
- Fear is for others, not for us; we seek to face all fears fully, so we are not at their whim or mercy, but often what others fear
- Fear moves from our problem to our ally. People fear what they do not understand, and we can easily become that fear for those who would harm us
- Sex is a sacred act of bliss, and in line with our discovery of powers

Symbols:

- The Black Rose is the symbol of the Stygian. It is only found on the altars and not on the crest of the Way
- The Black River symbol is also readily used and referenced in the rites
- The crest consists of the Death's Head Moth, the Dragonfly, and the heptagram, as well as the Child who sits at the bottom with a body of cosmic origin

- Initiates will often wear different aspects to symbolize different levels of their skill to display them to other members. The most common are the heptagram and Dragonfly. Obsidian/ Onyx, Jet, Snowflake Obsidian, Carnelian, or Amethyst are common in rings and jewelry
- The colors of the way are, of course, black and the deep blue of the flame, as well as red and purple.
- Cords are worn by certain levels to represent their position in rites/rituals or events
- The two other symbols used more for male energy are the bident or Stang and the wand. For females, it is the chalice and the sword.

Deities:

- The Dark Mother is the multifaceted and faced deity of the way, she offers the energy of Shakti, Nature, birth/creation, and destruction, wild and feral
- The Dark Father is the multifaceted and faced horned deity of the way. He offers the energy of Shiva, Power, focus, potential, and Universal balance
- They combine to an androgynous nature of the One, the Whole, the Source, and by this, they are the Cosmos, and we, we are them, and they are us if we tap the Egregore
- Pan, Charon, Hades, and Hermes are typical aspects seen in the Gods in their mythos
- Hecate, Queen Mab, Persephone, Kali, and the faeries (even the males) are typical aspects of the Goddess and her mythos
- Aspects of monotheists are avoided and seen as manifestations of society and not the deific entities of antiquity; we prefer the feral and living aspects
- The Kultus is a polytheistic experience, and there are a series of deities who manifest without order into the lives of the members when their time is right
- The Deities of the Stygian Way are not from known myths and legends; they were of the shadows, the dark, the ones people did not write about or refer to. Their manifestation is new and comes within a new crossroads of Chaos and Death Currents.

Sayings:

- The Dyad creates the initiate, and the initiate is autonomous. Through the river, they are washed clean of their blood and tears, and then they can be a true Guardian or Mistress
- Liberty from societal norms is the only real freedom
- Morality is a lever used to restrain; finding your ethics is required
- You come from the womb without shackles, they are put on by humanity, whether you see them or not, break them or remain enslaved
- Overthrowing all mental prisons must happen to be aware
- Pleasure and happiness are essential, and a proper human aim- Epicurean
- Intimacy and the beauty of art are part of the experience, indulge
- Free yourself from fear by breaking taboos and limits through experiences
- Question all authority, even those who teach within the way
- Skepticism and rationality are excellent tools; use them wisely
- Value experience over all things, even the texts, and especially other people
- Collective ideas are good if they expand your experience, but if they limit you, danger
- Forge your way without the fetters of identity; culture, history, status, birth, class, gender, or community, be "no one."
- In the end, you are the Universe; therefore, you must center the universe to go on with the work, the flesh is gone in an instant
- While you are in the flesh, be of the flesh
- Cultivate rare tastes and senses to the extent of your abilities
- Accentuate the beauty of what others see as perverse, exotic, or avant-garde
- When you do use your masks, do so in hedonistic glory, play out different roles and masks, and keep your favorites and refine them
- Lies are needed at times, but an ethical focus on your word can be used to your advantage
- Seek your own best interest, as no one else will
- Celebrate wins and failures the same; both allow for new information
- Immoral acts by others' standards can be virtuous and important to your development

Teachings:

- The study of books, texts, and scriptures is secondary to oral tradition
- The veneration of Sri Yantra as a map is used instead of the Tree of Life or other Kabbalistic sources as our primary tool
- Studies of tattvas, chakras, and kundalini are foundational
- The study of karmic, yogic, and dharmic living aspects are general concepts
- Connection to spirits, use of magick, conjuring, and weaving the Current are needed
- Transformative rites and spiritual experiences abound and are practical
- Circular breath, movement, and use of the body are daily
- The dyad is the principal tool: the apprentice and the teacher
- The Guardian holds the wisdom of the Current, the high priest of art
- The Mistress holds the keys and power, high priestess of the sword

Individual/Communal Work:

- Live freely and in tune with the body and its needs as one's temple
- Live in touch with ecstatic and joyful pleasures and experiences
- Adjust, work with, and understand other systems
- When living together, keep your openness and allow others full expression
- Transmission of sacred ideas is done communally or in a dyad
- Steps of Training:
  - Thrall: servant, entry-level seeking entry
  - Novice/Apprentice: accepted novice under the guidance of a teacher
  - Initiate/Apprentice: 2nd year, intermediate training
  - Stygian: accepted member of the Way, mastered the basics
  - Wanderer: the member who is in the world, working on their way
  - Guardian/Mistress: one who returned and is now a teacher and holder of wisdom

Tools and Skills

- Ashes to ash, the use of ash in rites is common

- Upon the altar are the symbols of the elements: fire- Goddess candle, air- incense, water- chalice or cup, earth- altar stone, and the void/ether is our sacred symbol
- The colors of the Current are black, red, purple, silver, and white
- Rocks/gems of the Current are jet, obsidian/onyx, moonstone, tiger's eye, amethyst, red jasper, and carnelian
- The Stang or bident, staff, and wands are of the male energy
- The Chalice, knives, cauldron, and bell are the female energy
- Divination is done through three primary tools: scrying, a pendulum, and cards or oracles of choice
- Meditation is done in chairs due to our specific methods, we do not sit on the floor
- Hypnosis is part of our training for ourselves, and for those we train
- Physical training is expected daily to reinforce the mind and spirit
- Because we do much of our work with others, we carry talismans and amulets for our protection, and we spend a lot of time with our personal jewelry
- We practice ways of shadowing our auras, our power, our presence, and our methods
- Our use of masks is tactical, psychological, and impactful to our outer world, and our inner work is ritualized and spiritual
- We obtain energy through many endeavors and often take up professions where we can maintain our lifestyle and focus

This is a rather long list to show the reader what this part of the book will discuss in more detail. All the methods, philosophical ideas, rites, and rituals are not formed in a dream but through direct interaction with deities and a history of practice for years. These were made for no one other than me. Even those within the Stygian Way will develop their systems and rites personally (other than the standards, which are few) and in their own ways. Of course, we will continue to use the basic ones that adhere to the Egregore, but it is clear that it and we are both very flexible. Some will want a group, a coven, a house, etc. Others will work in solitary life, and others will make fools of themselves by not attending to the basics and seeking some status or power they cannot hope to obtain by trying to skirt the process. There is no gate system or method I have found that keeps out those who want it cheap and easy other than closing the door when they arrive.

Because I have decided to write a book, I do not have any real gate options other than limiting what I write. Many of the teachers I have worked with over the years have echoed the same sentiment. We could offer the keys and all the secrets, and no one would ever access it. When asked why, they would say that those who are truly on the path would not read the book, convinced that it was a trick. The lazy would never do the work, and the adepts who would gain the most from it would take it and do it their way anyway. It is this last group I am writing to and for. The others will have little interest anyway. Why write a book for such a small audience? It is my belief that no one writes for them. There are always exceptions, and I feel I have come upon some of those books and am most grateful for those authors. Those books are not at your local store, not sold or found easily, and that is a shame. New publishers have sought to offer more of this material, but often at much higher prices. The good news is the quality and depth of some of their work is amazing.

In my later years, I have found a Gothic and deep black subculture that I deeply relate to and love. I have drunk from its fountain with delight. It is inspired by the horrors of film, art, literature, and music, and by the many genres of creatures who come to my door. My guardian and tulpa emerged from the ashes for me, the experiences with servitors, with spirits who sought to help, and guidance came from many cultures and for many reasons. Some have very personal relations to my work and others are open and can be seen by psychics. I will tell some of these stories in the pages to come.

CHAPTER TWENTY-FIVE

STORIES & EXPERIENCES

Experiences forge a deeper understanding. In this chapter, I will share some of the stories of my life and how they brought about the Stygian Way. I must say again, this is not my grand plan or from my mind. I believe the Stygian Way was in my since birth, and in the births before that. I believe it was to manifest this in this generation and that I am simply its vessel. The first few stories are around psychic readings and what I learned, and why.

I realized over a series of incidents with a partner that each time we went for a reading, if I was in the room, the reader would neglect to read my partner and read me instead. This became annoying for both her and me, so I went to the ritual chamber and began my work. I wanted to construct a shield, a holding pattern to cover my energy patterns, even my aura. I worked at it, and at first, I would forget and then be unable to pull back. I asked for a visual and used scrying to help. As I became more skilled at it, I booked an appointment with a very well-known elder. We met, and she could read nothing. Her psychic ability was quite renowned, and she was unsure what to do, and became frustrated. The moment I let it down, she gave me a dirty look, seeming aware that I had shut her out. I still did not allow her in completely, and she could only give a general reading. It was well worth the cost. I learned more from testing her than from the session.

In the following months, there were two examples where I went to readings, and the psychics were upset. They both told me I would not let them in, and they could not read me. I played with the pattern gently and allowed their entry, and then closed it again. It caused them to get angry. I realized at that point I could indeed control it. One of the psychics was just not very good, but I did share that I was working on this with the other one, who understood and thanked me for telling him. To be clear, I do not run around pissing off psychics. I did this with purpose and intent and discussed this with them after the sessions so as not to break their own beliefs in their work or cause any damage to them.

I wanted to be read on other occasions, and I would let down the wall. I recall the face of a woman who looked at me as I entered her small room. Her eyes opened, and she looked a bit afraid. I asked if she was okay, and she took a moment and said yes. Historically, I typically have a very devoted family member with me in my aura, but in the most recent years, she has only been there on occasion. It is the circling of my Current that is seen by the psychic. She took a moment, waited, and then could not take it.

She asked, "Are you a magician?"

I answered, "You could say that."

"Do you work with an Asian or some kind of tribe of people?"

"Yes," I said, smiling.

"Then there is the... thing, not sure what it is? It is small, gray?"

"He is not wholly gray to me, but yes, that is one of mine."

"What kind of magick do you do?"

"That is a very personal question," I told her, "I do not share that."

She sat for a moment and then turned up the cards. It was pretty good reading, but honestly, most of the readers see nothing, are usually not very good, and do not have any idea. Most of them do not even read the cards correctly. If they use another form of divination, then I spend a lot of time trying to understand it. Varied card decks throw me, but there is art there for a reason. Because this psychic did see deeper, we became friends, and when she learned the rest of the story, she felt very vindicated in her reading. She also helped me understand what I could not see or feel but was present.

In still another incident, I was offered a shamanistic reading. I was leery about it because so many people claim shamanism, and it is not. She appeared interesting, and we did not sit and talk but walked together instead. I was so honest with her that she seemed to understand me. She seemed unsure what to do with me, so she asked if she could ask some questions. I agreed.

"Do you believe in reincarnation?" she asked.

"Yes."

"Do you know any of your past lives? Have you done regression?"

"No."

She took a moment and then closed her eyes. She took a few moments and then looked up at me. She then told me I was a Chieftain in a past life, I was looking over thousands, and they would die for the tribe and me. I was filled with scars and cuts, and had times of bloodlust. I had a deep life as that leader, and he stood out to her. Another was a woman shaman, and in this life, I came back to not wage war but to be a priest. My dharma was made of cloth and not the blades of battle.

I cannot explain it, but while she was talking, I saw both the shaman and the Chieftain, and they were so real to me. I could touch them and smell them, and I knew them well. I had many lives before, and I had little interest in them. These two, however, have an influence on me and all I do. They were connected to the same deities with different faces that I engage with today. The idea that humanity is limited to this lifetime is a limit we set for ourselves. The Stygian Way seeks insight and scrying not just into the astral and to other realms but into our own lives and what has been for us. These two aspects combined are a powerful gathering of insight that furthers the work. The use of good psychics and mediums allows the Stygian to test their skills, their lives, and their insights across the realms. As always, I am not asking you to believe or share my beliefs. Experience speaks loudest. If you have had these experiences, I could not convince you otherwise. It also becomes clear that time is not on a line but a spectrum or cycle.

I have had many readings like this, but none spoke to me. You were a king! You will be wealthy! You will do great things. It meant nothing. We all get readings like that. No one really takes them seriously, and you shouldn't. But, on occasion, there are readers who really do see. This shaman was that for me. She was far from my home state and I only saw her once at a bookshop in the middle of nowhere Ohio. Yet, there was a deep connection. It wasn't all about me either. It is always the connection with family and experiences no one knows. When a psychic or shaman can talk about that, I am drawn in. They are never general experiences either. If you have those details, I will pay attention.

The second set of interactions is through coupling or taking on colleagues or partners. In each instance, it differs wildly. I will offer a few of my experiences. In one incident, I met with a Satanist and ceremonial magician. She was an interesting combination of a Thelemite and a witch. We spent a great deal of time together and manifested a ton of energy and insight together. We challenged each other and laid hands on one another. The results were interesting, and she left me too early for there to be more.

Another saw herself as a witch. She taught me herbs and was much older. Sex magick and power exchange happened. We used rope, leather, whips, and needles. She was wide open and came into my life in the middle of my kink exploration. Our journey into sacred sex and so much of what I had learned greatly enhanced my practices and knowledge. The experiments were massively helpful, and we learned a ton about ourselves and one another. Her body became an instrument I could play, and she knew how to entice and do amazing masses and rituals. I moved her from the circle to the ritual chamber. She moved me from the heavy and the dominant to being able to sway, dance, and join in ecstatic work better than anyone prior. We both had our dating partners, and we both had other lives outside this work. It upped our game by 100. The Great Work, for me, was a wonder and still is. What we did does not resemble that of the witches, and my partner found this to be very enticing. Where did I get all this? Did I make it up? This led me to initiate her into my Current. Silence is Golden.

The next player was a male. He was another witch but also a ceremonial magician. We became friends quickly because I got a taste of his energy in a ritual, and I was in. With him, I learned to be a bit of a vampire. After he fed on me, he taught me a few tricks around the protection I still use. He was a Gothic young male who was very attractive. I was very surprised by his interest in me. We would do rituals under the moon together, some of which were sky-clad. The work was needed for me to touch more of the feral side, and even though he understood energy, he did not see deity or any kind of spirit. He had no sight. He was one of the first people who taught me that there is a prejudice and misunderstanding around those who cannot see and believe no one can. He was also the first person to move energy and color it. The skill is well worth it and came up later for me when I learned Reiki.

Many years later, I went to train in hypnosis (see the chapter devoted to this for history). It was an intense twelve-week training. It included NLP (neurolinguistic programming) and was taught by therapists. I was hypnotized many times and often took the role of the client. I would sink as deep as I could into the work. I wanted it, and the instructor saw that and offered me more. I walked away from that program and was able to do self-hypnosis very easily. I was also able to induce trance in others, which helped a lot of my partners and students over the years. I never used it as a career and rarely offered it to others outside of my occult work. I see the benefit and use it for change and function within my discipline and behavior patterns. It also helps in dreams, astral work, and meditation. The two further training courses were to advance certain aspects and to gain experience in hypnosis from very good professionals.

You might see the link or wonder how any of these things fit together. They do fit together quite well. Trance, focus, and testing what others see and experience, testing my skills, readings of psychic people, and their ability to get in or not get through my walls are all needed information. All these aspects are referenced in my training, but do not speak to the interrelations of the masks. That topic is sensitive to me as I have not shared it before. Even with students, it is typically left to their imagination. I will offer a little here.

I learned the masks later in my occult life. It came up from left-hand path magicians who wanted to be left alone. I took their methods and added to them. They used physical masks, and I liked that in ritual, but I needed to expand it to the mundane. As a youth, I was into theatre and acting. I had pulled off roles and got people to believe my changes in the mundane world when I would visit different places. I would take on roles: flirt, the leech, the idiot, the comic, the stoic, and so on. It was interesting to watch people's reactions. Sometimes I was terrible at it. I learned the roles I liked and the ones I did not.

I recall moving this into daily life at a new restaurant or to pull myself further out of being an introvert. A partner asked me why I did it, and I explained it was yet another experiment. We all take on roles, but what if I were to dress differently, act differently, and manifest a different person? If I could manage this, it would be another aspect of Chaos Magick. It is another way to free myself from who I am supposed to be or what I am supposed to do, and augment my reality accordingly. Over time, it became a game I rightly enjoyed.

I added it to the kink in personas. I added it to the new dates when I realized they would be a waste of time to entertain myself. It was an intellectual game, and I learned a lot from the performances. I have digressed from this as age continues because it is no longer needed. It is a young man's game. As an older male, I know exactly who I am now. It is simple for me to take on roles I need to take, but they are all me. I believe I learned this through this experimentation.

I will add here that I recently listened to a video of Anton LaVey speaking on these same points, and I did not put them together until now, but it does work well. He was talking about this in the 60s with masks, roles, and the presence of mind to take on space and life you want and create it for your benefit. In a way, the video game lifestyle and generation seem to me to be an example of this in a modern sense. The move back towards so many playing RPGs (role-playing games) and so many aspects of losing yourself within a culture, genre, or place. I recall watching the musical *Cabaret* on stage in the 80s and having the same experience of people wanting to get away and leave their troubles behind. The world can be tough. Creating your reality can be very helpful, as are the masks of the roles you might play. The roles could be generated by the influence of others who decide for you what you will do and who you are. The Stygian gives that control to no one. All others are not to be trusted or allowed.

I highly recommend this game and the work it takes. It is disorienting at times. You fall out of yourself, and eventually, you run face-to-face into yourself. When you do, it is deep shadow work. It is not for the faint of heart. Those who play with this and who are already lost can go mad. For those with a firm grasp, it is invigorating and is a great way to spend your nights. It also shows you how much reality is not real. It shows you how much it is a matrix of sorts.

The senses have a major role that must be fully understood and fleshed out to maximize them. My sense work started in a strange place. I was born at a time in the 70s when my teenage years were in the midst of the ninja boom. Everything was ninjas then. In a set of books on ninjutsu in the 1980s, I began to practice the skills. It was the link to the body and mind I needed. I had no idea at the time what I was doing or why this kind of stuff was in a book on the ninja. I recognized the connection between the elements and the senses, but that was as far as I could discern. I explored all facets of my senses and, through that work, experienced food, sex, smell, and touch very differently from most people around me. It catapulted me into the senses. With each month of exploration, I expanded further and further. Eventually, it caught up with my occult work, and the marriage was on fire! I could not believe, when I picked up my notes a decade ago, how excellent the results were. When the two met, I recognized why elemental work, bodywork, touch, and scents had their place with touch. This work merged with Taoist aspects of meditation, moving energy, sexuality, and the work of elixirs.

When I sought to add sense work to the Kultus, I considered what other systems do. I understood them, but preferred the combination that I had developed from these sources because of the outcome. Our method differs from many other systems for a few reasons. We build the energy over the course of months through practice and experiment. We then add the potent energy work to the mix. Lastly, we focus our intent towards an ecstatic point of view. Stygians are very interested in feral or wild energy. While in the flesh, we work in the flesh. In the same way, we embrace aspects of yoga and Tantra. We must be able to extend ourselves in the Universal systems. The physical is also present to be able to keep the body alive, active, stretched, and healthy. This includes food intake, sleep, daily living, and water intake. Keeping to a rhythm and a lifestyle is foundational. For Stygians, that does include work to magnify the senses or to have an awareness of where they are dull or less than others. We need touch, taste, sex, joy, laughter, focus, intention, and scents to see fire, to lose ourselves in the mirror, to hear the sounds and vibrations, and to move and rock. We must experience and experiment. All these things are part of our senses and the needs of a Stygian. Not a want, a need. Without these, we believe we are not fully living.

This leads to the artistic nature of the Stygian. The Stygian is balanced in the world and on the other side. It falls into the ideas of the theatre, too. Aspects of the Moulin Rouge and the Bohemians are a beautiful rendering to consider. If I, as a Stygian, were wealthy, I would have and use a theatre to showcase all these things, from art to theatre to versions of burlesque and music. A Gothic old theatre with red drapes and rooms for small, intimate one-man or woman shows. If these ideas do not feel magical or mystical to you, then you do not understand the Stygian Way. It is embedded in the foundation to see things this way. Look deeper, or you are missing the Current and the point. This theatre would be much less for the public and much more for the players, artists, and people involved in the work.

If there were even more money and it were a different time, it would be even better to offer rooms and training in these same arts within the walls of the theatre or a nearby home. A commitment to this and removal from the overculture to stimulate the art and culture of the world's stage would be a masterful change from the fate and presentation of the world as it is. Moving us more towards a Renaissance of times and less towards the Middle Ages, where it seems we are moving. There is power in numbers and in people working towards the same ends. This is the peaceful revolution of art. That is the one I am interested in.

Why does it matter? It matters because if we change the faces and hearts of people, if we move towards actions, focus on art, music, and skills, and away from screens, numbing ourselves, and distraction, we are much more likely to be awake and change our fate. But alas, I am not rich or blessed with such wealth or with these kinds of friends that would honor the backing of such an endeavor. The magick, the dark, the foreboding, and the plays and films that could be made might help to transform the next generation from where they are headed to a brave new world where they can find control outside the doctrines and confines of politicians and universities. To a hands-on world of set building, directing, dance, film, and the beauty of all colors, voices, and ideas. A place where there is good communication, effective debate, and the training of meditation, focus, intent, and purpose. A world of magick and manifestation. That could be paradise. It is certainly the place of my dreams, even this late in life.

CHAPTER TWENTY-SIX

DREAMS & DELUSIONS

In 2013, 2015, and again in 2018, I sought to build a community. I fell in love with the idea of yurt living (wood, not canvas) or the idea of small homes or cabins set in a circle or some formation in a wooded area. As I expressed in prior chapters, I tried very hard to bring this to life, and it failed. The dreams had to change, and that is an important factor to discuss. The dreams of a communal group have been sidelined for the Current of the Technology of a Modern Chaos Reality. As an apprenticeship program, it differs from prior manifestations and hidden orders. I am sure it will remain very small, and that will always be my intent. How it will be executed is already being done by a few people. That may be all that happens to it, but my delusion is that what comes from the Kultus will make a difference.

Why am I sharing this? It is not to point out the issues in the community, to point fingers, or even to be negative. It is to challenge the occultists, Pagans, witches, and the like to have integrity. If you are not interested, do not fake it or suggest what you will not do. Be honest with yourself and others. There are deep divides in a lot of communities, and often, they circle this very issue. At this point, with the economy, with land and homes, and even building options, there is no way for me to envision a community. It is just too far beyond the fiscal possibilities. That saddens me, but I understand and accept it. If you are willing or have built a community like any of the ones I mentioned, please let me know, and I will help to support the work or join it myself. This is not ego-driven for me. I do not need to be in charge of the administration of any of it. I would deeply enjoy the ride if someone else were to take the wheel. I have run enough businesses and mentored and coached a large portion of my life. Believe me, I don't need to be in charge.

My vision is that it gets done in some form or fashion. I have put that out into the universe in this book, in spells, and in ceremonies and rites. I also know I am not alone. We need these communities so badly. We need options for people who want to live outside the societal ramifications. We need a connection to nature, to fresh air, while we can still get it. We need land that is not over-harvested or destroyed. We need the village in some form or another. Perhaps these are just my dreams, and they will never see the light of day, but I build them in the astral, so folks, at some point, they will manifest. I may have left this body in the dust by then, but it is coming, or perhaps it once was. Why do I see this need? I have seen many lower and low-income occultists and witches who just need opportunities. They want to make a difference, but they do not know how to get there. Our community often silos out and takes care of their small group or tribe and doesn't extend themselves. We must stop this and expand to come together along the same lines so we can be more secure as an unorganized organization.

The only dream I see possible at this point is the only one that is not communal. I have called it many things over the years. It leans back to France and the time of the Revolution. It is linked to a time when people were treated terribly, and they eventually could not take it anymore. Ironically, it was also a time of gorgeous art, literature, and artists doing some amazing works. The French salons came to me through the works of novelists and magicians like Joséphin Péladan. His history and work have been mostly lost in time, but have recently been revitalized through a few books that I enjoyed. It is this idea of a salon that I think would bring people together. How? I have been to several fairs, markets, and pop-up places that show up for the holidays or on other occasions. From Krampus, for Samhain, or just during the year. Music festivals and other kinds of storefronts and places have the feel of a salon in a modern sense. Even a trend towards Gothic gatherings, readings of plays, or literature with cocktails. Some have amazing flair and excitement attached, and others are small businesses that might never make it due to a lack of support, but are well worth that support if we want them to continue.

I believe the connection is through exchange and understanding. There must be speakers, entertainment, a theme, and a wonder to it. Within the year, I attended a reading and cocktail party that revolved around Edgar Allen Poe. This event had a great atmosphere and was beautiful. As I looked at the performers, servers, and the people around me, it was clear that everyone was enjoying the dress-up, the liquor, and the presentation. It was an adult situation, and no children were present. This is important. Perhaps a club, a location, a store that offers teaching, reading, and so on? That place could be a beacon for the community and, if done well on social media, be a beacon where people come from all over the country or the world. It is always important for the grassroots to support it within its community first. That would mean picking a community where the people are already. CA and NY typically carry the most alt lifestyle people, but are also the most expensive places to live. They have always been the key places, but if we look just below, there are key cities on lists of places that might work out great; Houston and Dallas, TX, are within the top 20 on some lists, and my city, Orlando, is #18. Although I have heard that Tampa is far more witchy and open. My exploration may open this storefront one day.

I admit these are my dreams; there is nothing like this in play so far as I am aware. I do know of many attempts from many, but still, nothing seems real. The closest thing I have encountered is in Salem and New Orleans. The Vampyre Balls of Father Sebastiaan is an ode to the French Salons in a way, and it does intrigue me. Janet Munin (2022) edited a short book titled *Polytheistic Monasticism: Voices from Pagan Cloisters*. I was one of the people on the forums and still am on some who are very committed to these ideas. I loved the book. I noticed quickly that all the writers seemed to be separate, small, and often single entities. We have a problem, and we must face it. Is it our own egos? We must have it our way. We must be the founders. I am not sure what the driver is, but if we do not learn to cooperate, to work together, and to move in the direction of a common cause, how can we ever expect any dreams to manifest?

A large part of the work of the Stygian is to exemplify cooperation in the world, to mark their flesh with ideas such as these. Don't misunderstand, it is not for the world, it is for the Stygian, their mask, and their work within the world. We also seek to influence in this way to intensify the unity of real disruption of the slavery of mankind's brain, not some other madness. The real enemy is not obvious. The real enemy is acceptance of the lies and culmination of fighting their wars and allowing their propaganda in like good little lemmings. Awake! The Stygian Way is open to you.

Any artist will dream; they must be creative. Whether it is the fantasy art of Frazetta, Vallejo, Brom, and Zawadzki, to the more dark and occult leanings of Hagen von Tulien, Marjorie Cameron, or H. R. Giger, there are many directions to carry art and many very interesting people within their fold. It is no mistake that Crowley and A. O. Spare were also artists in their own right. Art or poetry is not the end of artistic endeavor. Dream wide and open to what artistic work calls to you. Some musicians connect their occult leanings to their work, starting a lot of really bad bands and some good ones. Beauty can also be found in clothing design, in ceremonial clothing, and in the very idea of an occultist who is a practitioner working your fabric and helping with your vision can be very empowering. May the Gods bless Etsy. Perhaps it is the art of sculpture, and there is something inside the structure that adds to it, or it is a symbol or connection to the deities or spirits that inspire you to do this work. The ideas are endless, from jewelry to bodywork, to energy healing, to plants or herbs, and so on.

Allow your dreams to manifest, and if, like me, no one responds, do it anyway. I may never have the yurts and a farm in the country, but I will always have the beautiful vision of it and the inspiration to work hard on the Kultus. It is not about hope; it is about work. Make it happen. Don't wait or hope, this disempowers you, push! Work hard to reconcile your positive outcome, and if it is just you, be just you. If you get a partner for a season, then relish that partner. If you lose them or they move on, so be it. In the end, this is a lone game, a lone trial, and you cannot take anyone with you. When they get in with you, enjoy the ride with them, but know they are probably going to want to get out at some point. Do not coerce, but do not be coerced either. Keep dreaming, use meditation, and your astral temple to continue the dreams.

CHAPTER TWENTY-SEVEN

PRACTICES

The art of practice is different for each person. Do not read this as a set practice, only as an example. I have disclosed a set day before in general terms. This chapter will be more specific to the tasks and roles, what they look like, and a little more as to why. Practice is done for many reasons. It is to attain the skills sought out and to further them to a deeper growth and understanding. It is to open new doors. It is to normalize the work for the mind and the body but not to switch the brain to automatic. There must be enough differences to allow each set of practices to need attention and focus. That is why there is never a set practice. It must be revised and tinkered with all the time. There is something to be said for "muscle memory" and the beauty of a well-used ritual, but there is also a lot to be said for focused attention and intention. The best, for me, is a marriage of both. Both have their own purpose.

During the day, on three occasions, at high noon, 3 pm, and 6 pm, a bell will chime, and I will come into my body, feel my breath, silence everything, and ground. If I have nothing pressing, I will take those times for 2–8-minute meditations. Throughout the day, I will record notes or ideas on my notepad. The evenings are when the ritual chamber is very much alive. My work is based around the moon, so most of the work is done at night. I am lucky enough to work at home. When I have difficult meetings or people, I take a moment to resettle. I eat very little other than the first meal and have dinner at night. I drink lots of water and use supplements. I attend to the physical body during the day as well. That is when exercise, stretching, and attention to the body's needs are most often addressed. My practices include martial arts and body movements.

When night comes, I am regimented. I spend time socializing, and then I turn off. I begin with self-hypnosis and then move to meditation, pranayama, and mudras with various mantras, with a rosary or mala. If someone were to be looking on, they may mistake me for a yogi or Buddhist. The room is thick with incense and with candlelight only. The inside work is the most important, and that is where I spend about an hour or more. If there is a rite or ritual to do, I will then rise and do it either within the same trance state or in the state that results from the meditation. My materials are before me, on a bookshelf to my left, or in the next room for backup supplies. The room is a holy temple and ritual chamber. It is not touched by others. The exceptions are students, partners, and colleagues who might come over to do work together. If others do something in or by my ritual chamber, they are usually very uncomfortable unless they are within the Currents. That is a byproduct of my work.

I must add here that the idea of inner and outer, although I refer to these often in this work is an illusion. The Hermetic Principles apply and what is in is out, up is down, and so on. There is no real inner and outer. Most of the principles set evaporate at more advanced levels. Even the philosophy moves to a more obscure version, leading more to "why does it matter," or "it doesn't matter." In terms of what is seen or unseen, what is psychological, what is deific or spirit, or what is actual versus in the mind's eye. Experience is the one thing that is always present. What we do and our experience is the law bringer. It allows us to validate or discard. To do my work I must allow for that. There are no sacred cows and if you choose to hold them, it will be your undoing. Every time I wanted to hold on to something it always proved to be the one thing that held me back. It is imperative to change your mindset from a human collector of shit to a mystic that holds on to nothing. Letting go is for masters. It is the hardest part of the work because we are wired to be social creatures and we want to have stuff and be around people. If these things get in your way you will quit, stop working, or resist the very deities and spirits who are guiding you. If you are sabotaging your Daemon, it will depart, leaving you in your mundane existence.

The details of advanced work are as useless as can be. What I do may mean nothing to you. You must get the details from your deities, spirits, guides, and your own Daemon. Listening to mine is fruitless. When I see other teachers do that, my skin crawls. I used to have master teachers do this to me all the time, and those ways never worked for me. Of course not, this is a single-person project. If I am the Universe and you are your Universe, we cannot do things the same way. What works for you might explode for me. Deities and myths teach us this all the time. You take the seed from another, but if you continue to go back for seeds, you are planting their garden and not cultivating your own. It is not disloyal. It is not disrespectful to plant your own and innovate; it is your job to do so. It is disloyal and disrespectful if you simply copy from what I did, and that is enough, not to mention lazy.

My skin crawls from this because I have watched students create gods of their teachers and have made the vessel into the deity, and that never ends well because the flesh fails. It is supposed to. Don't be fooled by the masks; see them as masks. Accept them, and then there is no surprise. Your guru had sex with six of his students. Why is that surprising? If you build someone's ego bigger than the person, they seem to always buy into that vision and trip over themselves. Ironically, the work is to do the opposite, but we are human in our flesh, and that is flawed. It has its weaknesses. If we fortify against them, if we do not buy our own or sycophants' press, then we can be clear and see the truth. If we cloud it, well then, we move closer to pulling the shades back down and returning to an unawakened state. Somewhere in us, though, we know better, and that will get the better of us in the long run.

I once had a student for a year; he went very slowly. He invited me to his ritual chamber, and when I saw it, I was disappointed, and he saw it in my face. He asked what was wrong. I just stood there and waited. He did not get it, and that was worse, so I told him that he was being a robot. He went out and copied my ritual chamber. That meant to me that he had not grown or created his path, and he would indeed fail in his work. We had a long talk, and I passed him on to a teacher who wanted copies and not original thinkers. He was happier there. He was too early in his journey to be able to take the wheel. The Kultus is not for everyone. It is not a flaw. It is just where you are on the journey. I don't want to see a copy. I want to see expansion and your methods and then ask you why, and you know why.

In another example, I visited the ritual chamber of a female practitioner. She worked with me for some years and lived far away. My altar is quite dark in color and feel. I remember walking into her room and bursting out laughing. Rainbows, wide open light, pinks, reds, and shades of green were everywhere. The rug in front of her altar was made from a collection of baby heads from dolls. She was still dark, but she was dark in her way. When she saw me laugh, she was disappointed until I turned to her and hugged he. I told her how I loved it because it was all hers. That is what the Kultus is looking for. Don't copy and paste, be an artist, be you.

When I formed my small temple and called it the Technology of a Modern Chaos Reality as a Stygian, I did it to breathe life into this new Current and Egregore. The pull from other systems, the darkness, the music, the cultures, and the figures that tie to this Current make it potent even though it is new. Libertines are by nature potent, as are the artists favored in the Gothic themes of society. They are indeed returning thanks to modern films and antinomian themes. Rebels with a cause, my space is filled with these kinds of tricksters and playful entities. My personality and own peculiarities have always been in line with them: Pan, Hermes, Coyote, Bacchus, Loki, and the like. I offer this list to offer the idea of the deities and not who they are specifically. The other side is not trickster at all but more heartily dark mothers, bloodthirsty and wondrously powerful: Hecate, Kali, Nyx, and the like.

The mythos of the Stygian then extends to the River Styx, to the ferryman Charon, and to where part of the river leads, to Hades itself/himself. The ferryman then is a guide and a spirit of help for us. We use this method and way to gain access to all aspects of where our work and Current come from. It is not lost on the Stygian that it is a circle and mimics the circles of the path we are on and the walking between worlds, which is our primary calling and work. With Hesiod's tale or that of Homer or Dante, Styx is within the Greek myths proper. It is not the tales that inspired the Stygian Way. However, it was the work of gnosis and the awakening to the river that opened the Stygian Way. It was through the Underworld and the identity of several methods of travel all over the nine worlds that the astral walking and wanderer style of the river took me.

There is also an interesting trip when we learn that Pluto in 2013 had a moon named Styx and that another moon was called Nix (Nyx). It is also interesting that Hades himself is often referred to as Pluto. It is also interesting that it was removed from the list of planets. There is a deep association with cold, dark, and separate, all aspects of the work at its height. I believe that all great work happens backward, or if you like, in a full circle. You do a ton of practice and then realize it was there all along. It was staring at you, and you were not ready. When you are ready, it is a laugh. There it is! It makes so much sense now. We cannot know what we do not experience... this is the motto.

With this in mind, I will open up the idea of the practices of rites, rituals, and ceremonies a bit...

The presider sits deep in meditation upon the Blood Throne. As the meditation is completed, she rises with her staff and moves to the river; she waits on the shore. All aspects of the senses are piqued and explored. The presider stands between worlds and faces the altar. Three strikes to the ground with the staff, call to the ferryman. He arrives in his own time. When he does, she takes the coin in hand and strikes the bowl with a sound that reverberates when it is tossed in. The ferryman is paid. She enters his boat and is taken to the world, where her temple sits on the shore. The journey differs for many, but it is always dark, mist-filled, eerie, and for some, the ferryman speaks, and for others, he remains silent. At the shore, the ferryman turns to her and hands her back the coin, as our coins are different than others. She exists at the shore, removes her hood, and faces both the astral and mundane altar (some strip off the entire cloak).

She rightfully looks up, her Daemon present, and she sees the Dark Mother on the shore. She approaches the Mother and the altar. Then she offers gifts of incense, lighting the Goddess Candle, and taking up her blade, she ventures to the Mother. She uses the blade to illustrate her sigil, and then she talks and consults with the Mother, whom she knows well by now (introduced at initiation and every time since). With direction and intent, she determines the rites she has come to do. In this case, it is a power-raising rite, so she moves to the shore by the river where her circle is laid. Her hands rise, and she calls to the spirits to rise and come forth, her brethren, sisters, and others. The mentors, gurus, and peers, dead and alive, are welcome to travel and see her there. Her servitors, tulpa, and guardians are also present.

Positions are taken, and the mantras of the Stygian Rite are vibrated so we are certain nothing else has joined us. The brazier is lit, and incense is thrown into the fires (in symbol or if outdoors, actually done). The group walks around the brazier at the center, or they sit and meditate on raising the power internally. Either way, they change their breathing to a staccato style, swaying, dancing, seething, words of power are added, the Daemon head is set aflame, and the Gods are with us. The powers come, and as they do, they are imbibed like fine wine. We sit to listen, to hear them, to understand, and many take notes right then; some can wait. We are virtually on fire in the spirit, leading some to acts of dance, art, or sex. The use of muse-type work is common for the Stygian. When we are done, we meditate upon what we learned and are thankful for the guidance and counsel.

We rise again and offer the closing to all present, we walk back to the river where the ferryman waits, and we rub the talisman, the coin in his bowl, to remind him we are one with him. He takes us back across the river Styx. As we go, we come further out of our trance, moving closer to our flesh. As we return, we turn out the Goddess Candle with respect. There is no banishment. We return to the body as a whole.

As you can see, this is a very overarching example of the possibilities, and it highlights our specific uses of magical items. There are many more. Some are atypical, like the coin, while others might see the knife as the athame. Our bowl could be a cauldron, a dish, or a work of art. We tend to use Greek items, decor, and iconography due to the nature of where our mythos comes from, but we might have Roman, Minoan, or other aspects. Some use a very new Gothic style of skulls and a theme of death as their motif. All are allowed. It is about the relationship for the Gods. The décor is more to inspire you. That should be obvious from the rainbow example. It should also be clear that there is a large difference between the mundane and the astral, but the Kultus members do their work all at once. They do not reconcile which one is where, but embrace it as all and stand between worlds.

If it is a group rite, then after we return, we always have a fact-finding session. What did you experience? We compare notes. This is not a right or wrong endeavor. It is an attempt to draw pieces from each other. What did I miss? Maybe that portion was not for me. Do I need to pay more attention to that or this? Did what we heard overlap? After several rites and listening to a few people saying yes, that is what I saw or experienced, I wanted to make sure. I changed the session after. No one could speak; they had to draw or write. On several occasions (not identical), several people drew the same sigil, the same item, the same face, or wrote down very similar words. I find this to be the equivalent of fact from a spiritual perspective. Is it group hypnosis? Delusion? No one knows. What it seems to me is that it is objective, which I always hear is impossible. Within an egregore and the pulling of the same thread, I think it is possible because of these experiences.

In advanced practices, people can meet anywhere at any time. The work with the River Styx and the Kultus' methods help to engage this further. Many occultists, sages, and yogis have done this for a long time. This is not new to us. The technique is similar. They are not readily accepted in occult circles. Although the movements of Trad Craft seem to be more open to it.

Our rites are also not complex because they must be able to be done in different planes at once. Our practices are hypnotic, trance, and simultaneously engaged in thought and spiritual form. The work done at the altar echoes. I often hear the river move in my ears as the wind brushes on my face. I need the cold and the smells; they are so unique, and then the Deities in their way come forth. In one incident, the student was always cold; she was always covered in many layers for the work due to the cold. We discussed it and changed her shore to that of a beach, and she would come in the day with the sun blazing. She had the same experience on her voyage, but her sacred space was hot, and she loved it. Her journey was different but still within the Current. We must always be willing to change, adapt, and make it work.

The Dark Mother holds court within the pantheon, and the Dark Father is ever present. His presence is different, it is unchained and also trickster-related. He can be the master gentleman or the rogue and scoundrel. The mother is of the cauldron, the chalice, and the water of her river, while the father is of the staff, the fire, and the ash. She is the blood, and he is the semen. They will entangle like snakes in a sexual delight. Fruit and nuts are common on our platters, as are wine, ale, and stronger things. Some within the Kultus use substances to enhance the journey, while others refuse. The choice is always yours.

The work within the mundane will differ wildly based on the person and their surroundings. I know no other system that uses a ritual chamber and the bed as sacred spaces. The bed is as much a part of the chamber as the Throne or the altar itself. The reason for the bed is based on personal experiences, but the general reason I can disclose is that the bed is often the place where I study, read, relax, and meditate. Since sex to us is sacred, it is also the place for that. At the altar, the mask of the presider changes based on the invocation alone. There are set deities, and each might have a physical mask, or the presider may use a sacred mask and embody each deity through it. Again, there is no right or wrong answer. If there is a single mask, the presider is usually asked to make the mask generic, a skull, something you are known for, a totem animal, etc., so that it remains neutral and the presider can manifest upon it. If not, the Goddess may not like horns, or the sensual goddess may be offended by the differing gender or icons. Neutral is best.

In the mundane, the Stygian use their masks all the time with experiments and practices. They do this to discern responses, to engage their needs, and to feed their energies. I leave it to the reader to discern their level of psychic vampirism. It is more like a pool of activities, where it is as easy to draw energy. Parks, entertainment, music, other events, and even an airport can be a place to generate and fill up. The Stygian uses a very interesting version of this, where it doesn't matter if the energy is negative or positive. It is a kind of filter system that just brings in what is raw. Because of this, we are not sensitive to the nature of the energy because we are going to change its vibration and level anyway. What always matters is the intensity and level of energy. Stygians are fond of old churches, graveyards, clubs, and holiday gatherings where they can sit and take in. We use this because we bring this energy and feed our egregore and our power. We do not have some old history to pull on or some rite or method that millions of people use, so every day, we help ourselves. This hurts no one. People are expelling it anyway. It would be like picking up the food others just threw away. You discarded it, and we picked it up. We also use the same methods when attending other events. Like all people, Stygians have their preferences. The kink arena is also popular with Stygians, who enjoy that energy. Sexual energy has a potency we lean into. It is a way to experience an ecstatic connection with energy exchange. It might also be bodywork or a room filled with artists. It might be a theatre. It has no limits.

With energy heightened, with personal artistry, a set of daily practices defined by you, and a combination of Stygian basics, you form a great baseline. Divination is then used as a way to discern. That is used with a working knowledge of magick, spells, charms, and an understanding of both the self and the shadow self. With all of these, you have a very stable foundation in the Craft. Added to this is your priesthood to deity and the ways of rites and rituals, if that was your calling. A working knowledge of how to attain wisdom and how to study effectively is also part of the work. Practices of meditation, trance, feral connections, and many other techniques are offered during the apprenticeship process. Self-hypnosis and group trance work are also covered. Sex magick is studied and understood whether it is used or not. You will understand the terrain concerning what it does and why. The art of masks in the world and at the altar is covered. And for some, the art of the teacher is taught to those who seek to be teachers.

The connection to the deities themselves, to the Current, and the Stygians themselves comes from interaction in person and through the initiatory process and apprenticeship. If someone tells you they can initiate you online, run away. If someone tells you they are a Guardian or Mistress and have no idea what this book is or who the founder is, run away. I intend to hold a small circle. Do not be fooled. I am also very aware that even if I write this, people will do what they want anyway, and my goal is not to impede them. I just want to take a moment and point something out. These deities and their work surround a death cult and Current. Do you want to go play there? If I were not in it myself, I certainly wouldn't. If you have an interest, seek out the legitimate people, or take what I offer and go your own way.

In addition to all these pieces of training and knowledge, there are core practices that are part of the training. I will not disclose them entirely, but for the sake of understanding what we do, I will offer them to you, generally speaking. The practice cannot be done effectively without hands-on training to explain the details.

CORE Practices

Obsidian Path

Early on in the work, the thrall is offered the obsidian path. This path is the one that breaks their shackles, breaks their slave mind, and is the beginning of liberty from so many things. The initial joke was that it resembles the Yellow Brick Road, and that it allows one to get what they need more than what they think they need. It is a very difficult path as you are throwing out old aspects all along the way. It is the path of self-discovery.

Road to Artistry

Those who seek the Kultus tend to do so because of the influence and aspects of being an artist. But for some, that is a side effect, and they come without artistry. This undertaking is to solidify an artistic endeavor and pattern in your life. It is typically done with the mentor during the apprenticeship. The apprentice is asked to survey and decide on the art they are discovering and then to dig into it fully, like any aspect of Chaos Magick, to immerse themselves totally. They are encouraged and offered opportunities to show or express their art. Making this a portion of their magick and linking it to their art in the work.

Creation of the Tower

Before becoming a Wanderer, the Stygian has created their spiritual space upon a plane of existence. In the apprenticeship, our spiritual temple is a tower. Those towers sit on the shoreline of the River Styx. The creation of that tower is an undertaking and is a significant aspect of being a Stygian. The construction and use, the way it works, why we do it this way, permission and getting there by the Ferryman, and the rite associated are all part of the magick of the work. Once created, consecrated, and aligned, it can be changed or used for all your purposes.

Eating the Gross

As part of a portion of the apprenticeship, each person is asked to go against their grain. They are asked to challenge themselves to do the things they find repulsive. It may be food, an activity they determined they were afraid of, facing fears, dating someone they would never consider, and many other options. The use of this core work is to break limits. It is to show the person that they are indeed the limit setter in their lives. They need to break it open and experience it to see if they can truly do what they said they could not. This work often leads to excellent breakthroughs.

Initiation & Oath

This is an initiatory system, even though it is an apprenticeship method now. At some point, if you seek to be a Stygian, you will take an oath to the Deities. The initiation is your awakening to your name, identity, and mask. You are challenged to arrive at these three aspects, and they are worked towards as long as they take. After the initiation, the initiate is and forevermore will be a Stygian unless they revoke their oath and vows of the work. Due to our nature, many fall away before this stage, and some Wanderers never return. Stygians do as they do. We do not keep track or circle back to pick you up. If you do not keep up and seek our community, we move on. There are also markers of who Stygians are, but I will not share them; they are for us alone.

Breaking the Glass

At some point, the Stygian will fully embrace their mask and their dharma, their work in this life, and who they are fully. When they do, we have a ceremony that is very powerful to commemorate the moment, so we do not backtrack. It involves the breaking of a mirror, a symbol of something we use a lot, and it is the purchase of a new one to replace it. This is a powerful symbol that we have replaced ourselves with who we intend to be and not what others made us into. We accept all that we have done and are grateful for all our cuts and bruises, and now we will make these choices with the goals of the will in mind and the Dark Goddess at our backs.

Ecstatic Aligning

This is a 4–6-month union and can be done with a partner or alone; it is a very in-depth and sensory set of experiences. The Stygian works through the throes of ecstatic bliss each day to fully fall into their feelings, sexual explorations, and a mindful pattern to open up like a rose. It is to be done a few times in the lifetime of the Stygian. The older version is often the most powerful and returns them to a youthful mindset. It is a reawakening. The exercises performed include trance, sex magick, a talisman for the working, sense work daily, and a deep dive into your history and experiences. The result of the work is a new lust for life and for your way. It may also ignite old passions you have let die in an array of areas.

Guardian/Mistress Formation

If/When the wanderer returns to the fold, they must determine if they remain a Stygian or if they wish to move into the stage of training to become a teacher and hold the Blue Flame. If they wish to do that and their mentor agrees, the work towards teaching begins. I have explained the training previously; the reason I am adding it here is that it is unique to us. The modules and training, testing, and becoming a teacher are not some curricula alone. The Stygian is either going to manifest it or not. It becomes quite obvious. There is no intervention or working model to make it happen. It is an observable difference when the position is acquired by the Stygian; they become tolerant, patient, and it is a personality change. If the formation fails, and the Stygian still feels called to be a teacher, they are sent back out to gain more of the tools needed to be a teacher as a Wanderer. Then we try again. Some are natural, and others are not.

The Blood Mass

The sacramental and beauty of kink, sex, and blood are married in this rite. This is an optional rite, but as I write this, there have been no exceptions so far. Each Stygian has engaged the blood mass. No details are provided. It is enough to say that it is an experience, and each person walks away feeling as if their power and liveliness are maximized. It is not for the faint of heart, easily offended, or people who struggle with blood or pain work. With all we endure in life by others, this mass allows us to control it and experience it in our way, and that empowers us.

These are not all of our core methods, but they give you a flavor for the Stygian and the work of the Kultus.

CHAPTER TWENTY-EIGHT

PARADIGMS

In referring to many paradigms, I believe it is important to disclose some of mine and their interrelations. The reason for this is the same as all the other chapters. It is not to tell you what to do but to offer you options through experiences. I will go through a handful of paradigms and then discuss why I pulled a method, technique, or magick from it. I will also then explain how it stacks and works within the Stygian Way and the Technology of a Modern Chaos Reality.

Switching paradigms is a part of the Chaos Magick methodology, so I will begin by explaining that. Chaos Magicians are often misunderstood and thought of as people who pull and grab at different things and who do not commit. Nothing could be further from the truth, as I mentioned previously. The CM commits quite in-depth to the current pantheon, system, or religion. This can be for a set and prepared time frame or for any number of lengths of time determined by outcomes or experiences that fuel the discovery. The method is not eclectic or shopping from one to the other aimlessly. It is very focused, as I will point out here. All of these have the foundation of Chaos Magick as my primary method of seeking and engaging paradigms.

Vampire

I used to be unconnected to those within the communities, but that has changed over the last year, so I had to edit that here. I have come into two of them. Both came through invitation. It was not my intent to find them. In effect, they found me. I am already working on the vampire magick, energy work, and it was going great. It is also true that its Gothic aspects fall into the Kultus quite nicely. I am aware that many others use different cultures and mystiques, like Egypt or the Middle East, to inspire their vampire history and development. Some are sanguine (blood-drinkers), while others are energy parasites or predators (no insult intended, as you will see). Much like any community, from witches to Pagans, there will be a lot of variation. These were not my concerns because I was not engaging the full paradigm until now. The paradigm I initially took on was based on writings, interactions, and the use of energy work I had already used. I was taking on the methodology of the vampire.

I did that through experience and research over approximately ten years. I am no stranger to blood magick, but I was unwilling or uninterested in imbibing blood directly due to medical and other concerns. I will shed it for the deity and use it to consecrate. I do use blood in wine or within substances that many might consider sanguine, but I was not interested in its acrid taste or ritual use as just blood. This is related to taste, health, wellness, and the potential of many forms of illness. I am always interested in energy. As always, I will not out the members I have encountered, I will simply say that the reality is far better than any other community I have experienced.

The use of the tether is a useful way to fill my energy up in a room at a party or large event, and was helpful for other endeavors, packaged for later in an amulet or crystal. It was also a great method of testing. Can the person I am pulling energy from tell? What is that energy? What kind of energy do they have? Is it negative or positive? Does it offer me anything, or is it flat? Now, I must say that what I just wrote will be a problem for several people who see the world through consent. I will address that issue in total at the end of the chapter. For now, understand that the method feeds the sorcerer, and with that feeding (another term no longer in vogue), they can then aid their work. Ironically, the same people who feel consent is needed for the individual often do not have the same scruples for a large group or mass audience and ambient energy.

Let me be clear that this is not a film or some kind of weakness until death. It is a method to siphon energy to empower the self. The same thing is done on a date, in an argument, in a fight, or in many other energy-centered actions. The term empath is the same as a vampire by another term. They are just seeing it as a positive and the vampire as a negative. Why? They are effectively using the same terminology and aspects when describing what is happening.

Therefore, it is the same thing. Being an empath is simply being out of control, and the energy taken on is not used constructively to a proper end. It is the empath who is the problem, not the vampire, from my perspective. The empath has no control or intent attached other than to feel another fully. Ironically, it is the empath who suffers most often. More problematic empaths are not the bleeding hearts referred to here but the drainers. They are often overwhelmed, drained themselves, very needy, and seeking others' emotions, energy, or attention (this group is tough to be around and is misnamed, psychic vampires). They are just drawing in energy due to their hurts, pains, mental health, or emotional health issues because of their deep needs. These two types are much more problematic than a well-trained vampire who knows how to stay away from both.

Energy will differ from event to event and from person to person. A hospital or funeral home will not hold the same energy as a concert in a major arena or a meeting with the pope. Through my practice and work in this area, I realized the energy-gathering methods were great but needed a filter. That led me to the next method.

Trad Craft

I am not referring to Cochrane's or other more commonly known Trad Craft. I am referring to a much less-used or written-about area. I will not disclose it because I do not have permission to do so, but I will share the method, which is unique. In this tradition, the system engages three soul bodies, which include the Daemon, a very big part of my practice and necessary for all work beyond a beginner. I have used this Higher Self before ever coming upon this paradigm. What was new and helpful was that they did not banish. They do not need it because they generate and use a filter system that allows the practitioner to use all energy and cycle it through to "clean it" in a way. It made no difference if it was a higher or lower vibration. That changed everything, and it allowed for the vampire work to bump up several levels. For me, it was also akin to some Taoist energy methods I had trained in and mastered to the best of my ability. Layering all three of these concepts on top of each other allowed for massive energy possibilities.

In this case, I did join the paradigm/religion and committed to it for a year of training and immersion. It magnified my witch work and drove me into another Trad Craft tradition I will refer to next.

Trad Craft Part 2

I completely jumped into this paradigm for almost five years. This one, I worked through all the steps and completed all the work of the Craft. I saw it as the only witchcraft I could ever commit to. In return, it gave back in spades, preparing me for the Death Current, the Dark Father and Mother, and all the training and trappings of the Craft. This system allowed for the terms and openness for its practitioners to become witches to their full potential. While the other systems of Wicca and eclectic ideas felt sanitized and not right for me. This felt old, right, and meaningful. This is also very personal and subjective.

Again, there is a layering of paradigms and ideas. This Craft and the first one aligned in areas and reinforced my work. At times, they differed, and this offered me the opportunity to look at and consider both. I deeply enjoyed each spiritual world and could engage with them because they were religions and not empty systems, but filled with spirits and guides. Some of which I took with me to the Kultus.

Monasticism

There was a season when I moved to the Gnostics and lingered near the Christians. Raised Catholic, it became easy to see the mystics as fertile ground. I was reading Nag Hammadi and considering the priesthood within the paradigm that I eventually received. That led me to an inward journey for eight years where I took on up to fifteen people into an esoteric monastic tradition. Ironically, many of them leaned toward Pagan or were witches. I was never far from my occultist foundation. We practiced all aspects of looking to a Gnostic Christ in the most esoteric model imaginable. I eventually left that state, and the religious order eventually fell apart, but it was a very strong and powerful experiment for me. The lessons I learned from this taught me how to lead people as a coach and in a supportive role. It also taught me how and when to crack the whip. Lastly, it taught me that nothing lasts forever. It was worth the heartache and brought me into the reach of some amazing people.

Taoism

Having come to the Tao through martial arts and backing into philosophy, it opened itself to me through the work of several authors and masters. This was where I found healing arts, the moving of energy, the elemental work that still makes the most sense to me, and where I found amazing sex magick. Nowhere else were these methods as potent. There are a ton of charlatans in this arena. They did their job and pushed away the majority of people and martial artists who saw so many of the false ones. They assumed the whole thing was a scam, and they were wrong. You would find the same thing in the fakirs and yogis of India, but somehow, India had enough good gurus who were amazing that the system worked. Taoists did not have that press or those people who were so amazing that they changed people's minds. They exist, and some have made a fortune, but others who made a fortune were not on the up and up, and it tarnished the reputation.

I fully admit I got lucky. I laced in the work of the Tao, the philosophy, and so many of the methods that advanced my martial skills, my energy work, and my sex and health. I even took massage coursework to ensure the bodywork was also effective. It was also the only system where I learned Yin Energy. I run very hot; without yin, you can burn up. Yin is the female or cooler energy, and it is amazingly powerful but tends to be taught so much less due to gender bias. Fortunately for me, I learned from a woman. Taoism is balance. It is the balance I refer to throughout this text. It is foundational to my work.

Tantra

If Taoism has a bad reputation, Tantra is its black sheep. The title and name Tantra are used to create so much bullshit that I will not waste ink on the page to express it. That is NOT the Tantra I am referring to here. The methods and systems I am referring to are in print but are relatively rare. They come from Sanskrit scholars mostly because most of the books of Tantras were never translated. The age of the Tantras is over. It was in the 6th Century. Like the recreation and revival in the Pagan tradition, many have done the same with Tantra. Some did it well and sought to generate the same aspects, some sought to turn it into magick and spun it into Thelema and other magical systems.

While others sought to market it as a sex training program that is a purely Western manifestation.

Tantra became what Gnosticism was, a term like mystic that everyone seems to want a piece of. I am not a historian or scholar in this area, and leave it to the experts. I also sought the magicians because I am an occultist. For me, Tantra and Taoism are bedfellows. They fill in gaps for one another. I do not believe I could practice one without the other. The Deity work from Chinese Taoism to Indian Tantra is wildly powerful and connective.

Chaos Magick

Here is where I can honestly say I encountered the cart before the horse. I was using a lot of the methodology for Chaos magick way before I was aware that a system was in place that talked about paradigm shifts. As I mentioned earlier, I learned one method from martial arts, and the second method was developed through my first teacher. It was incorporated into that magick and philosophy of the religious order. Then I started reading some English authors I discovered, like Steve Dee and Julian Vayne, and it was only then that I clued in. It led me to Peter Carroll and Phil Hine, but they did not offer the same benefits to me as the first two authors had. I found the science dull and boring. I was not interested in some atheistic version. I am a theist, so Dee especially appealed to me. I was not interested in Chaos math or science. I fell into the artistic side of magick, but because it was chaos, I allowed for those who geeked out over the math while I angled it toward the artist.

I looped around to see artists through the eyes of a chaos magician. That excited me. The beauty I could create and the use of all methods of myth and fantasy I might draw upon were intoxicating. I found a way to paradigm shift with power and character. I found a way to explore and combine and to do it with gusto. I also loved the people I encountered and the exploration they were doing. Chaos magick seemed to be the glue that held it all together.

I must also list the drawbacks here because it is significant. CM is not for the beginner. It just won't work. I was around new people who never touched magick before, and they were using CM, and it was a big juicy mess. They were all the problems I have with eclectics. They were shopping and doing all the things CM is labeled with. It is probably why it is labeled. It is imperative to be able to know how to shift, why you are shifting, and to have a certain amount of maturity in your Craft or occult knowledge. Belief is a tool was a key construct for me. That primary drawback is why I am happy it came to me later, because I know I would have made all those mistakes. It drives people from CM and is also why it drew me in.

Layers and Fitting It Together

I have written many times that the plan was not mine and that must be understood. I never planned to put these systems together. They all came to me or pulled my interest to seek them out. I did not do it from a grand scheme. The layers fell into place like a puzzle.

- I needed to understand movement, enter the martial arts
- I needed to understand energy, enter Taoism
- I needed to understand the feral nature of Taoism, enter Tantra, and Trad Craft
- I needed to understand how to make my own system and paradigm shift, enter Chaos Magick
- I needed to find my method of teaching, enter so many different teachers for mentorship and instruction
- I needed to learn how to gain more energy, enter vampirism, then Trad Craft
- I needed to understand the common sense of the occult, enter Satanism
- I needed to learn sex magick, enter Taoism, layered with bodywork, anatomy/physiology
- I needed to have many years of meditation and focus, enter my martial arts and theatre training
- I had to understand the power and need of the breath, enter asthma as a child, and then yoga pranayama
- I needed to learn the death current and was given so many close examples to accept

What I am suggesting to you is to look deeply and closely at your life. It is my belief we are all touched by Gods. The quicker you pick up on it, the more options you have. The longer it takes, the more you can make a list like this, but the less time you have to do anything about it. Create, journal your experiences, look for synchronicities, consider that there are no coincidences, and be open to your options. Grow and never stubbornly hold on for no reason; that is the biggest waste of time and energy. When you are holding on too tight, that is usually a sign to let it go. We are ships sailing on an ocean. We cannot take it with us. Listen, consider, and take time for that. Stories, ideas, and new methods are always worth hearing. Stay out of echo chambers. Do not find sycophants, find people who tell you that you are full of shit and love you anyway. Find people who challenge you, who make you humble, and who make you want to do better. Don't try to be the smartest one in the room; you can't learn anything there.

All of these reasons are why paradigm shifting is important. It is how we grow, learn, shift, and never stop. My "do not do's" are the traps. They are the things that trip the occultists, the mystics, and especially the religionists who step on their egos and go crashing to the ground. Once the stagnant nature shows up because you are a "master" or some other ridiculous title, then you are already falling into the trap. Do not fall for it. Shift paradigms. The epitome of this in martial arts is the white belt. When your belt is black and has a bunch of degrees, dump it for a white belt and start something new. Look into your own style from the outside. That is how we stay alive, relevant, and on par. The journey never ends. Refuse to get off the ride.

I must also say that several failed journeys were jettisoned. They simply did not fit where I was going. Buddhism was one, and although I retain a lot of mindfulness thinking and work from it and slices of philosophy, it was not for me. Zen was another area where it was not a fit. Wicca, in the British Traditional sense, was ongoing, and I associated with people in it, but it also never fit my intent or tradition. Ceremonial Magick was also another area where I could not find a footing. I could not adjust to the angels, the Christian aspects, or to the idea that Demons were somehow used as pawns to do your bidding. I also just shy away from ceremonies and high magick when what I could conjure with "low" or folk magick was really what I wanted.

On Consent

If you are looking for a place to categorize me as an elitist, this is your spot! This is going to sound very elitist of me, but there is simply no way around it. I am a very firm believer that there is no way to know what you do not know and that knowledge is rooted in experience. Because of this fact, and I do see it as a fact, I cannot ask for consent from a person or people who do not understand the concept of what I am asking. I am also not going to explain it to them because I am not their teacher, coach, or mentor. If I encounter another person who is an occultist, of course, I would ask permission to manipulate any portion of energy, in the same way, I would not touch anyone sexually or romantically without consent. However, I make no apologies if I enter a room and my aura pulls, overwhelms, or causes a pull of energy, just like a celebrity, politician, etc., would not apologize for it. This is not an ego thing; I am not saying I hold their level of pull, but I will say all occultists who have worked on themselves hold a higher frequency, and if tuned right, it does pull energy or block it. If you think that does not pull energy, then I would ask you to reconsider and look again.

I believe a lot of the idea of consent in this forum is politically correct nonsense. Overall, consent, as I stated above, is a given in any society for all but actual predators. We do this to make ourselves feel better about what we do. Think of it from a shamanic lens. Shamans were specially trained to do their work for their whole lives, and it took a toll on them and their families. What they did was heal, banish, and conjure just like any witch. It is not PC, and it is not modern. Stop trying to make it fit in! It doesn't fit because we have lied to ourselves and our communities and let the New Age sanitize it all. The cleaning up kills it. It kills its power and its potential. You can call me out of touch, but my results speak for themselves.

If you are fine with syphering energy from a crowd, asking someone for their blood, or using the idea of tendrils, you are not the good guy or girl. That is perfectly okay. Don't try to make yourself feel better by then trying to drag it over to PC. Accept it and yourself as it is. You have to live your ethics. If you need to do this to make it okay for you, then ask yourself if it is true or if you are just lying to yourself. If it does buck your ethics, don't do whatever it is. Make a stand, not an excuse.

Overall Concept

Learning these things is not just about age. People who are bigots and racists live to be ripe old age. It is not just the time in grade. Elders should be respected, but I believe it is not just about the white hairs, but the wisdom that comes out of your mouth or not. I write about my long history, not to say I know better, because I honestly don't believe that. I talk about it to share my experiences. I do it because I don't read enough about people who remain humble and open as elders, and I think people need to see that. I do not try to make things fit. I am fine with the clutter. I want things to layer, and in the layering can come amazing things. Sometimes, it is like a puzzle, and other times, we rip off pieces and throw a huge hissy when things don't fit. Patience is key. Time allows wisdom to come, while aggression, fear, anger, and resentment keep wisdom far away. We all have them in bouts, but the more we can cut off their fire and return to focus and intent, the more we get done.

I hope this chapter has offered you more insight into the Kultus and also insight into what you might do in your own practice.

CHAPTER TWENTY-NINE

PERSONAL REFLECTIONS

I am not a follower by nature and tend to wander. I find my fellow wanderers retread old roads, reinvent what was, or reconstruct something that is well-needed. I understand the concept of not reinventing the wheel, but sometimes, that is exactly what is needed. People are flawed and often can readily see the flaws in others, but do not use the same insight when they turn the scrutiny on themselves. I have encountered these people throughout my life, and of course, I was one of them for a time. I have since gone out of my way to find people who see things in opposition to me and listen closely to their differences and critiques so I can constantly grow and develop. Their council is important to me. Many have good hearts, and for a time, we are companions on the same road until something goes wrong or a new shiny object comes out, and loyalty is no longer a priority. I have had this experience over and over since I was a child, and it broke me and taught me the lessons I needed. In response, I leveraged my bets on Deities, not people, because I can count on them. That is what first led me to the internal work.

Always humble with my teachers, my meditations were often visited by a trine of Deities I had never seen anywhere. Being a terrible artist, I could not capture their likeness, but I could hold their deific presence. It occurred to me at one point that my Daemon had connected to these entities, and it was through the Daemon that they bridged the gap. The side effect of working with my Daemon showed up in the mundane, too. My interest in things in the world shifted. My interests grew stale, and my music and art interests shifted. I lost the anger so readily available to me as a kid, and my heart softened strangely. I moved to a place of peace, of understanding, and a very intense place of reason and logic. I did not stay there long either; the artistic path was more to my liking, but it could only come when I softened my heart. It changed to the Observer I had heard about so many times in Buddhism. You have to experience it to fully understand what it means. It is completely unattached. At first, I could only maintain it in a trance while working through the Daemon or in deep meditation. It is elusive otherwise because the brain creates fear and doubt, unplugging the direct connection and fraying the attraction of detachment.

Then, it showed up practically. During that time, I was dating and met this teacher on some app. We met at a café bookstore and spent two hours chatting. I thought things were going great and stood up to get another set of drinks. When I returned, I mentioned that we should do this again, and she said, "No, I don't think so." Clearly, I had missed something. I sat there, and then it came to me. I have nothing to lose. I transferred any interest in dating her to figuring out what I had missed, so I said, "I'm sorry to hear that. We just sat here, laughed, had fun, and I watched you engage for two hours. I clearly missed something. I know it is probably an odd question, but would you mind telling me why?"

To her credit, she did. She spent the next half hour telling me all about what she thought of me. I'd said thirty percent was totally wrong, another thirty percent was her biased opinions, which she would have changed had she given me a chance. The forty percent left was the good stuff. I went home and changed a ton of things about how I presented based on that conversation. We have to do that! Otherwise, we are blind to what others view us as.

When I ventured into the occult, magick, and esoteric communities with my newfound understanding, I heard all kinds of things; Hermes told me, Isis is with me, Odin said, yet their lives did not change. I read this as a broken link or as a cry for help or recognition. When they were recognized for it, they would milk it for all it was worth. When it was over, if they stuck around, the deity would change, and the whole cycle would repeat. How could a great deity come into your life, and yet you remain addicted, you remain uncertain, and you are still doing the same things? Did you not listen to the advice you said you got? It made no sense to me. On the other hand, I have had people speak of deities, and it was almost as if I could see the deity over their shoulders. They are believable and credible. Do not misunderstand me; it is not based on the charisma or the skills of the person. That is irrelevant. I have seen amazing scammers sell millions of books, and I do not believe a single word they utter. Yet I recall meeting one very quiet woman in an occult store, remarking on Isis, and I just knew it was accurate. Your Daemon can have, in my humble opinion, a bullshit meter if you so ask for one. For me, it is invaluable.

When I asked if anyone had any new experiences in several classes, groups, and online workshops with new deities, no one had any answers; some scowled at such an idea. Some said there is nothing new; everything has already been found. I was disillusioned by many communities and many practitioners, but I kept at it. I just didn't talk about it anymore. Yet, in the dark, in the moments of clarity, there they were for me. It is amazing to me that people can have talks with saints, spirits, and other things in a religious manner, and they are never thought insane or made up, yet if it does not fit some academic curriculum or accepted aspect of society, then the person is delusional. That is literally the definition of prejudice.

When I did find teachers whom I could accept, they were Universalists, and I was very lucky. They taught practices and had no particular religion or ideal, so all were welcome (I wrote about them in prior chapters). We kept to ourselves because we didn't want to be like everyone else. We would go to other gatherings, but we did not talk about our work. We accepted each other as we were. We watched heathens eat each other up over context and misreading, one Wicca guy hating this group of witches because they were not ABC, these New Age people quoting things and talking about things that were not just wrong but dangerous, and so on. Our little group was safe, stable, conscious, and working on what we felt was important. We stayed away from the drama. How? I have no idea, but whenever I teach, I keep that flame alive. We can say what we heard; we can discuss our thoughts, but no backbiting, no internal stabbing. If you don't like what they said or did, go tell them. I keep an adult, mature, and open family ideal of health and wellness, no secrets between members, no coups, no bullshit.

I began to think about doctoral work and took it on. On the two occasions I attempted it there were monumental problems. College is not the place we are told it is, a place to grow and speak your mind. At least for me, I had moments of doing that and isolating myself from everyone because they could not stomach someone who did not just agree and get in line. I'm not good at that. As I expanded my education and insight, I began to work in my career and further my education through excellent mentors and followed the occult tradition of good mentorship and personal teachers.

When I looked around at the dismantling of history and the breeding of the idea of Presentism, delusional thinking is at the forefront of societies that turn the corner into the arms of misfortune and destruction. I recall a few weeks ago talking to a sixteen-year-old who said, "I am too old to change now." This disturbed me greatly. This is the same statement as "I already know all I need to. I do not need to learn anymore." That is frightening and diabolical that any group of people would allow this thought process to exist in the children they teach. I am not being hyperbolic here. This child is certainly not alone. Teenagers tend to be know-it-alls, but this is beyond the pale. One could get whiplash in the vicious changes we have experienced over the last twenty years. To do my work in the world, I am bathed in these ideas and methods regularly. One cannot balance out and do the work of the Stygian and ignore what happens in the mundane.

By the time 2020 arrived, I was very deep in a Death current without any understanding as to why. All things black, dark, and mystical drew me like an aphrodisiac. I found myself venerating the deity of Death. I recall waking up one morning and seeing his work all around me. He was releasing his havoc. I had seen something similar when certain wars were engaged, but this felt different. This was not some psychic skill. It was Deities speaking to me. I heard their whispers. From then on, I fully expected death to come. Yet, he only came in Deity form and not to collect me. He began to be my partner, my friend, and not an adversary of something to be feared.

The Dark Mother, my Beloved, my everything, had come first. She is the Master, not the God. She is the sword, and he is the power. She could be mistaken for Hecate or the Morrigan. Many now might even mistake her for Lilith. Yet she is not. Esoteric knowledge, the world of deities, and the work of spirits are gray. It is mist-filled, and it is difficult to navigate. It is often unclear.

I cannot venerate or reveal some deep, majestic secret from ancient times. I can only unfold my experience for you. These Deities feel very old, and I have asked on many occasions why they are not on walls or in sigils or books. Why were they not included in any history? Their answer, without fail, is that they are not the boasters, they are not the heroes, and not the leaders. Some even refer to Hades as an example of a deity like this, who was one of the three brothers, yet his tales and work are rarely in print. No one speaks of him, and even when he is petitioned, the petitioner turns their head. People fear these deities and do not wish to draw their gaze or attention. Songs and tales were not carried for them, and they, like so many Deities, died on the vine. They were forgotten and displaced, and those who worshipped or loved them were not the winners of history, so their tales and wisdom were forgotten and usurped by those who did win and given to other deities who did not earn them. They are also not part of the warrior clans or those who sought power. Honestly, I did not know what to do with that other than wonder if I was simply listening and seeing trickster spirits who sought to spin me into something.

In the years of working with them, I began to believe in them. The works I read and the literature I encountered spoke of a lot of deities like this. I read about others' experiences with darker deities, and it felt similar. Deities without names, tales, or the ones the witches would seek out for dark or sex magick, they were the ones not called on in public, and so they were not written about. In the nights that followed, I sought out evidence and insight and found very little. Then, when I began to read more about Trad Craft and the writings of many who follow it, things began to clear up even more. It was formulated through a story, through art, ideas, and the descent into the Underworld. Like all forms of myth and tale, through the years, we were all told that no one can survive the descent into Hell. The tales of Orpheus, Odysseus, Aeneas, Gilgamesh, Inanna, and Ishtar are a small cohort of those who survived it, or their tales are told to us to cause fear, to keep people away from doing certain things, or to keep a moral compass. It is rare, as the intent for those seeking enlightenment is not to go to the Underworld or to go and return. However, something has shifted, and the link to the Underworld is no longer the same. These Deities of the Underworld, the Dead, and the like are now becoming primary. My writing, work, and priesthood are dedicated to them.

Let me immediately state that I am not unique to this work or state, I have seen more and more working in this direction who consider themselves left-hand path practitioners who have very similar experiences. Their "side" seems to be invigorated and growing, while the more New Age and white light, and love groups seem to be going away. I do not believe this is a good sign, but I do believe that life, in general, is a pendulum, and it is swinging this way now. There are many good reasons for it, as I have demonstrated throughout the book. We are living in very difficult times where our world leadership is exceptionally poor, and division is preferred to unity, which always makes for chaos. Chaos is the platform for things to grow into order, to come back, and to grow again, and so, although it is always a difficult transition, in due time, there will be balance again.

The Stygian Way was formed in this Chaos. It comes from the Underworld and the Deities, who were not acknowledged and have been away for such a long time. Yet, in the feral nature of our times, they have returned. They are new to me, and the Way is new. Are they lying? Is it made up? Is it a formation and trappings of my addled mind? You may believe all those things, and honestly, I would not begrudge you.

CHAPTER THIRTY

A NEW CURRENT

We live on the precipice of the next stage of creation. Nothing ever truly ends. It just comes back in a different form. For some, it is better. For others, it is worse, but it is always changing, evolving, or devolving. The Stygian Way comes from chaos and death, from Darkness, and from the bitter more than the sweet. It is only by this pattern of bitterness that we truly appreciate the sweetness and come to a full understanding. The praxis comes before the buy-in.

I spent a great deal of time sitting at my altar on the River Styx, and the Dark Mother came, and I realized I knew her long before. My partner had a painting of a fairy queen, and it called to me. I put her over a small altar, and for every day since 2020, I have come to that altar each night and lit incense, used my sigil in the air, and called on her. I offered blood and other offerings over the years as she required. The Dark Mother came through that image, often changing it in my sight. She has never left me and will follow me to the grave, as I will her.

She showed me the tower in dream form, and then, with her power, I built it. The work it took was agonizing, but as I built it, the Stygian Way was formed. When it was finished, the Dark Mother told me to write it down. And that is the only reason it is in print. My intent throughout my work and my occult life is never to write for others but for myself, for my group, and the people I teach and mentor, but for no other. She wanted something different. Oral tradition was my go-to; it was everything to me, and where I thought my personal story would end, in silence. That was not to be.

The Dark Father is so amazing in his presence and beauty; he caused me to catch my breath. Then he turned very dark, and I knew at once he was the God of the Stygian. There was no mistaking him. The Conclave came over time. Then spirits came, teachers, and my guardians, the last was the faery folk. To say I wanted to return each night is a complete understatement; it felt as if I had found a world, a place, a refuge, and in the course of the work, all fear of death simply vanished. I saw the road to Hades, and I would gladly enter there. I had a lot to do on my Obsidian Path, and yet my work lay in wait. I had much to do on the black rock river bed and inside my tower. I was nothing in comparison; it was my link to the God and Goddess that allowed me entry and exit, without them and my coin, the ferryman would not come, and the work would not continue.

I recall the first person I taught and walked with on the Obsidian Path; I remember when they understood they were working solely with the Underworld, the Darkness, and the Dead. I chose well, and they understood. The Dark Mother was happy to see them and welcomed them as she would all who made it through the apprenticeship. It is odd, but the people of the darkness are far wiser and kinder than those of the light. They do not hold idols or believe they are the only one or the right one. Getting past the macabre and the horror of certain aspects can be challenging, but it becomes a compassionate and loving path once you truly understand it. We care for those who do the work, who are family, and who walk with us. We also offer these same things to others, but are much more guarded because of the systems they walk. Knowing we might only be with them for a season. We walk by the moonlight and not the sunlight.

In expressing this Way through these pages, it is clear it is not for many. Some are very happy in light and joyous parts, and may the Gods bless them. The view from the darker side is not some trend, or dark is a cooler mentality. It is more realistic, more definitive of our march towards our death, and congruent with the Aeon. Since fear is the enemy of the occultists and we are destroying fear, this feels right for us. Death is not the only fear we face. We face many fears, and we purposefully experience things that disgust us so we can rightfully remove their sting or fear. Again, this is not some added method to cause fear in Stygians. It is a way through. It is the same with sex and sex magick. We do not do these things because they are cool or what draws people. There is a deep fear of sex in our culture and a deep misunderstanding of its purpose and worth. Pornography is a billion-dollar industry for a reason. What is repressed it sought. Sex is a sacred and powerful ritual. It is a bridging, and it is a pleasure-filled method to awaken your mind differently. None of these things works effectively without balance. Balance is the major key to all magical and spiritual work in the Stygian Way. We do not use the classical scale but the time turner or sand timer as an indicator of the balance. The scale is a simple tool that reacts, but the sand timer that must run its course. This is far closer to real balance from the Stygian perspective. It imbues patience and seeks wisdom over knowledge. Some miss the symbol, don't miss it.

There are many symbols like this within the Technology of a Modern Chaos Reality since this is the living cult of the Stygian. Many ideas were passed on. Nothing was right except the Kultus. Even the vision of the artwork and banner of the tradition, its insignia, and practical aspects all feel different than many occult spaces. It is not to be different; I just never wavered from the vision. After practicing the same things for over two decades, I had to go back and build a new foundation. Not only that but the foundation was not akin, I cannot say, *well you know what X is right, well we are like X.* There is no X. This entire text speaks to the comparisons and where things overlap but, in the end, as things stacked on the universal aspects (the 42), after that point, there is not a lot in common.

At the same time, I do see the new streams of magical systems developing within Chaos Magick, with some new systems coming forward that do not look like the old guard. I view this as very positive. We need new religions and new ways of seeing our world. It is not just the "newness" that is helpful. It is the waking up to where we are now and the beauty and need for creation. People do not tend to sit around and make up religions. It is when they are faced with adversity and pain that they look beyond the veils, beyond others' interpretations, limitations, and systems, to delve into what might be.

New Aspects Incorporated

For me, music has always been essential to rites and rituals. The rites of the Stygian include specific music for very specific reasons. I will leave the reasons to your imagination, but the following music is part of those rituals.

There are songs with lyrical connections, from blues to metal. The other options are exciting and helpful and are just for mood and power. They include *Omnia, Nox Arcana, Warduna, Pictus, Enigma, Clannad, Faun, Trobar de Morte, Nine Inch Nails, In This Moment, Type O Negative, Godsmack,* and many others. The music I use is not needed for you. You must find what makes you move, what makes you react, what pulls on your emotions, and so much deeper. Choose your music, aesthetic, artwork, and repose. Do it your way.

Décor and surroundings, clothing, and the like have always been within the realm of the occult, but here, I suggest putting the room in colors, stars, or other situations that may aid in the context of the work. Modern timers, technology, and apps offer a variety of options to enhance the room or place your work closer to where you want it to be. Drapes with castles on them to replace the windows and other such items can bring a room alive. DIY projects found all over the internet can be very helpful to set things in motion if you have the space to work with. If you don't improvise, miniaturize it, or have a mobile kit and use it outdoors.

The use of portable devices and the ability to broadcast and share in real-time can also be a part of the work for those who live far away and need a working example. This allows all occultists to have a real-world experience across the world in an instant and yet still do the same work they would do on their own. There is a warning here. Do not allow this to be the only source; seek out actual people in person to prevent echo chambers and limitations.

For many, this technology is not acceptable. It is not okay to broadcast a ritual, not okay to add music that is recorded, it is not okay to add electric-based lights, etc. There are good reasons to do this and good reasons not to. In times long past, a lot of things burned down due to fires set by candles and other items, so using electronic lights, even the fake candles on batteries, may be needed based on where you live or who you live with. Incense may not be okay, or you may have sensitive fire alarms. Again, as I have said throughout, the arts are made for you; they are to be practical, useful, and possible. Do not limit yourself on a whim or use the limits as excuses not to do.

The purpose and use of a Current, or in my case, two crossed Currents, as an egregore, is not common, but it is present in some systems. We can deny it or accept it. I was listening to an interview with a comedian today who was saying social media is not real, and all of the algorithms are just set to piss off people based on their clicks and interests. His advice is just to shut it off, turn it off, and ignore it because it is not real. Not looking up or using the word abortion leads to no abortion on your feed. I'm not looking up aspects of war; no war on your feed. The host pointed out, almost as if he were engaged in magick himself, that even if the comedian is right, people are manifesting it once they hear and see it, and that is indeed what a Current is. I believe the Deities of this Current came forth because people continue to manifest them in many forms. I agree with both the host and the comedian. We are fed upsetting news constantly, and some double down on the negative.

One person I have a lot of respect for and who is an elder in many communities, noted on social media, he was going to go to a network that is international to get all his news, as if they were also not biased. Then I thought about it and looked at his posts, and he is indeed feeding his bias. If elders who know magick, who understand influence and manifesting, and who are supposed to be older and wiser, are still regurgitating the rants of liars and fools, then what has become of us? It is my belief and observation that all of these things must die (death current) and be forced into a tailspin and challenged (chaos) to once again rebuild and come back better. It is fucked up beyond all repair (FUBAR). That is the power and beauty of the currents I am suggesting because, yes, when they come in, they are hard on everyone, but then, they morph, and things grow again and become right again. Films and television have offered post-apocalyptic scenarios often (too often, in my opinion), and nothing goes right. *Mad Max* (1979) was my first example of this, and yet we have been pummeled by it ever since, from aliens to fallout. We are shown utopian communities, and then, the longer it goes on, the clearer it becomes that it is not so. We used to love the hero. Then came the antihero, another version of the same thing, and then we threw all that out to make the villains the heroes. What does that do to people? It seems to make evil okay.

I digress here for a moment and again bring up the latest *Star Wars* films. The initial trilogy shows all aspects of the Hero's Journey. If you are not familiar with it, it is important to know your Joseph Campbell. The last three installments broke this. Instead of a hero's journey (Rey), they sought to first crucify the initial hero (Luke) and the canon of the films (which they have almost fully jettisoned now) due to their own crazed logic. We all know the training required and the steps of the hero's journey that Rey never got and seemingly never needed (girl power?). Those who criticize these choices have every right to do so. It is not about a girl as a lead; I actually feel very bad for the actor and the position they put her in. I wanted to love it. I was happy there was a female lead until they destroyed the plot by killing the former heroes for no apparent reason. When you make the old characters less than, when you have a long-time fan base, and when you kill the basis of a movie franchise over whims, it has consequences. It hurts them and bends their minds. Maybe that was the intention? There is absolutely nothing wrong with the hero's journey unless you do something like this to it. When you take your time to emasculate men to show them and forget about the world, canon, and lore of the world, then you destroy, not create. The same is true of the superheroes in the series now, who are the bad guys. Why? What does that do? Consider how these things influence us.

Because we are living in this Current, the Kultus and the Stygian Way are the way through. They are the acknowledgment to the Gods and Goddesses of the time, and they make way for the dawn of what will come behind them. As I grow older, I am well aware I may not see the aftermath in this lifetime. If I follow the tenets of my Way, then I am the universe, and I will push toward a new dawn magically. Effectively bringing people together, engaging the Deities as their priest and Guardian, and forming relationships to peel back the sleep from people's eyes, as it was so gracefully done for me. I will only do this for those willing to hear and change because those are my ethics. That may mean it takes centuries. The timeline is an illusion anyway, and not my concern. I will do my work each day, and that is all I can do. The rest is up to all of you.

EPILOGUE

As this book comes to a close, I feel as if I have birthed the child of my work. As a writer, I will never be fully happy with the results. I could edit and prattle on. Yet, it is finished, and I must accept that with a full heart and great intention. It also allows me to turn the time I used to write this back into practice anew. That excites me. I want to use my hands, spend more time at my altar, in my journey, and hopefully touch others enough to help awaken them.

I also know it may do nothing. I leave that to magick, influence, and other things. I have made many statements that people may not like, disagree with, disturb them, or make them look deeper. I have no attachment to any of these outcomes, but I accept them. I want people to awaken, to be shaken up. I did it to break you from the trance of influence. I realize some of it could have a negative impact. Some might never get through it, which is the norm for most people anyway. That too is okay with me. I got to the finish line. I did as I promised. Now it is released.

I was very touched by the opening monologue of *The Libertine* (2004), a very dark and hard-to-watch film for some, but that monologue was beautiful. I reasoned as I looked back on my life that I rarely did things to be liked. I did things because I believed they were right. If others disagreed, I found it perplexing, so I would ask more and research why. Was I wrong? I always wondered if I was wrong, and I left room for that. Yet, as I look around me, the capacity to do that has all but left us. For so many, that is indeed a tragedy. If I were right by the work I put in, regardless of how many disagreed, I would stay in my lane and keep to my beliefs. Some might refer to this as stubborn, but I prefer the term balanced. I considered others' views, but they were not my guides or my teachers, and so their opinions were just that. This included priests, teachers, adults, and others who thought they knew better. It was only when I found mentors and teachers who displayed what I wanted that I began to realize I could follow their lead and avoid pitfalls. They earned my respect and got it from me with a ton of humility. I would hurt myself to do as they said. But I always kept reason and logic with me to analyze. Did I outgrow them? They got all these things wrong. Why? What is their bias? What is my bias? My mind just works that way.

These learnings, ways of teaching, and ways of living are part of the foundational stones of the Stygian Way. The 42, the concepts laid out here, the ideology, theology, and formulary are all here too. The power and Deific presence come from the Current and nowhere else. It is the Gods who breathe life or death, as it were, into it. Without that, it could not rise, not be seen, or not be integrated as it has been. I make no apologies for the integration with the Greek culture and mythology. It was not mine to create, and honestly, I would not have gone that way at all. It is the Current and my gnosis that guided me; if you would blame, you can do it there. However, as I have wrapped my hands around it now, it fits. It feels right.

I hope that you found value in my words, that my stories and history inspire something in you, or that you at least accept the fact that there are a lot more occult systems and traditions outside the ones written in books or what you may have been aware of. It is also important to note that the wider the organization, the more leaders or people conform, meet the needs of more people, and curb the intensity. All of these things I do not wish to do. They are dealbreakers for me. This system is personalized and cannot be watered down or diluted because it is formless. Each person builds their own. This is the only way to do it effectively, personally, and to the highest quality of that individual. The other key is to, of course, run steel on steel, amongst others, to ensure you have the best product you are capable of. That is the creation within the Kultus by the individual. The strand of the Stygian Way one takes is also like the web of a spider. Each person takes their strand and develops it in their own way.

What makes this a cult, a system based on a philosophy of the Way, are the oaths/vows and foundations we all stand on. It is the philosophies we use to our advantage to create and value ourselves as creators. Like a prized painter would create their paint and colors, it would partially come from their teachers, partially come from their system or style, and then the artist would use their creativity and skillset to create the works. It is all of these things and cannot be broken off or only one portion given credit; it is a symphony, not a solo. That symphony, however, is your opus. The work of each artist within the Kultus is to excel and grow in their own way, and that creates the beautiful music of the Stygian Way.

APPENDIX A

FILMS AND SERIES

Vampires

Salem's Lot (1979)	*Queen of the Damned (2002)*
Dracula (1979)	*Underworld (2003)*
Fright Night (1985)	*Van Helsing (2004)*
Fright Night II (1988)	*True Blood (2008-13) Series*
Bram Stoker's Dracula (1992)	*Hemlock Grove (2013-2016) Series*
Buffy the Vampire Slayer (1992)	*AHS: Hotel (2015-2016) Series*
Interview with a Vampire (1994)	*Preacher (2016-2019) Series*
Embrace of the Vampire (1995)	*The Carmilla Movie (2017)*
From Dusk till Dawn (1996)	*Dracula (2020) Netflix Series*
Buffy the Vampire Slayer (1997-2003) Series	*Interview with a Vampire (2022-) Series*
Blade (1998)	*Nosferatu (2024)*
Vampires (1998)	

Gothic, Magical, or Horror Films

Masque of the Red Death (1964)	*Bless The Child (2000)*
The Wicker Man (1973)	*From Hell (2001)*
The Exorcist (1973)	*The Skeleton Key (2005)*
The Omen (1976)	*Constantine (2005)*
Gothic (1986)	*Pan's Labyrinth (2006)*

Angel Heart (1987)	*Crowley (2008)*
The Crow (1994)	*Sleepy Hollow (2013-2017) Series*
Needful Things (1993)	*DaVinci's Demons (2013-15) Series*
Storm of the Century (1993)	*AHS: Coven (2013-2014)*
The Prophecy (1995)	*Penny Dreadful (2014-16) Series*
The Craft (1996)	*Salem (2014-2017) Series*
Wish Master (1997)	*A Dark Song (2016)*
The Devil's Advocate (1997)	*Taboo (2017) Series*
Fallen (1998)	*Chilling Adventures of Sabrina (2018-2020) Series*
Dark City (1998)	*The Pale Blue Eye (2022)*
Sleepy Hollow (1999)	*Wednesday (2022-) Series*
The Ninth Gate (1999)	*Mayfair Witches (2023-) Series*
The Cell (2000)	

Other

The Haunted Palace (1963)	*The Order (2003)*
Witchfinder General (1968)	*League of Extraordinary Gentlemen (2003)*
The Devil Rides Out (1968)	*The Libertine (2004)*
The Duelists (1977)	*Troy (2004)*
Caligula (1979)	*King Arthur (2004)*
Excalibur (1981)	*Casanova (2005)*
Robin of Sherwood (1984-1986) Series	*Rome (2005) Series*
Legend (1985)	*Kingdom of Heaven (2005)*
Marquis de Sade (1996)	*Sherlock Holmes (2009)*

Midnight in the Garden of Good and Evil (1997)	*Lie to Me (2009-2011) Series*
What Dreams May Come (1998)	*Spartacus (2010-2013) Series*
Merlin (1998) Miniseries	*Borgia (2011-2014) Doman Series*
Eyes Wide Shut (1999)	*Sherlock Holmes: A Game of Shadows (2011)*
Creul Intentions (1999)	*Venus in Furs (2013) French film*
Quills (2000)	*Black Sails (2014-2017) Series*
Gladiator (2000)	*The Magicians (2015- 2019) Series*
Moulin Rouge (2001)	*The Sandman (2022-) Series*
Brotherhood of the Wolf (2001)	*The Fall of the House of Usher (2023) Series*
Donnie Darko (2001)	*Wicked (2024), & Wicked for Good (2025)*

APPENDIX B

A LIBRARY OF IDEAS

Almost all of these books are in my library, but it is not a complete list. It is always changing and moving and often being added to. Some are very old, some are out of print, some are inaccessible, and others are brand new. The list is not for you to build a shopping cart with. It is to offer ideas and push you to consider what you need or want. I have read various volumes through and through many times. Others are simply for reference. Not all are for positive or useful reference; some are "how not to do it right." All the books I have referenced within this book are here. I will not break down each book and explain why; that is entirely up to the reader to explore.

TANTRA

Many of these books are excellent. Some are exceptional and speak to the real aspects of Tantra from India, and others are tales and stories from various kinds of people. Both are important to Tantra for different reasons. The rest are intended to work with magick.

Beth, David (Ed.) Ferocious: A Folk Tantric Manual on the Sapta Mantrika Cult. 2019.

Chinnaiyan, Kavitha M. Fractals of Reality, Living the Sricakra: Mystical Symbol, Practical Wisdom. 2022.

Chinnaiyan, Kavitha M. Shakti Rising: Embracing Shadow and Light on the Goddess Path to Wholeness. 2017.

Danielou, Alain. Gods of Love and Ecstasy: The Traditions of Shiva and Dionysus. 1982.

Danielou, Alain & Gabin, Jean-Louis. Shiva and the Primordial Tradition: From the Tantras to the Science of Dreams. 2007.

Dyczkowski, Mark S.G. The Doctrine of Vibration: An Analysis of the Doctrines and Practices of Kashmir Shaivism. 1987.

Dyczkowski, Mark S.G. (Trans.) The Stanzas on Vibration. 1992.

Dyczkowski, Mark S.G. (Trans.) The Aphorisms of Siva: The Siva Sutra with Bhaskara's Commentary. 1992.

Dyczkowski, Mark S.G. A Journey in the World of the Tantras. 2004.

Feuerstein, Georg. Tantra: The Path of Ecstasy. 1998.

Fries, Jan. Kali Kaula: A Manual of Tantric Magick. 2010.

Hine, Phil. Wheels Within Wheels: Chakras and Western Esotericism. 2024.

Hine, Phil. Yoginis: Sex, Death, and Possession in Early Tantras. 2018.

Johari, Harish. Breath, Mind, and Consciousness. 1989.

Johari, Harish. Chakras: Energy Centers of Transformation. Revised and Expanded Ed. 2000.

Johari, Harish. Tools for Tantra. 1986.

Levenda, Peter. The Tantric Alchemist: Thomas Vaughn and the Indian Tantric Tradition. 2015.

Kraig, Donald Michael. Modern Tantra. 2015.

Magee, Mike. Kali Magic. 2022.

Magee, Mike. Yakshini Magic. 2019.

Magee, Mike. The Book of the Brazen Angel

Magee, Mike. The Mysteries of the Red Goddess

Magee, Mike. Tantrik Astrology: A Manual of Sideral Astrology

Magee, Mike. The Grade Papers of the Magical Order of AMOOKOS

Mookerjee, Ajit & Khanna, Madhu. The Tantric Way. 2003.

Mookerjee, Ajit. The Arousal of the Kundalini: The Inner Energy. 1982.

Morgan, Mogg. Tantra Sadhana: A Practical Introduction to Kaula Magick. 2009.

Muller-Ortega, Paul E. The Triadic Heart of Siva: Kaula Tantricism of Abhinnava Gupta in the Non-Dual Shaivism of Kashmir. 1989.

Peters, Gregory. New Aeon Tantra: Secrets of Typhonian Magick & Western Tantra. 2024.

Peters, Gregory. Yogini Magic: The Sorcery, Enchantment, and Witchcraft of the Divine Feminine. 2022.

Power, John. The Rainbow Bridge: The Shakta Tantrika of the UttaraKaulas. 2020.

Power, John. Uttarakuru and the Return of the Goddess. 2016.

Power, John. The Nu Tantras of the UttaraKaulas. 2011.

Rinpoche, Kyabje Garchen. Vajrakilaya: A Complete Guide with Experiential Instructions. 2022.

Roy, Anamika. Sixty-Four Yoginis: Cult, Icons, and Goddesses. 2021.

Sargent, Denny. Tantra for All: The Path of the Nath Tantrika. 2021.

Singh, Jaideva. Para-trisika-Vivarana: Abhinavagupta: The Secret of Tantric Mysticism. 8th Reprint, 2017.

Sundar, Shyam Goswami. Layayoga: The Definitive Guide to the Chakras and Kundalini. 1999.

Svoboda, Robert E. Aghora: The Left-Hand Path of God. Brotherhood of Life Inc. 1986.

Svoboda, Robert E. Aghora II: Kundalini. 1994.

Taunton, Gwendolyn. Tantric Traditions: Gods, Rituals, & Esoteric Teachings in the Kali Yuga. 2018.

Tigunait, Pandit Rajmani. Sakti Sadhana: A Translation of the Tripura Rahasya. 2nd Ed. 2003.

Tigunait, Pandit Rajmani. Tantra Unveiled: Seducing the Forces of Matter & Spirit. 2007.

Tigunait, Pandit Rajmani. Sakti: The Power in Tantra, A Scholarly Approach. 1998.

Wallis, Christopher. Near Enemies of the Truth: Avoid the Pitfalls of the Spiritual Life and Become Radically Free. 2023.

Wallis, Christopher. The Recognition Sutras: Illuminating a 1,000-Year-Old Spiritual Masterpiece. 2017.

Wallis, Christopher. Tantra Illuminated: The Philosophy, History and Practice of a Timeless Tradition. 2nd Ed. 2013.

Williams, Craig. Desert Meditations: Gnostic Cartography, A Handbook of Agni Yoga. 2023.

Williams, Craig. Tantric Physics Vol. 1: Cave of the Numinous & Vol. 2: Sacred Body, Sacred Space. 2020.

Williams, Craig. Entering the Desert: Pilgrimage into the Hinterlands of the Soul. 2018.

Williams, Craig. Cult of Golgotha. 2018.

GENERAL RELIGION

This title serves as a catch-all and encompasses various aspects of spirituality that I deem important to the 42 aspects of the training. They are very diverse and include a great deal to chew on.

Adyashanti. The End of Your World: Uncensored Straight Talk on the Nature of Enlightenment. 2008.

Allione, Tsultrim. Feeding Your Demons: Ancient Wisdom for Resolving Inner Conflict. 2008.

Ardagh, Arjuna. The Translucent Revolution: How People Just Like You are Waking Up and Changing the World. 2005.
Aurobindo, Sri. The Integral Yoga: Sri Aurobindo's Teaching and Method of Practice. 1993.

Barks, Coleman (Trans.) The Essential Rumi: New Expanded Edition. 2004.
Brahinsky, David M. Reich and Gurdjieff: Sexuality and the Evolution of Consciousness. 2011.

Caplan, Mariana. Do You Need a Guru? Understanding the Student-Teacher Relationship in an Era of False Prophets. 2002.
Chetanananda, Swami. God Lived with Them: Life Stories of Sixteen Monastic Disciples of Sri Ramakrishna. 2014.
Cleary, Thomas (Trans.) Minding Mind: A Course in Basic Meditation. 1995.
Cleary, Thomas (Trans.) Opening the Dragon Gate: The Making of a Modern Taoist Wizard. 1998.

Dalai Lala, H. H. Toward a Kinship of Faiths: How the World's Religions Can Come Together. 2010.
Dass, Ram. Paths to God: Living the Bhagavad Gita. 2004.

Easwaran, Eknath (Trans.). The Dhammapada. 1985.
Easwaran, Eknath (Trans.). The Upanishads. 1987.
Easwaran, Eknath (Trans.). The Bhagavad Gita. 1985.

Freke, Timothy. The Mystery Experience: A Revolutionary Approach to Spiritual Awakening. 2013.
Freke, Timothy. The Hermetica: The Lost Wisdom of the Pharaohs. 1999.

Goleman, Daniel. The Meditative Mind: The Varieties of Meditative Experience. 1988.

Govindan, M. A. Babaji's Kriya Hatha Yoga: 18 Postures of Relaxation & Rejuvenation. 9th Ed.

Hixon, Lex. Coming Home: The Experience of Enlightenment in Sacred Traditions. 1995.

Huff, Benjamin. The Tao of Pooh & The Te of Piglet. 1992.

Jackson, Jake. The Four Branches of the Mabinogi. 2022.

Jackson, Jake. Egyptian Myths. 2018.

Jackson, Jake. Slavic Myths. 2023.

Jackson, Jake. Persian Myths. 2022.

Jackson, Jake. Myths of Babylon. 2018.

Jackson, Jake. Chinese Myths. 2018.

Jackson, Jake. Native American Myths. 2014.

Jackson, Jake. Japanese Myths. 2019.

Jackson, Jake. Polynesian Island Myths. 2020.

Jackson, Jake. Irish Fairy Tales. 2020.

Jackson, Jake. Celtic Myths. 2014.

Kempton, Sally. Meditation for the Love of It: Enjoying Your Own Deepest Experience. 2011.

Koshikidake, Shokai, & Faulks, Martin. Shugendo: The Way of the Mountain Monks. 2015.

Kriyananda, Goswami, Extraordinary Spiritual Potential. 1988.

Kriyananda, Goswami. Pathway to God-Consciousness. 1993.

Mann, John. Rudi: 14 Years with my Teacher. 1987.

Mitchell, Stephen. (Trans.) Tao Te Ching: A New English Version. 2006.

Ramacharaka, Yogi. Science of the Breath: A Complete Manual of the Oriental Breathing Philosophy of Physical, Mental, Psychic and Spiritual Development. 2018.

Rudrananda, Swami. Rudi: Spiritual Cannibalism. 4th Ed. 2009.

Shetty, Jay. Think Like a Monk: Train Your Mind for Peace and Purpose Every Day. 2020.

Smith, Houston. The World's Religions. 1991.

Villoldo, Alberto. Shaman, Healer, Sage: How to Heal Yourself and Others with the Energy Medicine of the Americas. 2000.

Villoldo, Alberto. Grow a New Body: How Spirit and Power Plant Nutrients Can Transform Your Health. 2019.

Villoldo, Alberto. Illumination: The Shaman's Way of Healing. 2010.

Villoldolo, Alberto. Yoga, Power and Spirit: Patanjali the Shaman. 2007.

Watts, Alan. Become What You Are. 2003.

Watts, Alan. Psychotherapy East & West. 1989.

PHILOSOPHY

Western and Eastern basics of philosophy are here; my library includes Stoicism, as well as various Western and Eastern variants, ranging from the Dhammapada to the Sutras, and more. But they are for reference and have little to do with the work of Magick or Stygian.

Allghieri, Dante. The Divine Comedy. 2025.

Aurelius, Marcus. Meditations. 2021.

Baudelaire. The Complete Verse, 2nd Ed. 2012.

Blake, William. For the Sexes: The Gates of Paradise. 2023.

Burns, Kevin. Eastern Philosophy: The Greatest Thinkers and Sages from Ancient to Modern Times. 2019.

Butler, Smedley D. War is a Racket. 2018.

Byron, Lord. The Major Works. 2008.

Camus, Renaud. The Great Replacement: Introduction to Global Replacement. 2024.

de Bono, Edward. I am Right, You are Wrong: From This to the New Renaissance: From Rock Logic to Water Logic. 1990.

Designing the Mind. The Book of Self Mastery Quotes: Timeless Words of Wisdom About Knowing, Changing and Mastering Yourself. 2020.

Desmet, Matthias. The Psychology of Totalitarianism. 2022.

Dickens, Charles. Complete Works.

Epictetus, Marcus. The Stoic Way of Life: The Ultimate Guide of Stoicism to Make Your Everyday Modern Life Calm, Confident & Positive. 2021.

Epictetus & Seneca. The Complete Guide to Stoicism. 2024.

Farnsworth, Ward. The Socratic Method: A Practitioner's Handbook. 2021.

Farnsworth, Ward. The Practicing Stoic: A Philosophical User's Manual. 2018.

Goethe. Faust. 1981.

Greene, Robert. Mastery. 2013.

Greene, Robert. The Concise 48 Laws of Power: New Edition. 2002.

Hawthorne, Nathaniel. Complete Works.

Heidegger, Martin. An Introduction to Metaphysics. 1959.

Heinrichs, Jay. Thank You for Arguing: What Aristotle, Lincoln, and Homer Simpson Can Teach Us About the Art of Persuasion. 2013.

Hitchens, Christopher. Why Orwell Matters. 2002.

Hitchens, Christopher. Thomas Paine's Rights of Man: A Biography. 2006.

Hitchens, Christopher. God is not Great: How Religion Poisons Everything. 2007.

Holiday, Ryan. Ego is the Enemy. 2016.

Holiday, Ryan. The Obstacle is the Way: The Timeless Art of Turning Trials to Triumph. 2014.

Holiday, Ryan. Stillness is the Key. 2019.

Kaufmann, Walter (Ed. & Trans.) The Portable Nietzsche. 1976.

Malice, Michael. The White Pill: A Tale of Good and Evil. 2023.

Malice, Michael. The Anarchist Handbook. 2021.

Malice, Michael, Dear Reader: The Unauthorized Autobiography of Kim Jong Il. 2014.

Milton, John. Paradise Lost. 1997.

Minford, John (Trans.) Sun Tzu's The Art of War: An Essential Translation of the Classic Book of Life. 2002.

Poe, Edgar Allen. Greatest Works of...

Ricci, Luigi (Trans.) Machiavelli, Niccolò: The Prince. 2021.

Russell, Bertrand. The History of Western Philosophy. 1972.

Saad, Gad. The Parasitic Mind: How Infectious Ideas are Killing Common Sense. 2020.

Schumacher, E. F. Small is Beautiful: Economics as if People Mattered. 2010.

Surprise, Kirby. Synchronicity: The Art of Coincidence, Choice, and Unlocking Your Mind. 2012.

Wilde, Oscar. The Greatest Works of... 2020.

CHAOS MAGICK

All of my experiences with CM come from across the pond, so there are a lot of UK books here. I also see Farber as a fit, but some may feel this is the wrong fit; he's on this list for me.

Carroll, Peter J. This is Chaos: Embracing the Future of Magic. 2025.

Carroll, Peter J. The Apophenion: A Chaos Magic Paradigm. 2008.

Carroll, Peter J. Liber Null & Psychonaut: An Introduction to Chaos Magic. 1987.

Carroll, Peter J. Liber Kaos. 1992.

Chapman, Alan. Advanced Magick for Beginners. 2008.

Dee, Steve. Chaos Monk. 2022.

Dukes, Ramsey. S.S.O.T.B.M.E., Revised. (1979) 2011.

Farber, Philip H. Brain Magick: Exercises in Meta-Magick and Invocation. 2016.

Farber, Philip H. Meta-Magick of the Book of ATEM: Achieving New States of Consciousness through NLP, Neuroscience, and Ritual. 2008.

Farber, Philip H. Future Ritual: Magick for the 21st Century. 1995.

Hawkins, Jaq D. The Chaonomicon: Quintessential Chaos for the Serious Magician. 2017.

Hawkins, Jaq D. Chaos Witch. 2022.

Hine, Phil. Condensed Chaos: An Introduction to Chaos Magic. 1995.

Hine. Phil. Prime Chaos: Adventures in Chaos Magic. 1993.

Humphries, Greg & Vayne, Julian. Now That's What I Call Chaos Magick: Vol. 1&2. 2004.

Lee, David. Life Force: Sensed Energy in Breathwork, Psychedelia, and Chaos Magic. 2017.

Lee, David. Chaotopia! Sorcery and Ecstasy in the Fifth Aeon. 2006.

Lee, David. Primordial Chaos. 2023.

Lee, David. Magical Incenses. 2020.

Metzger, Richard. (Ed.) Book of Lies: The Disinformation Guide to Magick and the Occult. 2003.

Smith, Dave. Quantum Sorcery: The Science of Chaos Magic. 3rd Ed. & Rev. 2021.

Spare, Auston Osman. The Writings of Austin Osman Spare: Anathema of Zos, The Book of Pleasure, and The Focus of Life. 2010.

Vayne, Julian. Getting Higher: A Manual of Psychedelic Ceremony. 2017.

Vayne, Julian. The Fool & the Mirror. 2018.

Vayne, Julian. Deep Magic Begins Here... Tales and Techniques of Practical Occultism. 2013.

Vayne, Julian & Dee, Steve. Chaos Craft: The Wheel of the Year in Eight Colors. 2016.

Vayne, Julian. Magick Works: Stories of Occultism in Theory and Practice. 2008.

Vitimus, Andrieh. Hands-On Chaos Magic: Reality Manipulation Through the Ovayki Current. 2019.

White, Gordon. The Chaos Protocols: Magical Techniques for Navigating the New Economic Reality. 2021.

Wyrd, Nikki & Vayne, Julian. The Book of Baphomet. 2012.

DIVINATION WORK

I only include the divination skills and work I do as part of the Stygian work, add your own as needed. I know many students add a ton of Runes work here, I own them but do not have the success I like, so rarely use them.

Achad, Frater. Crystal Vision Through Crystal Gazing. 2020.

Andrews, Ted. Crystal Balls and Crystal Bowls: Tools for Ancient Skrying & Modern Seership. 2005.

Belanger, Michelle. The Psychic Energy Codex: Awakening Your Subtle Senses. 2007.

Butler, W. E. How to Read the Aura and Practice Psychometry, Telepathy, & Clairvoyance. 1998.

Ellwood, Taylor. Scrying the Divine: Advanced Techniques for Spirit Communication and Behavior Alteration. 2023.

Goldberg, Ellen & Bergen, Dorian. The Art and Science of Hand Reading: Classical Methods for Self-Discovery through Palmistry. 2016.

Neos Alexandrina. The Diviner's Handbook: Writing on Ancient Practices. 2018.

Pagan Portals. Starza, Lucya. Scrying: Divination Using Crystals, Mirrors, Water and Fire. 2022.

Paxson, Diana L. The Way of the Oracle: Rediscovering the Practices of the Past to Find Answers for Today. 2012.

Tusk, Oscar. Through A Glass Darkly: The Practice of Catoptromancy or Divination by Mirrors in Traditional Witchcraft. 2022.

Tyson. Jenny. The Art of Scrying & Dowsing: Foolproof Methods for ESP and Remote Viewing. 2022.

GENERAL OCCULT

The entire corpus of the rest of the occult titles I value is here. For those in the know, there are notable missing items, and that is on purpose.

Acher, Frater. Holy Heretics. 2022.

Acher, Frater. Black Abbot White Magic: Johannes Trithemius and the Angelic Mind. 2020.

Acher, Frater. Holy Daimon. 2018.

Auryn, Mat. The Psychic Art of the Tarot: Opening Your Inner Eye for More Insightful Readings. 2024.

Auryn, Mat. Mastering Magick: A Course in Spellcasting for the Psychic Witch. 2022.

Auryn, Mat. Psychic Witch: A Metaphysical Guide to Meditation, Magick, & Manifestation. 2020.

Albert, K. K. & De Biasi, Jean-Louis (Ed.) Peladan, Josephin. How to Become a Mage. 2019.

Bardon, Franz. Initiation Into Hermetics: Vol.1 Of the Holy Mysteries. 1998.

Bardon, Franz. The Practice of Magical Evocation: Vol. 2 Of the Holy Mysteries. 2001.

Bird, Stephanie Rose. Sticks, Stones, Roots, & Bones: Hoodoo, Mojo, & Conjuring with Herbs. 2021.

Boland, Yasmin. Moonology: Working with the Magic of Lunar Cycles. 2016.

Cecchetelli, Michael. The Holy Guardian Angel. 2014.

Chaitow, Sasha. Son of Prometheus: The Life and Work of Josephin Peladan. 2022.

Churton, Tobias. Occult Paris: The Lost Magic of the Belle Epoque. 2016.

Clark, Rawn. A Bardon Companion, 2nd Ed. A Practical Companion for the Student of Franz Bardon's System of Hermetic Initiation. 2010.

Cooper, J.C. An Illustrated Encyclopedia of Traditional Symbols. 2008.

Cowan, Tom. Shamanism: As a Spiritual Practice for Daily Life. 1996.

Crowley, Aleister. Book 4. 1980.

Crowley, Aleister. 777: And Other Qabalistic Writings of… 1998.

Crowley, Aleister. The Rites of Eleusis.

Crowley, Aleister. Eight Lectures on Yoga. 1991.

Day, Christian. The Witches Book of the Dead, 10th Anniversary, Expanded & Revised. 2021.

Dey, Charmaine. The Magic Candle: Facts and Fundamentals of Ritual Candle Burning. 1982.

Duquette, Lon Milo & Shoemaker, David (Ed). Llewellyn's Complete Book of Ceremonial Magick: A Comprehensive Guide to the Western Mystery Tradition. 2020.

Duriel, Durgadas A. The Little Work: Magic to Transform Your Everyday Life. 2020.

Duvendack, Bill. Spirit Associates: Your User-Friendly Guide to Spirit Guides, Allies and Teachers. 2021.

Duvendack, Bill. Astrology in Theory & Practice. 2018.

Ellwood, Taylor. The Quest for Mature Masculinity: How to Become an Embodied and Present Man. 2024.

Ellwood, Taylor. Walking with Magical Entities: How to Create and Work with Servitors, Egregores, and Thought Forms to Get Consistent Results. 2020.

Ellwood, Taylor. Inner Alchemy: Energy Work and the Magic of the Body. 2018.

Emrys, Avallach. The Path of the Sacred Hermit: Exploring Monasticism in a Modern Pagan Spirituality. 2023.

Farmer, Steven D. Animal Spirit Guides: An Easy-to-Use Handbook for Identifying and Understanding Your Power Animals and Animal Spirit Helpers. 2006.

Farrar, Janet & Bone, Gavin. Lifting the Veil: A Witch's Guide to Trance-Prophecy, Drawing Down the Moon, and Ecstatic Ritual. 2016.

Filan, Kenaz & Kaldera, Raven. Talking to Spirits: Personal Gnosis in Pagan Religion. 2013.

Filan, Kenaz & Kaldera, Raven. Drawing Down the Spirits: The Techniques of Spirit Possession. 2009.

Fries, Jan. Nightshades: A Tourist Guide to the Nightside. 2012.

Fries, Jan. Seidways: Shaking, Swaying and Serpent Mysteries. 2010.

Fries, Jan. Living Midnight: Three Movements of the Tao. 1998.

Frisvold, Nicholaj De Mattos. Seven Crossroads of the Night: Quimbanda in Theory and Practice.2023.

Gonzalez-Wippler, Migene. The Complete Book of Amulets and Talismans. 1991.

Harner, Michael. The Way of the Shaman. 1990.

Heller, Steven, & Steele, Terry. Monsters and Magical Sticks: There's No Such Thing as Hypnosis? 2007.

Hulse, David Allen. The Eastern Mysteries: An Encyclopedic Guide to the Sacred Languages & Magickal Systems of the World; The Key of It All, Book I. 2nd Edition. 2000.

Hulse, David Allen. The Western Mysteries: An Encyclopedic Guide to the Sacred Languages & Magickal Systems of the World; The Key of It All, Book II. 2nd Edition. 2000.

Hyatt, Christopher. The Big Black Book: Become Who You Are- There are No Guarantees. 2020.

Hyatt, Christopher S. Undoing Yourself: With Energized Meditation and Other Devices. 2006.

Hyatt, Christopher S. & Willis, Jack. The Psychopath's Bible: For the Extreme Individual. 2003.

Hyatt, Christopher S. The Psychopath's Notebook: In Four Parts. 2008.

Hyatt, Christopher S. & Black, S. Jason. Tantra Hyatt, Christopher S. & Black, S. Jason. Pacts with the Devil. 1997.

Hyatt, Christopher S., & Iwema, Calvin. Energized Hypnosis: A Non-Book for Self-Change. 2005.

Hyatt, Christopher S. & Duquette, Lon Milo. Taboo: Sex, Religion & Magick. 2001.

Hyatt, Christopher S. & Duquette, Lon Milo. Sex Magic, Tantra and Tarot: The Way of the Secret Lover. 1991.

Hyatt, Christopher S. To Lie is Human: Not Getting Caught is Divine. 2004.

Hyatt, Christopher S. Secrets of Western Tantra: The Sexuality of the Middle Path. 2010.

Kaldera, Raven. Dealing with Deities: Practical Polytheistic Theology. 2012.

Kaldera, Raven & Krasskova, Galina. Neolithic Shamanism: Spirit Work in the Norse Tradition. 2012.

Kraig, Donald Michael. Modern Magick: Twelve Lessons in the High Magical Arts. 2010.

Kynes, Sandra. Llewellyn's Complete Book of Correspondences: A Comprehensive & Cross-Referenced Resource for Pagans & Wiccans. 2025.

Leitch, Aaron (Ed.) Ritual Offerings. 2014.

Leitch, Aaron. Secrets of the Magickal Grimoires: The Classical Texts of Magick Deciphered. 2005.

Levenda, Peter. The Dark Lord: H.P. Lovecraft, Kenneth Grant and the Typhonian Tradition of Magic. 2013.

Matthews, John. The Celtic Shaman: A Practical Guide. 2001.

McCarthy, Josephine. Magical Healing: A Health Survival Guide for Occultists, Pagans, Healers, and Tarot Readers. 2019.

McCarthy, Josephine. The Work of the Hierophant. 2009.

McCaughry, G. Aurora. 2018.

Mickaharic, Draja. Spiritual Cleansing: A Handbook of Psychic Protection. 2012.

Mickaharic, Draja. Magical Techniques: Unusual Techniques in Practical Magic. 2002.

Mickaharic, Draja. A Century of Spells: More than 100 Time Tested, Easy to Use Spells that Really Work. 1990.

Mistlberger, P. T. The Three Dangerous Magi: Osho, Gurdjieff, Crowley. 2010.

Mistlberger, P.T. Rude Awakening: Perils, Pitfalls, and Hard Truths of the Spiritual Path. 2013.

Mistlberger, P. T. The Way of the Conscious Warrior: A Handbook for the 21st Century Men. 2019.

Mistlberger, P. T. The Dancing Sorcerer: Essays on the Mind of the Magician. 2020.

Mooney, Thorn. Traditional Wicca: A Seeker's Guide. 2018.

Morrison, Dorothy. Utterly Wicked: Hexes, Curses and Unsavory Notions. 2020.

Munin, Janet (Ed.). Polytheistic Monasticism: Voices from Pagan Cloisters. 2022.

Murphy, Amantha, & O'Connell, Orla. The Way of the Seabhean: An Irish Shamanic Path. 2020.

Nema. Maat Magick: A Guide to Self-Initiation. 1995.

Nema. The Way of Mystery: Magick, Mysticism, & Self-Transcendence. 2003.

Nema. Feather and Firesnake: The Maat of Kundalini. 2010.

Neos Alexandrina. Hardy, Michael (Ed.). Ascendant II: Theology for Modern Polytheists. 2019.

Neos Alexandrina. Hardy, Michael (Ed.). Ascendent: Modern Essays on Polytheism and Theology. 2019.

Newcomb, Jason. The New Hermetics: 21st Century Magick for Illumination and Power. 2004.

Nixey, Catherine. The Darkening Age: The Christian Destruction of the Classical World. 2017.

Pagan Portals. Corak, Robin. Persephone: Practicing the Art of Personal Power. 2020.

Pagan Portals. Dillon, Steven. Polytheism: A Platonic Approach. 2022.

Pagan Portals, Draco, Melusine. Pan, Dark Lord of the Forest and Horned God of the Witches. 2016.

Pagan Portals. Forest, Danu. Gwyn Ap Nudd: Wild God of Faerie, Guardian of Annwen. 2018.

Pagan Portals. Leaver, Samantha. Hellenic Paganism. 2021.

Pagan Portals. Teixeira, Jennifer. Temple of the Bones: Rituals to the Goddess Hecate. 2021.

Pagan Portals. Patterson, Rachel. The Cailleach. 2016.

Pamita, Madame. The Book of Candle Magic: Candle Spell Secrets to Change Your Life. 2021.

Pennick, Nigel. The Spiritual Power of Masks: Doorways to Realms Unseen. 2022.

Pennick, Nigel. The Ancestral Power of Amulets, Talismans, and Mascots. Folk Magic in Witchcraft & Religion. 2021.

Pennick, Nigel. Secret Signs, Symbols, and Sigils. 1996.

Poisson, Denis. Hidden Paths. 2023.

Rankine, David. Becoming Magick. 2003.

Robichaud, Paul. Pan: The Great God's Modern Return. 2021.

Rysdyk, Evelyn C. Spirit Walking: A Course in Shamanic Power. 2013.

Rysdyk, Evelyn C. The Norse Shaman: Ancient Spiritual Practices of the Northern Tradition. 2016.

Rysdyk, Evelyn C. & Banstola, Bhola Nath. The Nepalese Shamanic Path: Practices for Negotiating in the Spirit World. 2019.

Sanders, Maxine. Firechild: The Life and Magic of Maxine Sanders. 2008.

Stavish, Mark. Between the Gates: Lucid Dreaming, Astral Projection, and the Body of Light in Western Esotericism. 2008.

Stavish, Mark. Egregores: The Occult Entities that Watch Over Human Destiny. 2018.

Three Initiates. The Kybalion: Hermetic Philosophy, Centenary Ed. 2018.

Von Tulein, Hagen. Occult Psaligraphy: The Hidden Art of Papercutting. 2013.

Wachter, Aiden. Changeling: A Book of Qualities. 2021.

Wachter, Aiden. Weaving Fate: Hypersigils, Changing the Past, & Telling True Lies. 2020.

Wachter, Aiden. Six Ways: Approaches & Entries for Practical Magic. 2018.

Warwick, Tari (Ed.). Corpus Hermeticum: The Divine Pymander; Original Manuscript of Hermes Trismegistus, 3rd Century A.D. 2015.

Wasserman, James. In the Center of the Fire: A Memoir of the Occult 1966-1989. 2012.

Wasserman, James (ed.). Aleister Crowley and the Practices of the Magical Diary. Rev. and Expanded Ed. 2006.

Wasserman, Nancy. Yoga for Magick: Build Physical and Mental Strength for your Practice. 2007.

Webb, Don. How to Become a Modern Magus: A Manual for Magicians of All Schools. 2023.

Whitcomb, Bill. The Magician's Companion: A Practical Encyclopedia Guide to Magical & Religious Symbolism. 1997.

Wilson, Robert A. Wilhelm Reich in Hell. 2007.

Wilson, Robert A. Prometheus Rising. 2005.

Wilson, Robert A. Quantum Psychology: How Brain Software Programs You and Your World. 2011.

HYPNOSIS/PSYCHOLOGY

Hypnosis is a big portion of the work and that includes NLP but also includes aspects of how the mind works. All of these issues include mindfulness and the magick books of Hyatt.

Bandler, Richard. The Ultimate Introduction to NLP: How to Build a Successful Life. 2017.

Dispenza, Joe. You are the Placebo: Making Your Mind Matter. 2014.

Heller, Steven, & Steele, Terry. Monsters and Magical Sticks: There's No Such Thing as Hypnosis? 2007.

Hunter, C. Roy, & Elmer, Bruce N. The Art of Hypnotic Regression Therapy: A Clinical Guide. 2014.

Kabat-Zinn, Jon. Full Catastrophe Living: Using the Wisdom of Your Body and Mind to Face Stress, Pain and Illness. 2009.

LaBay, Mary Lee. Past Life Regression: A Guide to Practitioners. 2004.

Nongard, Richard. Excellence in NLP and Life Coaching: How to Structure Success and Create Influence at an Expert Level. Subliminal Science Press. 2021.

Nongard, Richard & Hazlerig, James. Speak Eriksonian: Mastering the Hypnotic Methods of Milton Erikson. 2014.

O'Connor, Joseph & Seymour, J. Introducing NLP: Psychological Skills for Understanding and Influencing People. 2002.

O'Hanlon, William H. Taproots: Underlying Principles of Milton Erikson's Therapy and Hypnosis. 1987.

O'Hanlon, Bill. A Guide to Trance Land: A Practical Handbook of Ericksonian and Solution-Oriented Hypnosis. 2009.

Rossi, Ernest L. & Cheek, David B. Mind-Body Therapy: Methods of Ideodynamic Healing in Hypnosis. 1988.

Willis, Jack. Reichian Therapy: A Practical Guide for Home Use. 2013.

Yapko, Michael D. Mindfulness and Hypnosis: The Power of Suggestion to Transform Experience. 2011.

Yapko, Michael D. Trancework: An Introduction to the Practice of Clinical Hypnosis. 2nd Ed. 1990.

DARK OCCULTISM

This category includes the LHP, issues of Black Magic, aspects of Western Magick outside the norm.

Abrahamson, Carl. Anton LaVey and the Church of Satan: Infernal Wisdom from the Devil's Den. 2022.

Aquino, Michael A. The Satanic Bible: 50th Anniversary Revision. 2018.

Aureavia, Hagia. Mystery Babylon: Being the Bhaktic and Ecstatic Rites of Babylon. 2016.

Belanger, Michelle. The Dictionary of Demons: Expanded and Revised. 2021.

Blish, James. Black Easter and The Day After Judgment. 1981.

Brand, Damon. Magickal Protection: Defend Against Curses, Gossip, Bullies, Thieves, Demonic Forces, Violence, Threats, and Psychic Attacks. 2015.

Brand, Damon. Words of Power: Secret Magickal Sounds That Manifest Your Desires. 2015.

Brand, Damon. Magikal Seduction: Attract Love, Sex and Passion with Ancient Secrets and the Words of Power. 2015.

Brand, Damon. Magikal Checkbook: Attract Money Fast with Ancient Secrets and Modern Wealth Magick. 2014.

Dimech, Alkistis & Grey, Peter. The Brazen Vessel: Collected Works 2008-2018. 2019.

Grey, Peter. Apocalyptic Witchcraft. 2013.

Grey, Peter. Lucifer: Princeps. 2015.

Grey, Peter. The Red Goddess. 2007.

Grey, Peter. The Two Antichrists. 2021.

Guiley, Rosemary Ellen. The Encyclopedia of Demons and Demonology. 2009.

Hall, Nicholas. Chaos & Sorcery. 1998.

Kelly, Michael. The Magical Vision of Anton LaVey. 2022.

Kelly, Michael. Apophis. 2009.

Leved, Fr. Nate. Seven Scrolls of the Black Rose: The Restoration. 2012.

LaVey, Anton S. The Satanic Bible. 1969.

LaVey, Anton S. The Satanic Rituals. 1972.

LaVey, Anton S. The Satanic Witch. 1989.

Malphas. The Black Ship. 2012.

Mason, Asanath. Draconian Ritual Book. 2016.

Page, Richard K. Luciferian Ego Sum. 2018.

Page, Richard K. Discovering the Divine. 2017.

Page, Richard K. Exegesis of Lucifer. 2015.

Simon. Necronomicon. 1977.

Webb, Don. Uncle Setnakt's Essential Guide to the Left Hand Path. 1999.

Webb, Don. Uncle Setnacht's Night Book. 2016.

Webb, Don. Overthrowing the Old Gods: Aleister Crowley and the Book of the Law. 2013

SEX MAGICK & SEX

This includes magick, sex therapy, fetish, and approaches to sexuality.

Adoum, Jorge. (Rocha, Monica D. Trans.) Sex to Divinity: Religions and Their Mysteries. 2021.

Anand, Margot. The Art of Everyday Ecstasy: The Seven Tantric Keys for Bringing Passion, Spirit, and Joy into Every Part of Your Life. 1999.

Anand, Margo. The Art of Sexual Ecstasy: The Path of Sacred Sexuality for Western Lovers. 1989.

Brotto, Lori A. Better Sex Through Mindfulness: How Women Can Cultivate Desire. 2018.

Brame, Gloria, William, & Jacobs, Jon. Different Loving: The World of Sexual Dominance & Submission. 1993.

Brame, Gloria. Come Hither: A Commonsense Guide to Kinky Sex. 2000.

DeNaglowska, Maria. Advanced Sex Magic: The Hanging Mystery Initiation. 2011.

DeNaglowska, Maria. The Light of Sex: Initiation, Magic, and Sacrament. 2011.

Easton, Dossie & Hardy, Janet. The Ethical Slut: A Practical Guide to Polyamory, Open Relationships & Other Adventures 2nd Ed. 2009.

Elliott, Carolyn. Existential Kink: Unmask Your Shadow and Embrace Your Power. 2020.

Ellwood, Taylor & Lupa. Kink Magic: Sex Magic Beyond Vanilla. 2007.

Flagg. Forked Tongue: A Handbook for Treating People Badly Revised. 2019.

Flowers, Stephen E. & Crystal D. Carnal Alchemy: Sado-Magical Techniques for Pleasure, Pain, and Self-Transformation. 2013.

Greaux, Jacquie Noelle. Better Sex Through Yoga. 2007.

Harrington, Lee. Sacred Kink: The Eightfold Path of BDSM and Beyond. 2016.

Harrington, Lee. Spirit of Desire: Personal Explorations of Sacred Kink. 2016.

Hyatt, Christopher S. & Black, S. Jason. Tantra Without Tears. 1999.

Hyatt, Christopher S. & Duquette, Lon Milo. Sex Magic, Tantra and Tarot: The Way of the Secret Lover. 1991.

Hyatt, Christopher S. Secrets of Western Tantra: The Sexuality of the Middle Path. 2010.

Kaldera, Raven. Dark Moon Rising: Pagan BDSM and the Ordeal Path. 2006.

Kaldera, Raven. Pagan Polyamory: Becoming a Tribe of Hearts. 2005.

Kraig, Donald Michael. Modern Sex Magick: Secrets of Erotic Spirituality. 1999.

Nagoski, Emily. Come as You Are: The Surprising New Science that Will Transform Your Sex Life. 2021.

Newcomb, Jason. Sexual Sorcery: A Complete Guide to Sex Magick. 2005.

Randolph, Pascal B. & De Naglowska, Maria. Magia Sexualis: Sexual Practices for Magical Power. 2012.

Schreck, Nikolas & Schreck, Zeena. Demons of the Flesh: The Complete Guide to Left Hand Path Sex Magic. 2002.

Tempest, Jareth. The Filthy Grimoire: Sex, Sigils, and Servitors. Magick for Having Better Sex More Often. 2022.

Thomas, Sophie Saint. Sex Witch: Magickal Spells for Love, Lust, and Self Protection. 2021.

Versluis, Arthur. The Secret History of Western Sexual Mysticism: Sacred Practices and Spiritual Marriage. 2008.

West, Michael W. Sex Magicians: The Lives and Spiritual Practices of.... 2021.

Yudelove, Eric S. Taoist Yoga and Sexual Energy: Transforming your Body, Mind and Spirit. 2000.

Yudelove, Eric S. 100 Days to Better Health, Good Sex & Long Life: A Guide to Taoist Yoga & Chi Gong. 1997.

DEVOTIONALS

In CM, we change paradigms, so we need things like devotionals, and I find these to be very helpful. It is my set and only a sampling. There are so many options. These must be paired with either a good esoteric research set of books or academic research to fully expand and understand the entire paradigm to make it effective.

Krasskova, Galina. Sacramentum: A Devotional for Dionysus. 2016.

Neos Alexandrina. Krasskova, Galina (Ed.) Ferryman of the Souls: A Devotional to Charon. 2014.

Neos Alexandrina. Hurley, Callum (Ed.) Lunessence: A Devotional to Selene. 2016.

Neos Alexandrina. Sophia, Diotima (Ed.). Out of Arcadia: A Devotional Anthology in Honor of Pan. 2011.

Neos Alexandrina. Roy, K. S. (Ed). Guardian of the Road: A Devotional Anthology in Honor of Hermes. 2012.

Neos, Alexandrina. Written in Whine: A Devotional Anthology for Dionysos. 2008.

Neos, Alexandrina. Shipman, Zachariah (Ed.) Among Satyrs and Nymphs: A Devotion to Hellenic Nature Spirits. 2022.

Neos, Alexandrina. Munin, Janet. (Ed.) Queen of the Great Below: Anthology in Honor of Ereshkigal. 2010.

Pagan Portals. Moss. Vivienne Heckate: A Devotional. 2015.

TRAD CRAFT

I am a practitioner and a strong believer in these traditions as well as the folk traditions that follow with them. I offer a small but potent set of books I love.

Amaranthus. Feasting from the Black Cauldron. 2017.

Artisson, Robin. Soon Comes Walpurgis: A Collection of Macabre and Disturbing Tales. 2016.

Artisson, Robin. The Clovenstone Workings: A Manual of Early Modern Witchcraft. 2020.

Artisson, Robin. An Cawdarn Rudh: A Companion of Invocations and Charms for An Carow Gwyn. 2018.

Artisson, Robin. An Carow Gwyn: Sorcery and the Ancient Fayerie Faith. 2018.

Artisson, Robin. Letters from the Devil's Forest: An Anthology of Writing on Traditional Witchcraft, Spiritual Ecology, and Provenance Traditionalism. 2014.

Artisson, Robin. The Resurrection of the Meadow. 2010.

Black, Laurelei. The Red Thread Academy: Year 1: Foundations Course Manual. 2021.

Black, Laurelei. The Red Thread Academy: Year 2: Practicum Course Manual. 2022.

Black, Laurelei. The Red Thread Academy: Year 3: Mastery Course Manual. 2023.

Chambers, Ian. The Witch Compass: Working with the Winds in Traditional Witchcraft. 2022.

Coyle, T. Thorn. Crafting a Daily Practice: A Simple Course on Self-Commitment. 2022.

Coyle, T. Thorn. Make Magic of Your Life: Passion, Purpose and the Power of Desire. 2013.

Coyle, T. Thorn. Evolutionary Witchcraft. 2005.

Coyle, T. Thon. Kissing the Limitless: Deep Magic and the Great Work of Transforming Your-Self and the World. 2009.

Daimler, Morgan. The New Dictionary of Fairies: A 21st Century Exploration of Celtic and Related Western European Fairies. 2020.

Evans-Wenz, Walter. The Fairy-Faith in Celtic Countries. 2017.

Faerywolf, Storm. The Satyr's Kiss: Queer Men, Sex Magic, & Modern Witchcraft. 2022.

Faerywolf, Storm. Betwixt & Between. 2017.

Faerywolf, Storm. Forbidden Mysteries of Faery Witchcraft. 2020.

Finnin, Ann. The Forge of Tubal Cain. 2008.

Foxwood, Orion. The Flame in the Cauldron: A Book of Old-Style Witchery. 2015.

Foxwood, Orion. The Tree of Enchantment: Ancient Wisdom and Magic Practices of the Faery Tradition. 2008.

Foxwood, Orion. The Faery Teachings. 2003.

Frisvold, Nicholaj De Mattos. The Cunning Craft: A Tortuous Path of the Wise Art. 2025.

Freuler, Kate. Magic at the Crossroads: The Devil in Modern Witchcraft. 2024.
Freuler, Kate. Of Blood and Bones: Working with Shadow Magick of Dark Moon. 2023.

Gary, Gemma. Silent as the Trees: Devonshire Witchcraft, Folklore & Magic. 2017.
Gary, Gemma. The Devil's Dozen: Thirteen Craft Rites of the Old One. 2015.
Gary, Gemma. The Black Toad: West Country Witchcraft and Magic. 2011.
Gary, Gemma. Traditional Witchcraft: A Cornish Book of Ways. 2008.
Grimassi, Raven. Hereditary Witchcraft: Secrets of the Old Religion. 2019.
Grimassi, Raven. What we Knew in the Night: Reawakening the Heart of Witchcraft. 2019.
Grimassi, Raven. Grimoire of the Thorn-Bloodied Witch: Mastering the Five Arts of Old World Witchery.2014.

Horne, Roger J. The Witch's Art of Incantation: Spoken Charms, Spells, & Curses in Folk Witchcraft. 2023.
Horne, Roger J. The Witches' Devil: Myth and Lore for Modern Cunning. 2022.
Horne, Roger J. Cartomancy in Folk Witchcraft: Divination, Magic, and Lore. 2019
Horne, Roger J. Folk Witchcraft: A Guide to Lore, Land, & Familiar Spirit for the Solitary Practitioner. 2021.
Horne, Roger J. A Broom at Midnight: 13 Gates of Witchcraft by Spirit Flight. 2021.
Howard, Michael. Liber Nox: A Traditional Witch's Grimarye. 2014.
Howard, Michael. Welch Witches and Wizards. 2009.

Johnson, Kenneth. The Craft of Tubal Cain: Traditional Witchcraft and the Legacy of Robert Cochrane. 2024.
Johnson, Kenneth. Witchcraft and the Shamanistic Journey. 2022.

Kelden. The Witches Sabbath: An Exploration of History, Folklore, & Modern Practice. 2022.

Keldon. The Crooked Path. An Introduction to Traditional Witchcraft. 2022.

King, Nathan. Awakening the Witch Blood: Embodying the Arte Magical. 2024.

Leland, Charles. Aradia: Gospel of the Witches. 2010.

Mason, Darragh. Song of the Dark Man: Father of Witches, Lord of the Crossroads. 2024.

Meredith, Jane & Parma, Gede. Magic of the Iron Pentacle: Reclaiming Sex, Pride, Self, Power, & Passion. 2016.

Morgan, Lee. People of the Outside: Witchcraft, Cannibalism, and the Elder Folk. 2024.

Morgan, Lee. Sounds of Infinity. 2019.

Morgan, Lee. Standing and Not Falling: A Sorcerous Primer in Thirteen Months. 2019.

Morgan, Lee. A Deed Without a Name: Unearthing the Legacy of Traditional Witchcraft. 2013.

Oates, Shani. Tubelo's Fire: A Grammarye of Robert Cochrane's Early Years. 2025.

Oates, Shani. The Robert Cothrane Tradition: CTC: Tubal's Mill Revised. 2018.

Oates, Shani. The Devil's Supper. 2021.

Oates, Shani. Crafting the Arte of Tradition. 2018.

Oates, Shani. Tubelo's Green Fire: Mythos, Ethos, Female, Male, and Priestly Mysteries of the Clan of Tubal Cain. 2010.

Oates, Shani. The People of Goda. 2012.

Paddon, Peter. A Grimoire for Modern Cunningfolk. Revised Ed. 2012.

Parma, Fio Gede. Ecstatic Witchcraft: Magic, Philosophy & Trance in a Shamanic Craft. 2024.

Parma, Fio Gede. The Witch Belongs to the World: A Spell of Becoming. 2023.

Parma, Fio Gede. By Land, Sky, & Sea: Three Realms of Shamanic Witchcraft. 2010.

Pearson, Nigel. Treading the Mill: Workings in Traditional Craft. 2020.

Pearson, Nigel. Wortcunning: A Folk Magic Herbal. 2018.

Sanchez, Tara. Urban Fairy Magick: Connecting to the Fae in the Modern World. 2021.

Swain, B. J. Familiar unto Me: Witches, Sorcerers, and Their Spirit Companions. 2023.

Swain, B. J. Luminarium: A Grimoire of Cunning Conjuration. 2020.

Swain, B.J. Living Spirits: A Guide to Magic in A World of Spirits. 2018.

Wisner, Kerry. The Art: A Grimoire of Traditional Witchcraft. 2023.

WSL, Marshall. The Red Mother. 2024.

WSL, Marshall. Cunning Words: A Grimoire of Tales and Magic. 2023.

GOTH, VAMPIRES & The Dark Side

This Current has always been in my purview since I was a teen. I find it to be intoxicatingly beautiful and needed for the Technology of a Modern Chaos Reality. The Stygian Way does not need it, but the full Kultus would be less without it. These books are very helpful and powerful for the journey. It includes for me many titles on the LHP and darker aspects of magick.

Baddeley, Gavin. Gothic Chic: A Connoisseur's Guide to Dark Culture. 2006.

Baddeley, Gavin. Goth: Vamps and Dandies. 2010.

Belanger, Michelle (Ed.) Vampires in Their Own Words: An Anthology of Vampire Voices. 2007.

Belanger, Michelle. Walking the Twilight Path: A Gothic Book of the Dead. 2023.

Breverton, Terry. Phantasmagoria: A Compendium of Monsters, Myths, and Legends. 2011.

Cagliastro, Sorceress. Blood Sorcery Bible Volume 1: Rituals of Necromancy. 2011.

Cagliastro, Sorceress. Blood Sorcery Bible Volume 2: Striking the Target: The Practitioner and the Statis Practice, Iron-Blood-Magnetics. 2013.

Connolly, S. How to Draw Friends and Sacrifice Toxic People: Black Magick for Glamour, Influence and Letting Go. DB Publishing. 2022.

Digitalis. Raven. Goth Craft: The Magickal Side of Dark Culture. 2007.

Douris, Steele A. Spirits, Seers, & Seances: Victorian, Spiritualism, Magic, & the Supernatural. 2023.

Gambino, Paul. The Art of Gothic Living: Dark Décor for the Modern Macabre. 2024.

Grimm, Jacob & Grimm, Wilhelm. The Complete Grimm's Fairy Tales. 2025.

Huggens, Kim (Ed.) Memento Mori: A Collection of Magical and Mythological Perspectives on Death, Dying, Mortality and Beyond. 2012.

Kale. Steven. French Salons: High Society and Political Sociability from the Old Regime to the Revolution of 1848. 2004.

Kilpatrick, Nancy. The Goth Bible. 2004.

Marques, Luis. Violet Throne: Legacy of the Aset Ka. 2017.

Robb, John. The Art of Darkness: The History of Goth. 2023.

Voltaire. Aurelio. Gothic Life: The Essential Guide to Macabre Style. 2024.

Wilson, Peter L. Peacock Angel: The Esoteric Tradition of the Yezidis. 2022.

Wynd, Viktor. Dark Fairy Tales. 2025.

GREEK

Betz, Hans D. (Ed.) The Greek Magical Papyri in Translation Including the Demotic Spells, 2nd Ed. 1992.

Burkert, Walter. Greek Religion. 1985.

Butler. Hans D. (Ed.) Homer. The Iliad & the Odyssey. 2008.

Dunn, Patrick. The Orphic Hymns: A New Translation for the Occult Practitioner. 2021.

Dunn, Patrick. The Practical Art of Divine Magic: Contemporary & Ancient Techniques of Theurgy. 2019.

Graves, Robert. The Greek Myths I. 8th Ed. 2000.

Graves, Robert. The Greek Myths II. 8th Ed. 2000.

Jackson, Roy. Greek Mythology: Myths and Legends of the Gods, Titans, Zeus, Olympians, and More! 2nd Ed. 2014.

Luck, Georg (Trans.) Arcana Mundi: Magic and the Occult in the Greek and Roman World: A Collection of Ancient Texts, 2nd Ed. 2006.

Mierzwicki, Tony. Hellenismos: Practicing Greek Polytheism Today. 2018.

Ogden, Daniel. Greek and Roman Necromancy. 2001.

Reece, Gwendolyn. The Waters of Mnemosyne: Ancient Greek Religion for Modern Pagans. 2024.

Shaw, Gregory. Hellenic Tantra: The Theurgic Platonism of Iamblichus. 2024.

Skinner, Stephen. Techniques of Graeco-Egyptian Magic. 2016.

Taunton, Gwendolyn. The Path of Shadows: Chthonic Gods, Oneiromancy, & Necromancy in Ancient Greece. 2018.

Waggoner, Jamie. Hades: Myth, Magic, & Modern Devotion. 2024.

Warrior, Valerie M. Greek Religion: A Sourcebook. 2009.

Wender, Dorothea (Trans.) Hesiod. Theogony and Works and Days. Theognis, Elegies. 1973.

Winter, Sarah K. I. Kharis: Hellenic Polytheism Explored. 2nd Ed. 2008.

Martial/Health/Wellness

Anderson, Bob. Stretching: For Everyday Fitness and Running, Tennis, Racquetball, Cycling, Swimming, Golf and Other Sports. 1980.

Chia, Mantak. Awaken Healing Energy Through the Tao. 1983.

Chia, Mantak. Chi Self-Massage: The Taoist Way of Rejuvenation. 1986.

Chia, Mantak. Tendon Nei Kung: Building Strength, Power and Flexibility in the Joints. 2009.

Chia, Mantak. Chi Kung for Prostrate Health and Sexual Vigor: A Handbook of Simple Exercises & Techniques. 2013.

Chia, Mantak & Winn, Michael. Taoist Secrets of Love: Cultivating Male Sexual Energy. 1984.

Chia, Mantak. The Secret Teachings of the Tao Te Ching. 2005.

Chia, Mantak. Chi Nei Tsang: Chi Massage for Vital Organs. 2007.

Chia, Mantak. The Taoist Soul Body: Harnessing the Power of Kan and Li. 2007.

Chia, Mantak. The Alchemy of Sexual Energy: Connecting to the Universe from Within. 2009.

Chia, Mantak & Jan, Andrew. Tai Chi Wu Style: Advanced Techniques for Internalizing Chi Energy. 2013.

Chia, Mantak & Chia, Maneewan. The Multi-Orgasmic Couple: How Couples Can Dramatically Enhance their Pleasure, Intimacy, and Health. 2000.

Ferguson, Pamela. The Self-Shiatsu Handbook. 1995.

Franklin, Eric. Relax Your Neck Liberate Your Shoulders: The Ultimate Exercise Program for Tension Relief. 2002.

Hogan, Scott. Built From Broken: A Science-Based Guide to Healing Painful Joints, Preventing Injuries and Rebuilding Your Body. 2021

Judith, Anodea. Eastern Body Western Mind: Psychology and the Chakra System as a Path to the Self. 2004.

Jwing-Ming, Yang. The Root of Chinese Chi Kung: The Secrets of Chi Kung Training. 1995.

Jwing-Ming, Yang. Qi Gong for Health and Martial Arts: Exercises and Meditation. 1998.

Lundberg, Paul. The Book of Shiatsu: A Complete Guide to Using Hand Pressure and Gentle Manipulation to Improve Your Health, Vitality, and Stamina. 1992.

Mate, Gabor & Mate, Daniel. The Myth of Normal: Trauma, Illness, & Healing in a Toxic Culture. 2022.

Mitchell, Damo. A Comprehensive Guide to Daoist Nei Gong. 2018.

Morris, Glenn J. Path Notes of an American Ninja Master. 1993.

Novak, Janice. Posture: Get it Straight! 2nd Ed. 2006.

Ohashi, Wataru. Do-It-Yourself Shiatsu: How to Perform the Ancient Japanese Art of Acupuncture Without Needles. 1976.

Tedeschi, Marc. Essential Anatomy: For Healing and Martial Arts. 2003.

Vineyard, Missy. How You Stand, How You Move, How You Live: Learning the Alexander Technique: To Explore Your Mind-Body Connection and Achieve Self-Mastery. 2007.

Worwood, Valerie A. The Complete Book of Essential Oils and Aromatherapy: Over 600 Natural, Non-Toxic & Fragrant Recipes to Create Health, Beauty & a Safe Home Environment. 1991.

THE POSSIBILITY OF THINGS TO COME

As the book ended, as is the nature of the Stygian, a lot changes. I went back and had to edit some of that in. If I continued to do that, I would never release the book. I had to decide that I would release a series of Treatises following this book to give a good example of growth and movement. This is the first book I will release as the first in a series. I leave that in the hands of the Gods and to the readers.

The writing and interchanges with Deities are ongoing. This is a living religion and philosophy, and it is forever moving forward. I have greatly appreciated the people who read, assisted in editing, and the art. In the aftermath, in the kind words of readers, and in the possibility of things to come, I feel this tradition or system is there for those who want it, have experienced it, and have become Stygian.

Thank you all for reading and experiencing my world and that of the Kultus. May your work result in awakening.

Publications from Liminal Gate Press

liminalgatepress@gmail.com

www.liminalgate.co.uk

The word liminal comes from the Latin word līmen which means 'threshold'

Tattwa Magick for Beginners

by Tim Brown

Following Earth, Water, Fire, Air, and Spirit — the building blocks of the universe and of the self. This practical guide introduces the ancient Vedic system of tattvas and shows how they can be integrated into Western Magickal practice.

Through meditations, visualisations, pathworkings, and rituals, you will learn how to work directly with the tattva symbols as gateways into inner realms of transformation. Clear explanations, practical exercises, and original illustrations guide you from the basics through to advanced techniques such as scrying and elemental pathworking.

Along the way, you will explore both the similarities and differences between the Vedic and Hermetic traditions, gaining insight into how the elements can reshape your magickal practice.

This book bridges the gap between Eastern philosophy and Hermetic magick, making the subtle energies of the tattvas accessible to modern magickians, particularly those who work with the Golden Dawn system of magick.

Whether you are new to magick or seeking to expand your elemental work, Tattva Magick for Beginners offers a structured yet flexible path into the heart of elemental wisdom.

A Dream of the Seraphim: Guides, Ethereal Messengers and Celestial Beings Drawn from the Psyche

by Maggie Blake-Reece

'What lies just beyond our grasp in the realms of sleep?'

This is a book of dreams and psyche, one which unfolds to the reader in three distinct movements that reflect facets of the author's personal journey. The dreams and visual renderings, the stories which were born from within those dreams, and the theological and psychological research and reflections that followed as a means to better understand the messages received.

This book is not doctrine nor a declaration of truth, it is instead a living archive of visions and questions, a project undertaken in pure devotion and at its heart lies a search for meaning and connection.

Let the drawings speak to you, the stories stir the imagination, and the reflections challenge your perceptions of known reality.

www.ingramcontent.com/pod-product-compliance
Lightning Source LLC
LaVergne TN
LVHW010051110826
845155LV00028B/290

* 9 7 8 1 9 1 9 5 1 2 2 0 4 *